Breathing

Aesthetics

Aesthetics

Breathing

DUKE UNIVERSITY PRESS   Durham and London   2022

Breathing

Aesthetics

Tremblay

Jean-Thomas

Library of Congress Cataloging-in-Publication Data
Names: Tremblay, Jean-Thomas, author.
Title: Breathing aesthetics / Jean-Thomas Tremblay.
Description: Durham : Duke University Press, 2022. |
Includes bibliographical references and index.
Identifiers: LCCN 2021058321 (print)
LCCN 2021058322 (ebook)
ISBN 9781478016229 (hardcover)
ISBN 9781478018865 (paperback)
ISBN 9781478023494 (ebook)
Subjects: LCSH: Ecocriticism. | Environment (Aesthetics) |
Respiration—Political aspects. | Respiration in literature. |
Respiration in art. | Feminism and the arts. | Arts and
society. | Queer theory. | BISAC: LITERARY CRITICISM /
Semiotics & Theory | NATURE / Environmental Conservation
& Protection
Classification: LCC PN98.E36 T74 2022 (print) |
LCC PN98.E36 (ebook) | DDC 700.1—dc23/eng/20220621
LC record available at https://lccn.loc.gov/2021058321
LC ebook record available at https://lccn.loc.gov/2021058322

Cover art: © Henrik Sorensen. Courtesy Getty Images.

For Sam, who reminds me that function follows form

Contents

Acknowledgments

There is a concept that appears in this book's third chapter: prepositional breathing. We owe it to the Caribbean Canadian poet M. NourbeSe Philip. The locution "I breathe," Philip notes, would not be possible without the prepositional act of "breathing for." Respiratory autopoiesis—the self-maintenance and self-renewal of organisms—necessitates a hospitable milieu. To breathe-for is to generate such a milieu. It is to create the conditions not only for other people's survival but also for their flourishing. When others breathe for us, holding our breath with anticipation and running out of breath with exhaustion feel tolerable. I wish to express my gratitude to the following guides and companions who have had the generosity to engage in prepositional breathing, and who in doing so have made the genesis of this project, and life around it, possible.

For their early mentorship, and for regarding me as a person with ideas when I had few, I thank Sophie Bourgault, Dalie Giroux, Susie O'Brien, and Mary O'Connor.

What would become *Breathing Aesthetics* began—through many false starts, then some less so—in the University of Chicago's Department of English Language and Literature and Center for the Study of Gender and Sexuality. Lauren Berlant, chair of my dissertation committee, has taught me the value of scholarship that opens its objects up instead of containing them, even if there might not yet exist a world to welcome it. Near Lauren, I've experienced the thrill of unlearning my defenses against curiosity. (Revisiting these statements after Lauren's passing, I struggle to convert the present perfect into the absolute past proper to the eulogy. The learning is ongoing.) On my committee also sat Patrick Jagoda, the fiercest ally there is, and Jennifer Scappettone, whom it would be etymologically accurate to call a coconspirator. Pre- and postgraduation, I've benefited from the sharp, Chicago-style insights of such faculty members as Maud Ellmann, Rachel Galvin, Elaine Hadley, Tim Harrison, Alison James, Joseph Masco, Jo McDonagh, Debbie Nelson, and Ken Warren. Very, very special thanks to Adrienne Brown, Sianne Ngai, Julie Orlemanski, Kristen Schilt, and Jennifer Wild. For long, absorbing conversations and the more than occasional gossip session, I thank Michael Dango, Annie Heffernan, Lauren Jackson, Rivky Mondal, and Katie Nolan. Members of the staff in English (Racquel Asante, Angeline Dimambro, and Hannah Stark) and at CSGS (Gina Olson and Sarah Tuohey) provided invaluable resources and fostered academic communities to which it felt good to belong. Lex Nalley and Tate Brazas became, more than coworkers, dear comrades.

I wrote and rewrote most of this book in my first, whirlwind years as a junior faculty member in New Mexico State University's English Department. Thanks to Brittany Chavez, Rose Conley, Ryan Cull, Ruth Garcia, Meg Goehring, Harriet Linkin, Tracey Miller-Tomlinson, Rabiatu Balaraba Mohammed, Brian Rourke, Liz Schirmer, Tyson Stolte, and, most of all, Susan Enger.

Exchanges with theorists of the ventilatory—Aleesa Cohene, Ashon Crawley, Brad Harmon, Stefanie Heine, Jack R. Leff, Arthur Rose, Clint Wilson III, and especially Hsuan L. Hsu—have been nothing short of vivifying. It is a privilege to think and work alongside a cohort of interlocutors that far exceeds institutional limits; among them are Kadji Amin, Benjamin Bateman, Tyler Bradway, James Cahill, Alberto Fernández Carbajal, Will Clark, Jorge Cotte, Ranjodh Singh Dhaliwal, Rachele Dini, Sarah Dowling, Adam Fales, Joey Gamble, Brian Glavey, David Hollingshead, Annabel Kim, Travis Chi Wing Lau, Christina León, Paul Nadal, Matthew J. Phillips, Jordan Stein, Ricky Varghese, and Christopher Walker. Coediting and cocurating with Rebekah Sheldon, Drew Strombeck, and Michelle Velasquez-Potts have made me enjoy collaboration to an extent that would stupefy my younger self—*growth!* And in Steven Swarbrick, fellow Scorpio, I have found a dream cowriter; his influence is palpable across this book. Portions of this monograph have been presented in various venues. Thanks to Nan Z. Da for inviting me to share my research with the University of Notre Dame's Americanist Seminar, and to Ricky Varghese for including me on the "Sex and the Pandemic" line-up.

Dodie Bellamy, CAConrad, Renee Gladman, Kevin Killian, and Sheree Rose, whose works are discussed in this book, have been kind enough to correspond or chat with me. They needed openness and patience to watch me stumble toward an idea about their work, and they had them. Thanks to the archivists at the University of Southern California's ONE National Gay and Lesbian Archives (Bob Flanagan and Sheree Rose Collection), the Ohio State University's Rare Books and Manuscripts Library (Bob Flanagan Collection), and the Spelman College Archives (Toni Cade Bambara Collection).

That *Breathing Aesthetics* has landed at Duke University Press continues to inspire in me both incredulity and gratitude. Early conversations with the visionary Ken Wissoker laid the book's foundations and structured its argument. Joshua Gutterman Tranen has guided me from a partial, haphazard manuscript to a completed book with verve, flair, precision, and a healthy dose of humor. Josh is taking the publishing industry by storm, and we're all the better for it. Lucid, detailed reports by Nicole Seymour and Sarah Jane Cervenak enabled a meaningful revision of the manuscript. I hope that these meticulous readers will notice their positive impact on the book. Thanks to Liz Smith, Karen Fisher, Emily Lawrence, Courtney Leigh Richardson, and, for the index, Matthew J. Phillips. Beyond Duke, I wish to thank Elspeth Brown, Rebecca Colesworthy, and Dani Kasprzak for judicious advice on the publishing process.

Thanks to my family—especially Renelle, Pierre, Amy, and Michael—for conjuring optimism and bestowing strength. Katie Hendricks, Omie Hsu, Chase Joynt, Eva Pensis, Miranda Steege, and André-Luc Tessier are dear friends. Despite the distance separating some of us, I have felt and relied on their presence throughout the writing of this book. A handful of fellow travelers have been not only trusted confidantes but also trusted readers, and their willingness to revisit problems and rethread arguments in my company has made everything lighter. Dan Guadagnolo's savvy and sagacity have proven miraculous. Hannah Manshel, thank you for remaining my fellow traveler. Ari Meyer Brostoff models "being a writer" with (comedic) rigor. Rachel Kyne lives as she reads: tenderly and thoughtfully. And Jules Gill-Peterson, my kin: the life and career worth fighting for are with her.

My ultimate thanks are to Sam Creely. Sam, my co-navigator and my North Star (my mixed metaphor), has made their way, and helped me find mine, through the following pages more times than I can count. To long hikes, long reads, and, hopefully, a long life together.

PORTIONS OF CHAPTER 2 are derived from Jean-Thomas Tremblay, "Aesthetic Self-Medication: Bob Flanagan and Sheree Rose's Structures of Breathing," *Women and Performance: a journal of feminist theory* 28, no. 3 (2018): 221–38, https://doi.org/10.1080/0740770X.2018.1524621. An early version of chapter 3 appeared as Jean-Thomas Tremblay, "Feminist Breathing," *differences: A Journal of Feminist Cultural Studies* 30, no. 3 (2019): 92–117. Thanks to those journals' editors and readers.

Excerpts from Orlando White's "NASCENT," from LETTERRS (2015), are reprinted by permission of Nightboat Books. Excerpts from *The TV Sutras*, © 2014 Dodie Bellamy, are reproduced with the permission of the author and Ugly Duckling Presse. Excerpts from CAConrad's "POETRY is DIRT as DEATH is DIRT," "QUALM CUTTING AND ASSEMBLAGE," and "(Soma)tic Poetry at St. Mark's Poetry Project, NYC," from *A Beautiful Marsupial Afternoon: New (Soma)-tics* (2012), are reproduced with the permission of the author and Wave Books. Excerpts from Bob Flanagan's *The Pain Journal* (2000) are reproduced with the permission of Semiotext(e). Excerpts from Linda Hogan's "Old Ocean, She," "Morning's Dance," and "The Other Side," from *Dark. Sweet. New and Selected Poems* (2012), are reproduced with the permission of Coffee House Books. Excerpts from *Scree: The Collected Earlier Poems, 1962-1991*, © 2015 Fred Wah, Talonbooks, Vancouver, BC, are reproduced by permission of the publisher. Excerpts from Renee Gladman's *Event Factory* (2010) are reproduced with the permission of Dorothy, a publishing project. Excerpts from Trisha Low's *Socialist Realism* (2019) are reproduced with the permission of Coffee House Books.

Introduction. Ecologies of the Particular

Breathing is inevitably morbid. This postulate may seem counterintuitive; after all, respiratory modulations often attest to energy or vigor. Steady breathing and held breath evidence stamina and athleticism, while deep breaths provide a sense of balance or presence. Moreover, breathing is key to autopoiesis, or the self-maintenance and self-renewal of living systems. But breathing makes life out of an orientation toward death. To be a breather is to be vulnerable; this is an existential condition. As long as we breathe, and as long as we're porous, we cannot fully shield ourselves from airborne toxins and toxicants as well as other ambient threats.[1] Becoming conscious of our breathing confronts us with our finitude. Not only have we been inhaling and exhaling both benign and malign air particles, but our awareness of this predicament does not grant us the means to remedy it.

The respiratory process through which life and death loop into each other as on a Möbius strip is best summed up by the notion of "negative refueling," which in Michael Eigen's psychoanalytic nomenclature labels the inseparability of affective "nourishment" from emotional "toxins" or "poisons."[2] Eigen illustrates a theory of emotions with an anecdote about breathing: "I think of a wonderful philosophy teacher who had emphysema. In his first semester of retirement, he decided to teach in Switzerland, after years in New York. He died soon after arriving in Switzerland. I imagined his lungs could not take fresh air, after years of adaptation to toxins."[3] For Eigen, affective dynamics are analogous to respiratory dynamics: we incorporate and rely on productive and destructive affects, just as the professor's survival appears conditional on his habitual exposure to toxins and toxicants. Eigen's anecdote, meant to clarify figurative nourishment, doubles as a perspicacious statement on life in increasingly toxic environments—a life marked by the "vertiginous discovery of poison and nourishment mixed beyond discernment."[4] In this book, I grapple with this vertigo and stick around to see what respiration teaches us once the shock of the affiliation between life and death has dissipated.

That vulnerability is an existential condition does not mean that everyone experiences it consistently or equally. *Breathing Aesthetics* tells the story of how the respiratory enmeshment of vitality and morbidity has come to index an uneven distribution of risk in the late twentieth and early twenty-first centuries. Under racial and extractive capitalism and imperialism, breathing has emerged as a medium that configures embodiment and experience as transductions of bio- and necropolitical forces—forces that optimize certain lives and trivialize or attack others.[5] The intensified pollution, weaponization, and monetization of air and breath since the 1970s amount to a crisis in the reproduction of life. Within this crisis, breath, a life force to be marshaled individually or collectively, reveals its contingency on environments, broadly conceived, that exhaust their occupants at different rates. Accordingly, articulations of survival become predicated on the management and dispersal of respiratory hazards.

The difference between breathing that kills and breathing that both enables and imperils life has to do with *mediation*: the linking of seemingly disparate or contradictory positions and processes by way of aesthetics. The term *aesthetics* featured in this book's title does not, then, signal the limits of my inquiry. The aesthetic isn't one of many, equally valid domains in which to study the contemporary dynamics of breathing. Instead, it is the aesthetic mediation or aestheticization of breathing that structures threat and injury into something like individual and collective persistence. I posit the existence of an aesthetics of breathing, rather than subsuming engagements with breathing under an all-encompassing aesthetics of sociopolitical and environmental peril, in order to underscore a distinct mode of creation and expression whose fluidity and translucence defy the codes of aesthetic judgment. As Hsuan L. Hsu explains, smell, a corollary of respiration, poses a problem for aesthetic inquiry: "the human body's most sensitive tool for detecting invisible chemical threats across space is also deeply ambiguous, fraught with uncertainty, socially constructed, culturally neglected, and resistant to representation."[6] Dora Zhang similarly writes that "the up-in-the-air quality" of theorizing about the atmosphere is "occasioned by the fact that this phenomenon defies our desire for conceptual integrity and resists our usual models of causality."[7] An aesthetics of breathing trains us to focus on exchanges between bodies and milieus. It also trains us to be receptive to a range of processes and phenomena that are related, yet irreducible, to speech and action.

Such a training is manifest in Theresa Hak Kyung Cha's DICTEE (1982) and Orlando White's (Diné) LETTERRS (2015), two celebrated experimental works that cultivate our attention to a breath that never exactly coincides with speech acts. In one case, breathing might, but doesn't necessarily, flow into an utterance; in the other, breathing exceeds the utterances whose sonority it modulates. In both, signs of cultural vitality circulate through airways shaped by the deleterious pressures of colonialism, racism, and sexism. Early in DICTEE, a vignette titled "DISEUSE," French for fortune teller or psychic, features an account of the facial minutiae of breathing. A character—perhaps Cha, perhaps the *diseuse*, perhaps an individual to whom the *diseuse* is attuned—seeks to make an utterance from a position of gender, racial, and colonial subordination. Born during the Korean War, Cha, along with her family, migrated, first to Hawai'i and then to San Francisco, in the 1960s. Unable to speak, DICTEE's unnamed character resorts to mimicking the process, letting out "bared noise, groan, bits torn from words" along the way.[8] These breathy noises correspond to what Cha, in an artist's statement, calls the "roots of language before it is born on the tip of the tongue."[9] Free-indirect discourse in DICTEE reveals a character who tries to estimate her pitch, her reach: "she hesitates to measure the accuracy"; "she waits inside the pause."[10] The character speculates a sequence of adjustments that may conduce to speech: "The entire lower lip would lift upwards then sink back to its original place. She would then gather both lips and protrude them in a pout taking in the breath that might utter some thing. (One thing. Just one.) But the breath falls away."[11] Should the breath not fall away, the character might be able to convert the air she takes in "rapidly," "in gulfs," into a momentum that would conclude "the wait from pain to say. To not to. Say."[12] She "gasps from [the] pressure" of not-quite-speaking, "its contracting motion."[13] When she cannot contort her breath any further, and I, as a reader, cannot hold my breath any longer, the speech act happens, at last: "Uttering. Hers now. Hers bare. The utter."[14] That utterance is DICTEE, all of it. With the convulsive formulation, "The wait from pain to say. To not to. Say," the narrator lays out a paradox: breathing at once affords a thrust or rhythm and signals the pitfalls of a character's effort to turn this force into language. Variations in the intensity of breathing, that is, register a painful effort to speak through oppression while offering respite from the pain of speaking of oppression. By introducing a subject of respiration, one we get to know through her breathing (and not the inverse), Cha makes the conditions of minoritarian life's possibility coextensive with its conditions of impossibility. For this character, living on and losing steam constitute a false dichotomy. Although it signals an exchange between a character and her milieu, breathing is here described in solitary terms. DICTEE leaves us with the question of how breathing, a shared activity if there ever was one, might figure collective life.

White's LETTERRS—stylized to emphasize the errant quality of a poetry that dissents from colonial structures of language—grapples with this question. LETTERRS, like DICTEE, focuses on breath to dilate anticolonial communication.[15] Whereas DICTEE examines breath in extreme close-up, LETTERRS moves between individual and communal respiration. The collection's opening poem, "NASCENT," slows down a newborn's first breath and cry:

> It begins at a diacritical spark   of breath   and soma.
> Vowel stress   nasal enunciation   the tenors of existence.[16]

White space prolongs caesuras. Its incorporation into the line suggests whiteness's saturation of Native people's breathing under settler colonialism. At the same time as it records an experience of colonialism, breath here animates an anticolonial poetics. In DICTEE breath precedes language, and in LETTERRS breath gives language its diacritics—its accents and tones. Breath's diacritical operation, mentioned at the beginning of the sprawling "NASCENT," recurs some four pages later:

> Pronunciation marks are proof
>
>   of one's own cultural sentience.
> Those authentic reverberations
>
>   above the cap height where breath
> pressures tongue against teeth,
>
>   below the baseline where throat
> exhales the long accent vowel,
>
>   in that moment it echoes through
> nose, quivers as phonemic air:
>
>   the ogonek tickle of   łį̨į̨.'"[17]

The respiratory gymnastics described in this sequence of dropped lines culminates with the utterance of the "ogonek tickle" or diacritic hook in "łį̨į̨'" (horse in Diné Bizaad). Phonemes, these units of sound that distinguish one word from another, reside in the air. This isn't to say that evidence of "cultural sentience" evaporates or becomes amorphous in White's poems. On the contrary, air is a conduit between the guttural and skeletal adjustments that produce breath and a destination that, throughout LETTERRS, alternately appears as the "collagen / of thoughts," "the cochlea of thought," "the narrative of bone," "bone-shaped artifacts," "where the calcium hardens," "the notochord of thought," and "backbone a sentence."[18] Breath leaves the skull to reossify as sharable artifacts like a thought, a sentence, and a narrative. Toward the end of "NASCENT," breathing's role in the mediation of a commons is reflected by the aerial manifestation of a Diné *we*: "vibration waves in air / until we materialize."[19]

The "breath [that] falls away" in *DICTEE* and the "diacritical spark of breath" in LETTERRS function as figures for, and fickle archives of, historically and culturally specific iterations of negative refueling. Both breathing lessons telegraph efforts to make do through oppression and occupation. Cha and White model respiration as the negotiation of ambient or climatic colonialism, with White's Diné poetics more specifically documenting life within what the anthropologist Kristen Simmons (Southern Paiute) terms "settler atmospherics."[20] Simmons, a water protector who in 2016 protested the Dakota Access Pipeline at the Standing Rock Indian Reservation, explains that the settler state puts Indigenous peoples, tribes, and nations "into suspension": it uproots and immobilizes them through the ongoing operation of capitalism, militarism, and racism.[21] Calling to mind the aerial emergence of Indigenous solidarity in White's lines, "vibration waves in air / until we materialize," Simmons notes that "those in suspension," managed through riot control agents like tear gas and pepper spray, "arc toward one another—becoming-open in an atmosphere of violence."[22] Water protectors, Simmons's account goes, had to turn to each other and breathe together as they cried or choked in the cold. The environmental and military violence opposed by water protectors at Standing Rock recapitulated a long history of colonial interferences with breathing. In the nineteenth century, the popularization of spirometry, a pulmonary function test, corroborated colonial and racial hierarchies of aliveness. As Lundy Braun recounts, biased medical models, developed in part in colonial India and on US plantations, equated lung capacity with "vital capacity" to justify the enslavement and oppression of Black and brown people.[23] The uranium mining and nuclear tests that took place on or near reservations a century later contributed to abnormally high lung cancer rates among Indigenous populations.[24] From medical pathologies to radiological and chemical weapons, colonial bio- and necropower have reproduced themselves by seizing breath and constraining Indigenous life.

The emergence of breath as both a record of injury and a political vernacular can be traced through Black studies. Anti-Blackness, as Lindsey Dillon and Julie

Sze note, circulates as "particulate matter"; it is ambient, and not just figuratively so.[25] Christina Sharpe argues that "aspiration," or "keeping breath in the Black body," takes place through and against asphyxia as the condition of Blackness.[26] Sharpe's history of Black asphyxiation begins with the drowning of enslaved people thrown overboard in the Middle Passage and culminates with the killing of Eric Garner. On July 17, 2014, white New York Police Department officer Daniel Pantaleo put Garner, a Black resident of Staten Island, in a deadly choke hold for allegedly selling "loosies" or single cigarettes. Garner suffered from asthma, a condition that, according to epidemiological data, disproportionately affects African Americans.[27] Asthma was so central to Garner's life that after his passing his mother, Gwen, would line a memorial to her son with inhalers.[28] In 2017, Garner's daughter Erica, who following her father's death staged die-ins and became a prominent critic of police brutality, would die of complications due to a heart attack, itself triggered by an asthma attack.[29] Garner's last words, "I can't breathe," were also those of Elijah McClain and George Floyd, two other Black men killed by police just a few years later.[30] On August 24, 2019, in Aurora, Colorado, three police officers—Nathan Woodyard, Jason Rosenblatt, and Randy Roedema—arrested McClain, who had reportedly been listening to music and dancing while walking down the street. They held McClain on the ground for fifteen minutes, applying a carotid control hold. After paramedics injected him with a sedative, McClain suffered a cardiac arrest. He was pronounced brain dead on August 27 and was removed from life support on August 30.[31] On May 25, 2020, Derek Chauvin, a white Minneapolis police officer, killed George Floyd, whom he had arrested for allegedly passing a counterfeit twenty-dollar bill. Chauvin pressed his knee to Floyd's neck for almost nine minutes as three other officers prevented onlookers from intervening.[32] In the wake of these public executions, "I can't breathe" and "we can't breathe" have become rallying cries in the fight against the institutions that orchestrate Black death.

Massive protests erupted in 2014 in response to the killing of Garner, and again in 2020 in response to the murders of Floyd, McClain, Breonna Taylor, Ahmaud Arbery, Tony McDade, Dion Johnson, and others. "Black Lives Matter May Be the Largest Movement in US History," read a memorable *New York Times* headline in July 2020.[33] The 2020 protests coincided with the COVID-19 outbreak, which was declared a Public Health Emergency of International Concern on January 30 and a pandemic on March 11. Many of the symptoms associated with the infectious disease are respiratory, from cough to shortness of breath to loss of smell. Complications such as pneumonia and acute respiratory distress syndrome also imperil breathing. Although it is, as of this writing, too early to assess the disease's long-term effects, researchers have pointed to limited lung capacity, kidney complications, and neurological problems such as inflammation, psychosis, delirium, nerve damage, and strokes.[34] Higher infection and hospitalization rates within Black communities have shed light on insufficient preventive health services, unaffordable medical care, and highly concentrated respiratory hazards in low-income and minority-heavy areas—all of which amount to structural and environmental racism.[35] Police violence and structural and environmental racism are two mutually reinforcing modalities of the necropolitics of anti-Black asphyxiation. One temporality is accelerative, and the other chronic; both are catastrophic.

Ashon Crawley's study of breath and Blackness is, like Sharpe's, haunted by Garner's death. Crawley reads "I can't breathe" as a refusal of the conditions that negate Black life.[36] Decades before Crawley, the West Indian psychiatrist and philosopher Frantz Fanon turned to breathing to anatomize the formation of a Black unconscious under colonization and imagine a collective release from enslavement. In *Black Skin, White Masks* (1952 in the original French), Fanon unforgettably writes, "It is not because the Indo-Chinese has discovered a culture of his [*sic*] own that he [*sic*] is in revolt. It is because 'quite simply' it was, in more than one way, becoming impossible for him [*sic*] to breathe."[37] In late 2014, Fanon's claim was widely shared on social media, as an extension of "I can't breathe." By then, the subject of the claim had switched from the Indo-Chinese to the Black *we* whom Fanon had sought to activate. "We revolt simply because, for many reasons, we can no longer breathe," now read the pronouncement.[38] In *A Dying Colonialism* (1959 in the original French), his account of the Algerian war, Fanon gives a name to the struggle against colonial pressures: "combat breathing."[39] Subjects engage in combat breathing when they must direct all their energies toward surviving state violence. Under such conditions, revolutionary action is a matter of life and death. Crawley shares with Fanon a political ontology of Black respiration that outlines a transition from debilitating to galvanizing breathing. The Blackpentecostal practices of shouting, tarrying, whooping, and speaking in tongues, Crawley offers, conjure *"black pneuma,"* or a "fugitive inhalation of oxygen plus more and fugitive exhalation of carbon dioxide plus more," to "enunciate life, life that is exorbitant, capacious, and fundamentally . . . social, though it is also life that is structured through and engulfed by brutal violence."[40] Through breath, Crawley and Sharpe affirm the possibility of Black life from its conditions of impossibility—a tension that recalls the paradox animating the anticolonial aesthetics of DICTEE and LETTERRS. By turning to Blackpentecostalism's repertoire of aesthetic practices, Crawley defies respiratory obstructions with the creative possibilities of rhythmic and synchronic breath.

Across the contexts I've begun to map out, breathing traffics between the structural and the experiential. Breathing constitutes a sensory realm where bio- and necropolitical forces operating on the population scale are embodied. This isn't strictly a top-down process; breathing is a negotiation. For Cha's character in *DICTEE*, to breathe is to be hailed, nonverbally, coercively, into a subordinate position—but it is also to generate the rhythm and momentum needed to address subordination. In Sharpe's account of Black aspiration, an experience of violence morphs into a wish, an orientation toward the future. White and Crawley, for their part, show not just how populations are forced into shared breathlessness but also how solidarity arises from untenable conditions. White's Diné *we*, materialized from "vibration waves in air," and Crawley's commons, held together by "*black pneuma*," do not neutralize atmospheric threats; they rearrange, reconfigure, reorder them. Aesthetic experimentation cannot realistically solve breathing, or disentangle it from its status as evidence of vulnerability to violence or neglect. Aesthetic experimentation can however produce a breath that exceeds this status. The cultivation of such excess makes breathing, more than an index of crises, a resource for living through them.

Since the 1970s, writers, filmmakers, and artists have experimented with breathing with extraordinary frequency in an effort to shuffle the terms by which they relate to the milieus they inhabit. The breathing aesthetics rubric after which this book is named proves expansive; I've written elsewhere about the panicked oscillation between loss and triumph in popular music's bombastic respiratory anthems.[41] Here I devote most of my attention to minoritarian works created by marginalized figures who tend to contest the genre and media conventions traditionally valorized by artistic and academic institutions. I say most of my attention because not every case study relays the book's radical commitments; the logic of exemplification isn't always straightforward. For instance, some of the figures who populate this book—from the antiheroine of Todd Haynes's *Safe* (1995), who appears later in this introduction, to the singer-songwriter Kate Bush, in whose company we begin chapter 1—problematize aspects of a relation between breathing and whiteness that I seek to expose and displace. This said, I wouldn't qualify such figures as hegemonic just because they benefit, in some ways, from systems of domination. So much is true of many other figures, real and fictional, who show up in this book—figures whose identities ought not to be understood in monolithic terms. I use the attribute *minoritarian* to refer not to fixed positions but to an impulse, be it artistic or analytic, to contest the forces that make the world more breathable for some people than for others. A focus on minoritarian practices reveals, in Kyla Wazana Tompkins's words, "the art—and the artfulness—that emerges from the everyday life of socially deviant peoples, people rendered deformed by capital, or simply understood as deformed within normative aesthetic frames."[42] As I answer Sasha Engelmann's call to "engage the key affective and aesthetic dimensions of air, where aesthetics is taken to mean the broader, not necessarily human organisation of the sensible," I insist on aesthetic criticism's status as social and political commentary, rather than an exemption from it.[43] My guiding principles throughout *Breathing Aesthetics* are that respiration's imbrication of vitality and morbidity is differently felt by differently situated people, and that minoritarian works best exemplify the function of aesthetics in registering and partially, only partially, diffusing the risks of breathing.

Breathing in Crisis

Breathing Aesthetics examines responses to a crisis in breathing that intensified around the 1970s. My proposed periodizing notion—crisis in breathing—does not imply a simple historical shift from easy to strained breathing. For one, as I've previously stated, breathing is inevitably morbid. Any fantasy of a past wherein breathing was strictly invigorating would be just that: a fantasy. What I label a crisis in breathing is the present-day configuration of the enmeshment of life and death. This configuration is typified by the increased pollution, weaponization, and monetization of air and breath, the consequences of which are unevenly distributed. By framing the crisis in breathing as a problem of the long 1970s, I posit exceptional, episodic, and chronic respiratory obstructions as metrics of a crisis in the reproduction of life that has worsened since that pivotal decade.

One shorthand for the crisis in the reproduction of life is *precarity*. Lauren Berlant outlines precarity as a problem both existential (we are contingent beings; life proceeds more or less without guarantees) and historical (economic and political conditions accelerate the wearing out of human beings).[44] Judith Butler distinguishes between precariousness, a function of our vulnerability and exposure that is given some political form; precarity, the differential distribution of precariousness; and precarization, an ongoing process that makes the precarious endemic, which is to say irreducible to a single event.[45] What Berlant sees as historical precarity and Butler as precarization refers by and large to the collapse, in the long 1970s, of the economic and political structures that had previously carried, at least for select populations, some of the burden of life's self-perpetuation. To economic and political structures, we should add environments; as Pramod K. Nayar's neologism "ecoprecarity" suggests, fragilized ecosystems and species extinction evidence a crisis in the reproduction of human and nonhuman life.[46] As I use it, the concept of precarity tallies, among other things, the effects of the climate crisis precipitated by capitalism.

Some scholars—though neither Berlant nor Butler—see precarity, specifically ecoprecarity, as a great equalizer, heralding a condition that equally afflicts all organisms. This is the case of the philosopher Michael Marder, whose twist on the precarity concept, the "global dump," entails the inescapable absorption by all of pervasive toxicity.[47] In the twenty-first century, Marder summarizes, "being is being dumped."[48] He goes on:

> It is not that the dump is over there, at a safe distance from the well-off members of affluent societies, who live at several removes from polluted water sources and open-air landfills. Radioactive fallouts know no national boundaries, microplastics are as ubiquitous in tap and bottled water as mercury is in fish, and smog does not stop at the municipal borders dividing the city's poor neighborhoods from the rich. The toxicity of the air, the clouds, the rain and the snow; of the oceans and their diminishing fish and crustacean populations; of chemically fertilized soil and the fruit it bears—this pervasive and multifarious elemental toxicity is also in us.[49]

Although Marder claims that "the arrows of toxicity do not discriminate among those they hit in a 'toxic flood,' [or] the anthropogenic emission into the environment of over 250 billion tons of chemicals a year," there is copious evidence to the contrary.[50] As Dorceta E. Taylor reports, noxious and hazardous facilities are concentrated in minority and low-income communities; this is one of the forms that environmental inequality takes in the United States.[51] While I agree with Marder that no one is fully protected from toxicity—I made a similar statement, earlier, in reference to the porosity of breathers—I maintain that toxicity does discriminate, and it does know boundaries. Marder mistakes existential vulnerability for proof of the flattening of class, racial, and gender hierarchies. And while it is true that all living organisms breathe some toxins and toxicants, the quality of air is not uniform across a given city's neighborhoods, let alone on a national or global scale. The aerial reproduction of inequalities and hierarchies corresponds to what Hsu terms "atmospheric differentiation."[52]

The contemporary crisis wherein breath functions as a metonym for uneven precarities marks the confluence and acceleration of such historical processes as the weaponization, monetization, and pollution of air. An overview of these processes is in order. Although the weaponization of air precedes the 1970s, militarized police forces have deployed chemical weapons (CWs)—rebranded as riot control agents (RCAs)—with increasing frequency since that decade. Peter Sloterdijk argues that the proliferation of gas warfare in the early twentieth century made environments, rather than bodies, primary military targets.[53] Sloter-dijk simplistically casts bodies and environments into an either-or situation. If chemical and radiological weapons—from the phosgene, chlorine, and mustard gas of World War I to the nuclear bombs and missiles of World War II—have targeted environments, they have done so to attack bodies more efficiently. Making breath a prey in its own right synchronized occupation (atmospheric saturation) and injury (asphyxiation). International protocols and agreements, including the Biological Weapons Convention of 1972, a supplement to the Geneva Protocol of 1925, have sought to regulate the use of biological agents and toxicants. The 1993 Chemical Weapons Convention (CWC) forbade the use of RCAs as a method of warfare. These accords have been imperfect, and their reach limited. The slow burn of carcinogens, whose power to debilitate and kill eludes spectacle, exceeds the purview of these agreements. Moreover, the CWC still authorizes the use of RCAs for domestic law enforcement in "'types and quantities' consistent with such [a purpose]."[54] No types and quantities of toxicant are consistent with the purpose of law enforcement, insofar as the rubric of law enforcement is called upon to justify extralegal acts. Tear gas, as Anna Feigenbaum notes, is often employed as a "force multiplier"; it induces disorientation, debilitation, and panic, increasing the effectiveness of other kinds of force, including baton beatings and bird shot.[55] The deployment of tear gas by city and university police has become a fixture of the repression of political struggles.[56] By appropriating CWs, police agencies have borrowed from the military rulebook on what types of violence register as "less lethal." Filling the lungs with toxicants and burning the esophagus restrict alertness and mobility. Tear gas may trigger asthma attacks and aggravate other respiratory afflictions. Such strategies make respiration acutely morbid but not fatal. Not necessarily or immediately, at least.

Within the current crisis in the reproduction of life, respiration indexes privilege and disprivilege. With the 2017 installation *Breath (BRH)*, Max Dovey satirizes the monetization of breath and air by using spirometry to mine cryptocurrencies.[57] Cryptocurrencies like Bitcoin and the aptly named Ether (exchanged through the decentralized computing platform Ethereum) convey the fantasy of an immaterial capitalism, where frictionless transactions make value appear out of thin air and disappear just as easily. But finance capitalism seems immaterial only if we ignore its drain on energy resources. Its massive technological infrastructure pollutes the air and hinders respiration. To extract value from breath, Dovey developed a proof-of-work algorithm that solved a series of encrypted mathematical puzzles to verify transactions. The rewards were minimal. In four weeks, Dovey's machine mined £0.02p.

Not only is there little money to be made from breathing, but we must now pay to breathe. The "breathfulness industry" ascribes therapeutic and monetary value to conscious respiration. In a piece titled "The Business of Breathing," Kelly Conaboy relates her incursion into twenty-first-century "capitalist respiration."[58] After sampling an array of luxury breathing sessions, Conaboy comes to an inevitable conclusion: "I don't see breathing's rise in popularity as a bad thing, though that is admittedly an odd sentence to have to write."[59] Stretching breathing sessions into a 24/7 regimen of monitoring and adjustment, manufactured products such as costly wearable technologies record vital signs to integrate user and device holistically.[60] The Spire Stone, quasi-mystical in name, promises that its interface supplies an objective measure of optimizable breathing. A sleek pager, the stone converts the "realtime bio-signals" of "respiratory sensing" into "useful and actionable" data.[61] Whereas in DICTEE variations in the intensity of breathing have to do with unrealized speech and action, Spire assures its customers that every datum draws the missing vector between breath and action. The Canadian company Vitality Air, whose product isn't so much manufactured as packaged, differently abstracts life force from breath and air. The company bottles fresh air from the resort town of Banff, Alberta, which it then ships to Chinese, Indian, Korean, and now North American customers. Vitality Air's sales pitch, indicative of the importance of resource extraction and circulation to the settler state's sovereign imaginary, assigns each breath monetary value ("We pack the air pretty tight into these little cans. Through compression, we get you more breaths of air and oxygen for your money"); presents the air's freshness as a quality that can expire, such that breaths of recently bottled air have higher value ("We all go outside for 'fresh' air, so how fresh is canned air? With our products, we stamp every one with the exact bottling date"); and casts (air) quality as an exportable, distinctly Canadian natural resource and civic virtue ("Our values of quality, service and innovation are all grounded in our roots as Canadians looking to be leaders in our market").[62] Vitality Air, as the company's motto promises, "enhances vitality one breath at the time."[63] The good news is that we can now buy our *élan vital*. The bad news is that we must now buy our *élan vital*.

The contemporary crisis in breathing is, above all, an environmental crisis. From a historical standpoint, breathing enters indefinite crisis when air is polluted faster than it is purified. Dating large-scale environmental transformations is a tricky endeavor, and something as vague as pollution's irreversibility might be assessed by competing measurements. We can at least say with confidence that the modern environmental movement, as it has evolved in the late twentieth and early twenty-first centuries, enables us to diagnose a crisis in breathing and link it to attrition (a dearth of breathable air) as well as saturation (an excess of toxins and toxicants). In the United States, the implementation of the Air Pollution Control Act of 1955 and the better-known Clean Air Act of 1963, the establishment of the Environmental Protection Agency (EPA) in 1970, and the celebration of the inaugural Earth Day that same year indicate a growing concern for, if not necessarily a willingness to adopt measures that would remedy, breathable air's scarcity. The analytic "late industrialism," which Chloe Ahmann and Alison Kenner borrow from the anthropologist Kim Fortun, identifies "the trouble in the air as a predictable outcome of industrial order."[64] Respiratory inequalities testify to an atmospheric differentiation that isn't "the accidental [byproduct] of industrial prosperity" but "its necessary underside."[65] Systemic asphyxiation is by design, and within the present crisis this design is coming into sharper focus.

The transformations I've sketched—from the weaponization of the air to its monetization, to its pollution—amount to a major shift in what it means to be a breather. The uneven distribution of risk renders unconvincing any conception of the breather as a universal subject. The anthropologist Tim Choy illustrates this point in an ethnography of ecological endangerment in Hong Kong. Choy treats breathers as scaled-down condensations of "air's poesis" who differently accrue the unaccounted-for costs of capitalist production and consumption, including climate-related injury and debility.[66] The breather, as anthropological subject, operates as a catachresis of sorts in Choy's study. Unable to hold together the experiences it purports to generalize, the breather demands to be particularized. Inspired by Choy, I follow breathers across the milieus they occupy in order to register precarities—in the plural form—that overlap but are not isometric. Whenever I refer to *we* or *us* in this book, I, too, do so catachrestically. I use these pronouns to make propositional statements about breathing as an existential phenomenon or a shared activity. But the collective subject behind these statements is differential: a contingent and provisional assemblage of incommensurate experiences.

Epiphenomenal Bodies

Breathing Aesthetics displaces sexuality studies: away from the body, and between bodies and milieus; away from speech and action, and in variations of breathing's intensity that may or may not rise to the status of event. Many of the contexts, aesthetic and critical, that this book occupies are feminist, queer, and trans, for those are categories, along with race and ethnicity, that expose the constitution and construction of bodies. The crisis in breathing prevents us from presuming the integrity of the body as a unit of analysis. As Annabel L. Kim observes, "The ease with which *body* takes a definite article—The Body—is a testament to how naturalized and seemingly self-evident its existence as a thing is, and to how we take for granted the body's epistemic accessibility and a certain democratization of experience (the body—now here's something that everyone has and experiences)."[67] Kim sheds light on the ironic, silent agreement behind uses of The Body in cultural criticism: we tend to ignore that our concept for real experience—experience that, we somehow believe, resists abstraction or aggregation—presumes a universal metaphysics. Kim's call for a defetishization of The Body appears especially suited to the study of respiration, a process that reveals bodies as contingent, constituted by exchanges and transactions. *Breathing Aesthetics* takes up Kim's challenge and locates its examination of gendered and raced embodiment and experience in the flows and frictions between environmental and disability studies. I superimpose these heuristics to chart what I call *ecologies of the particular*: accounts of respiration that move across scales, assessing the broad impact of environmental harm without minimizing or universalizing the experiences of people living with respiratory disorders.

The notion that bodies are epiphenomenal to the atmospheres they breathe goes by many names in environmental studies and the life sciences. The cultural geographer Derek P. McCormack calls "envelopment" the emergence of forms of life out of atmospheres, those elemental space-times that are simultaneously affective and meteorological. Envelopment corresponds to "the process of partial enclosure through which a difference within and between bodies immersed in atmospheres is generated, a difference sufficient to allow for a relation of mediation to occur."[68] McCormack's account of envelopment approximates what Gilbert Simondon, in his philosophy of ontogenesis, names "individuation." According to Simondon, the individual is but one phase of the metastable, nondyadic individual-milieu couple.[69] As Jason Read notes, noncoinciding individuations take place on multiple scales at once: collective individuations coexist with physical and psychic individuations.[70] In a logic of intensification, we undergo individuation by inhaling and exhaling the atmospheres we occupy. We become ourselves, if you will, by incorporating a milieu into which we are also pouring ourselves. Both epitomized by breathing, the concepts of envelopment and individuation show that corporeality is always "transcorporeality," Stacy Alaimo's term for the constitution of human bodies' materiality by the more-than-human world.[71]

Disability studies, too, regards bodies—and bodily normativity and nonnormativity—as, among other things, the product of environments. It has become customary to sort through disability discourses based on the model they ratify: either a medical model, treating bodies as the loci of disability, or a social one, pathologizing the built environments that disable individuals and, for that reason, necessitate intervention in the form of social justice advocacy. Tobin Siebers proposes, as an intermediary between these competing models, the "theory of complex embodiment," which "raises awareness of the effects of disabling environments on people's lived experience of the body, but . . . emphasizes as well that some factors affecting disability, such as chronic pain, secondary health effects, and aging, derive from the body."[72] While it may read as common sense, this theory makes an important intervention by formulating disability as mediation—a relation between bodies and environments. Such insight proves illuminating in the case of respiratory afflictions like asthma, allergy, and cystic fibrosis, all of which are tied to genetic factors but are exacerbated by environmental factors. Kenner contends that the asthma and allergy epidemics ought to be addressed alongside climate crisis, for higher asthma and allergy rates mean that more people will be acutely affected by extreme weather events as well as long, intense allergy seasons.[73]

While environmental and disability studies have both elaborated paradigms that conceive of embodiment and experience as epiphenomenal to a mediation of which breathing is exemplary, these critical projects are not exactly congruent. Environmental illness, for instance, reveals a certain chasm between ecological and disability logics. Disability studies at least somewhat departs from medical pathologies to activate an identity politics whose program is to expose and rectify disabling environments. People living with environmental illness, by contrast, may not be granted access in the first place to a pathological realm they may then exit for political reasons. For people with multiple chemical sensitivity (MCS) or idiopathic environmental intolerance (IEI), a syndrome associated with a severe sensitivity to pollutants, medical pathology would mean recognition and relief; it would stabilize causes that appear too environmental, thus slippery and evasive. Studies estimate that 80 percent of persons with MCS/IEI identify as women—though the uneven recognition of the syndrome by medical experts, the variability of symptoms, and a reliance on self-diagnosis complicate the production of statistical data.[74] Because their experience is rarely validated by doctors, people living with MCS/IEI must double as experts, amassing and trading unofficial knowledge about their responses to environmental conditions.

The self-diagnosis questionnaire that opens Dodie Bellamy's essay "When the Sick Rule the World" formalizes just how difficult it is to trace the contours of an environmental illness. Without official pathologies and etiologies to work with, Bellamy sets out to draw connections between a symptom like shortness of breath and such potential causes as exposure to chemicals and toxic metals, low air quality and strong smells in the workplace, mold in the home, and overdue maintenance work on air filters and ducts. I use punctuation, but Bellamy does not. Only a question mark concludes the three-page questionnaire: "have you ever smoked if so for how long have you ever lived with others that smoked if so for how long and how old were you how often do you eat fish what types of fish do you eat?"[75] The historian of science Michelle Murphy argues that the sick building syndrome, a relative of MCS/IEI prevalent in enclosed workplaces, poses a problem postmodern in form: a problem that lacks an essence.[76] Whether or not environmental illnesses have an essence, Bellamy is determined to search for one in the particulate and gaseous. Environmental illness prompts Bellamy to generate forms, such as the breathless questionnaire, for addressing injury outside of the (admittedly limited and ambivalent) comforts of pathology and identity afforded by the rubric of disability.

Todd Haynes's independent film *Safe*, which narrates the deterioration of Carol White's (Julianne Moore) health as she comes to terms with what is likely MCS/IEI, hoards symptoms and potential remedies with a maximalism that matches Bellamy's. Carol exhibits hypohidrosis or low sweating; she faints near cans of indoor paint and cleaning supplies; she has an asthma attack while driving through fumes; she feels run-down; she's stressed out and tired; her nose bleeds while she's getting a perm; she has a headache; she convulses and vomits after hugging her husband, who has just sprayed aerosol deodorant; she can't sleep because of "the air, the smell"; she has skin rashes; she's feeling under the weather; she has a panic attack and wheezes after eating ice cream; she forgets where she is; her mouth swells during an allergy test; she coughs; she has a seizure; she feels dizzy on an airplane; she sobs; she has trouble expressing her feelings; she's nauseous. Carol tries out an array of healing protocols, first in Southern California's San Fernando Valley, where she resides, then at Wrenwood, a zero-chemical rehab facility outside of Albuquerque, New Mexico. She adopts an all-fruit diet; ingests unspecified pills; "slows down a little"; stays in bed; attends support group meetings; creates an oasis conducive to air quality control; undergoes homeopathic treatment; controls her "toxic load"; fasts; carries an oxygen tank; "gives herself to love"; and "just breathes." Breathing suffuses both Carol's symptomatology and her treatment plans. It's the problem and, maybe, part of the solution. Even though Carol struggles to ascertain her illness's causes, her racial and class privilege—not so subtly underscored by her last name—grant her access to a costly treatment facility. In one early scene where cinematographer Alex Nepomniaschy's camera monitors her irregular breathing, Carol occupies the center of a frame whose background features Latinx domestic workers and house painters (figure I.1). Their bodies are cropped by the kitchen bar, but we know from a prior shot that they are directly manipulating noxious chemicals (figure I.2). As Alaimo and Nicole Seymour have separately noted, *Safe* invites us to notice whose strained breathing qualifies as a problem, and whose, were it in focus, might be dismissed as an ordinary effect of racially stratified work cultures.[77]

Safe's climactic scene dramatizes the imperfect alignment of environmental and disability rhetorics. Through Haynes's lens, MCS/IEI, which a poster visible in one shot names an "allergy to the twentieth century," partially allegorizes the fear of contagion prevalent during the HIV/AIDS crisis. *Safe* stages the HIV/AIDS moral panic's worst nightmare: the infiltration and dissolution of white heterosexual domesticity by an overpowering threat. At Wrenwood, a worn-down Carol brings MCS/IEI and HIV/AIDS together in a birthday speech delivered in a high-pitched voice and with erratic gesticulation: "I don't know what I'm saying, just that I really hated myself before I came here. So, I'm trying to see myself, hopefully, more as I am, more positive, like, seeing the plusses. Like, I think it's slowly opening up, now, people's minds, like, educating, and . . . AIDS . . . and . . . other types of diseases. And it *is* a disease because it's *out there*, and we just have to be more aware of it. People. More aware of it. And even ourselves. Like, reading labels and going into buildings and stuff." In Carol's address, met with blank stares, MCS/IEI and HIV/AIDS cohabit uneasily. Carol's juxtaposition of MCS/IEI with a medically recognized virus/syndrome and her attempt to derive a political statement from this juxtaposition occasion an epistemic crisis and the collapse of speech. The recurrence of "like" signals demonstration and exemplification, but what counts as argument or evidence is unclear. Breathy hesitations and false starts are corollaries of Carol's effort to make sense of an affliction that is "out there," "in the air"—an affliction that makes itself known through her breathing but eludes her as a marker of identity and an object of pedagogical and political discourse.

The methodological challenge of thinking *disability* in concert with *environment* is perhaps best summed up by Sarah Jaquette Ray and Jay Sibara. An "eco-crip theory," they show, would have to reconcile the widespread effects of environmental collapse with models of disability that, even when they account for the environment's role in constructing disability, tend to center individuals who identify or are identified as disabled.[78] Jasbir Puar offers one answer to this problem by supplementing the rubric of disability with debility and capacity. Debility, Puar explains, has to do with "the slow wearing down of populations instead of the event of becoming disabled."[79] In a case study on debility that

Figures I.1 and I.2. Stills from *Safe* (1995), directed by Todd Haynes. Criterion Collection.

illustrates the differential distribution of harm along ethnic and racial lines, Puar contends that the West Bank is controlled largely through checkpoints and "the Gaza Strip . . . suffocated through choke points" that obstruct the course of the workday and "[slow] down . . . Palestinian life."[80] Puar states that "the capacity to asphyxiate is not a metaphor," but it may be more accurate to say that choking evidences literal and figurative debility: a reduction in animation or life force as well as a hindered capacity to be mobile and earn a living.[81]

In a review of Puar's *The Right to Maim: Debility, Capacity, Disability* (2017), David T. Mitchell and Sharon L. Snyder contest Puar's critique of disability activism's demand for recognition from a state that debilitates subordinated populations through military occupation. Mitchell and Snyder observe that disability activism's and disability studies' attention to the ways "impairment disqualifies an individual from access to common participation in a multitude of activities" relays, rather than "a fetishization of citizenship," a commitment to uncovering "how expectations of physical, psychological, and sensory capacities are unexpectedly grounded in the bedrock definition of participatory democracy."[82] Yet Mitchell and Snyder's polemical claim that "debility studies might be ultimately understood as disability studies without disability" exaggerates Puar's stance.[83] Puar insists that the notion of debility does not diffuse or departicularize disability. Neither does it imply that everyone is, to some extent, disabled. Disability, debility, and capacity exist in tension, at times convergent and at times divergent. Mitchell and Snyder's criticism betrays a reluctance to evaluate disability studies' reliance on individualistic models of impairment that, as Ray and Sibara have noticed, are not calibrated for environmental morbidity and lethality, the effects of which are measurable on the population scale.

Some of the writers, filmmakers, and artists featured in *Breathing Aesthetics* identify as disabled; others don't. Others still might identify as disabled but haven't made this identity public. Throughout this book, I maintain not only that it's possible to uphold debility as a category of inquiry without detriment to disability but that the contemporary crisis in breathing demands it. A nexus where life is seized and manipulated, breathing marks the gray zone between individual and mass impairment where the boundary between disability and debility is perpetually negotiated. By approaching disability and debility as mutually constitutive, I map out ecologies of the particular. Although this phrase may appear pleonastic—ecology, a relation of interconnection and interdependence, inevitably asks us to articulate the particular vis-à-vis the general—the repetition is valuable. As a methodological principle, an ecology of the particular resists the idea that toxification and other environmental calamities homogenize, and as such departicularize, experience. An ecology of the particular can accommodate two or more truths: while air and breath channel bio- and necropolitical regimes that compromise the vitality of entire populations and ecosystems, it is also the case that the impact of these regimes is unevenly distributed and registered with particular acuity by marginalized individuals, including persons with disabilities.

Breathing Aesthetics

The act of breathing is omnipresent. And, as I've argued, respiration at once materializes and figures the uneven distribution of risk in the late twentieth and early twenty-first centuries. So how could there not be an aesthetics of breathing? Perhaps less obvious is the perimeter of a breathing aesthetics—what objects count as exemplary of something as ubiquitous as respiration. Today's aesthetics of breathing ratifies a gradual disentanglement of breath from universal experience within philosophy and theory. For the Stoics, *pneuma* designated a universal breath or life force that in its highest form constituted the psyche or soul. *Qi*, in Taoism, and *prana*, in Hinduism, label vital forces that flow through bodies and are manifest in respiration. Throughout scientific modernity, as human beings have, in Steven Connor's words, "taken to the air," breathing has come to be understood as an index of geographically and historically specific conditions.[84] For example, Tobias Menely deciphers traces of Anthropocene thinking, or of human beings' consciousness of their status as a geological force, in the atmospheric lexica of Thomas Hobbes, Karl Marx, Walter Benjamin, and Theodor Adorno. These figures, for whom atmospheres could no longer accommodate fantasies of unlimited replenishment, prompt us to comprehend the "catastrophe of the present" as an "accretion of the past, a thickening of the air."[85] The genealogy of "Anthropocene air" traced by Menely answers, for the most part proleptically, Gaston Bachelard's 1943 call for a "*physiologie aérienne*" (aerial physiology) that accounts for the relation between breathing beings and the "*douceur et violence, pureté et délire*" (softness and violence, purity and madness) of the wind.[86]

Luce Irigaray has lamented that Western philosophy's engagements with breath and air have been too few and far between, and that its metaphysics has in fact been predicated on elemental repression. Martin Heidegger, she contends, flattens the air-filled "*ouvert*" (open or clearing) that makes possible a metaphysics of presence.[87] Since the 1980s, Irigaray has regularly swapped the "interval," her concept for a force of life irreducible to the two or more individuals who keep it alive, with the "*souffle*" (breath or blow). Remedying the interval's stagnant connotation, breath heralds the emergence of new forms of life that are embodied but not possessed.[88] To cultivate breath is to usher in a world where "words are ethereal [or aerial]" and "the sensible remains sweet and carnal: living, pulsating."[89] Air is a "fluid density which leaves space for every growth[, m]atter that, not yet divided in itself, permits sharing."[90] It is as, among other things, a corrective to Emmanuel Lévinas's philosophy that Irigaray designs a style of relation not premised on facial recognition. But while Lévinas is best known for his ethics of the face-to-face encounter, his "pneumatism" conceives of breath, specifically the instant of suspension between inhalation and exhalation, as something of a temporal counterpart to the interval that Irigaray figures in spatial terms.[91] In the breathlessness that both unites and separates breathing in and out, we encounter otherness and find ourselves in the realm of ethics.[92] Following Lévinas, Lenart Škof elaborates a philosophy of the "mesocosmic breath"—a breath that is endowed with spiritual properties and accommodates an "ethics of otherness . . . that will open up new grounds for future exchanges of *mild* gestures, such as compassion, patience and care."[93] With Petri Berndtson, Škof has edited a volume announcing a "new respiratory philosophy" of relation and encounter, one that promises to account for the uneven availability of breathable air.[94]

Inspiration provides a starting point for determining what distinguishes an aesthetics of breathing from a philosophy of breathing, which is to say what constitutes a breathing aesthetics beyond a set of thematic or ethical concerns. Theories of inspiration accredit aesthetic works to a life force breathed into, then breathed out by, artists.[95] The object of inspiration has evolved from a divine alterity that overtakes the subject (for Plato, in his musings on the Greek *enthousiasmos*), to an external force that kindles a potential already located in the subject (for Percy Bysshe Shelley), to a vector that moves poets, as mystics or prophets, beyond their historical conditions (for Allen Ginsberg, whose transcendentalism was inflected by New Age beliefs).[96] By the 1950s and 1960s, the poetic avant-garde pushed the inspiration concept one step further by taking an interest in the ways breathing's physiology concretely shaped meaning and syntax. The urtext of what Nathaniel Mackey, in the essay "Breath and Precarity," calls the "pneumatic turn" is Black Mountain poet Charles Olson's 1950 manifesto, "Projective Verse."[97] In this manifesto, Olson calls for a poetry that magnifies the "possibilities of breath, of the breathing of the man [*sic*] who writes as well as of his [*sic*] listenings," in order for verse to catch up to the present.[98] Within this model, poems are formal extensions of the energy that animates poets.[99] Accordingly, poetic breath might signal a vitality in jeopardy. Mackey provides, as an exemplar of compromised vitality's rhythmic manifestation, Robert Creeley's writing and reading styles: "Creeley's emphatic, signature pause following lines as short as one or two words, one or two syllables even, his veritable pronunciation of each and every line break, conveyed a trepidatious, anxious apprehensiveness. His insistent, asthmatic employment of caesura, his halting, hesitant delivery . . . accorded with a radical loss of assurance regarding such basic amenities and givens as identity, relationship, knowledge, perception and language."[100] "Projective Verse" coincided with poetry's evolution into a performing art; as Christopher Grobe writes, the poetry reading yoked the *I* "more tightly than ever to its living, breathing referent."[101] Mackey compares marshaling poetic breath to playing wind instruments. Circular breathing, a technique that jazz players in particular must acquire to produce a continuous tone, enables Mackey to move between midcentury breath poetics and a contemporary moment wherein asphyxia has imposed itself as a defining aspect of Black life.[102] Mackey's tentative juxtaposition of these two strikingly different contexts suggests that breath, as an index of endangered vitality, communicates individual crises as well as structural ones.[103] This said, poets of Black precarity might not have the luxury of opting into a breath poetics; their verse is inevitably, in Fred Moten's words, "preoccupied / with breathing."[104]

The traditions just surveyed imply that poetry has a privileged access to breath. And yet scholars of literary fiction, film, and even video game also assume, often with convincing examples in hand, that theirs is the respiratory form or medium par excellence. In a study of respiratory afflictions in French fiction, François-Bernard Michel supplies a dogmatic formula for the relation between the author's breathing and breath as literary content or form. Michel's injective functions are unequivocal: Raymond Queneau gave life to asthmatic characters because he was allergic to grass pollen; Marcel Proust exhibited a literary sensitivity to the weather because he suffered from asthma.[105] Michel insists on the *"unicité du symptôme respiratoire"* (unicity of the respiratory symptom): literary eruptions of undermined breathing, he believes, always refer to the inflammation or obstruction of the author's airways.[106] Michel overstates the synchrony between an author's respiration and breathing as it manifests on the page, and other critics have taken a less deterministic approach to the emergence of respiratory symptoms in fiction. In a pair of judicious studies of the respiratory geopolitics of postcolonial novels, Arthur Rose argues that the way characters breathe reveals two negotiations: an atmospheric one (characters, for instance, register the impact of asbestos exposure in shipbuilding and shipwrecking episodes) and a generic one (literary genres entail distinct affective conventions as well as breathing conventions).[107]

The insight that generic conventions include styles and modes of breathing impels screen studies' engagement with breath. For David Scott Diffrient, the still-breathing bodies of actors playing dead disclose one of horror cinema's paradoxes: that those who are tasked with maintaining the artifice of fictional death almost inevitably betray it.[108] Horror cinema's respiratory tropes are easily recognizable; threatened characters hold their breath to avoid detection or run out of breath in an attempt to escape. Linda Williams has identified horror as one of three "body genres"—the other two being melodrama and pornography—wherein excess or grossness urges bodily reactions on the part of spectators.[109] Visually, this excess exudes from spasmic bodies beside themselves with terror, despair, or pleasure. Aurally, excess comes across in "inarticulate cries" and sobs.[110] Although Williams doesn't mention it, breathing constitutes a prime channel for these sensationalized disarticulations and inarticulations. According to Williams, the potency of the "spectacle of a body caught in the grip of intense sensation or emotion" is measured by the spectators' impulse to partake in the excess and mimic the characters' expression.[111] It is no surprise that theorists of breath in screen cultures such as Davina Quinlivan have concerned themselves with the interplay between on- and off-screen breathing.[112] By attuning themselves to the distress or elation of characters, spectators might reproduce, intentionally or not, the breathing they witness. Or a more sinuous mimetic circuit might develop. As Ian Bryce Jones contends, respiratory interpellations by video game interfaces aren't always met with compliance on the part of players, inasmuch as some games thematize or incorporate into their very mechanics the potential disobedience of rogue breathers.[113]

My point in using the generic label *breathing aesthetics* is that respiration is not the exclusive dominion of poetry or fiction, of film or video game. This isn't to say that all art exists on the same plane in this study. The respiratory tactics and strategies for living through precarity inventoried in this book are not only historically, culturally, and environmentally situated but also genre- and medium-specific. Works, like *DICTEE*, *LETTERRS*, and *Safe*, that fall under the breathing aesthetics header meet two criteria: first, they exhibit an attunement of content and form to respiration (though not necessarily the artist's breathing or the spectator's); and second, they relay a conceptual engagement with the sociopolitical and environmental dynamics mediated by breathing.

The aesthetics of breathing provides an opportunity to review the assumptions that inform ecocritical approaches to art. Some ecocritics assess the worth of aesthetic objects based on their ability to rouse environmental awareness or consciousness. Ursula K. Heise and Lawrence Buell, for example, separately underscore the role of literature and cinema in helping individuals and groups to become aware of large-scale ecological shifts and to project an environmentalist agenda onto a planetary canvas.[114] Likewise, Zhang offers that "sensitizing ourselves to the affective climates around us allows us to be more deliberate about creating the kinds of atmospheres amid which we want to live."[115] This scholarship accomplishes the important task of highlighting the ways art makes environmental challenges immediate and promotes sound behavior. At the same time, we should not overestimate the capacity of readers or spectators exposed to the inextricability of vitality and morbidity relayed by the aesthetics of breathing to step out into the world and transform it through sheer force of will. It would require a leap of faith to believe that all reactions to this aesthetics—from exhaustion to disorientation, to panic, to titillation—fulfill a civic purpose.[116] Across *Breathing Aesthetics*, I consider awareness and consciousness from a technical standpoint (witnessing someone's labored breathing makes me aware or conscious of mine) without sublimating them into civic or moral positions. In doing so, I account for a range of aesthetic responses not so easily subsumed under such qualities as being more conscious or being more deliberate.

Readers will notice the occasional commixing of literal and figurative breathing as well as intentional and unintentional breathlessness in both the art I showcase and my analysis. Some instances of mediation covered in *Breathing Aesthetics* organize or disorganize actual respiration. Others manage the range of figurative meanings that respiration takes on. Others still set out to do both, tweaking breath's figurative work in hopes of producing a corporeal effect. Due to its ubiquity and its importance to scientific and cultural conceptions of life, breathing constitutes an especially busy intersection in the traffic between the literal and the figurative. Even though I regularly differentiate between breathing as experience, form, and symbol, the direction of this traffic isn't always clear, nor is it always intuitive. What looks to me like a symbolic engagement with breath might not feel like an abstraction to its originator. For instance, in Ana Mendieta's film work, brought up in chapter 1, an ostensibly intentional performance of difficult breathing symbolizing historical trauma might just as well be a slight accentuation of a respiratory difficulty that the artist, whether or not she was present to it, would have experienced as an unintentional symptom of such trauma. In any case, even deliberately erratic respiration can cause confusion and disorganization that exceed what an artist is capable of managing. While I acknowledge that there exists a distinction between not being able to breathe and performing not being able to breathe, I, as a spectator and a critic, am not always in a position to locate this distinction with accuracy. The same can be said of some of the individuals who turn breathing into (an) art.

Another question pertaining to intention deserves to be addressed: whether the writers and artists assembled in this study understand themselves to be contributing to a respiratory archive. The title of this book does not refer to a unified movement or program, and in my curation I oscillate between compiling works intended to address a contemporary crisis in breathing (for example, the practices of respiratory notation in chapter 2) and exposing the ways works not generally associated with respiration also address this crisis (the ceremonial poetry and fiction of healing in chapter 3, or the speculative city writing in chapter 4). The purpose of the case studies is to track how a number of works differently articulate the relation between respiration and art and, consequently, redefine the very idea of an aesthetics of breathing.

To feel out the contours of the aesthetics of respiration and start building this book's archive, I now turn to Fred Wah's *Breathin' My Name with a Sigh* (1981). This is a book of poetry, but one that is not tethered to the program laid out by midcentury breath poetics. Wah's work is indicative of a minoritarian formation of the aesthetics of breathing proper to the crisis in the reproduction of life that has raged since the last decades of the twentieth century. *Breathin' My Name with a Sigh* contains untitled poems that range from short onomatopoeic couplets to plumper stanzas verging on prose poetry. The preface offers a statement on the book's ontology:

> This is a book of remembering. I am trying to clarify what the language carries for me, the ontogeny. Somehow a selection of the information of a life is made and placed in such a way as to allow it to generate a truth otherwise impossible to locate. But the book is a "draft," since each incision (the beachwood, bookwood, and so runes, etc.) changes the whole thing it is part of. To select out a pattern of things having to do with any of it has to do with all of it. One of my teachers told me "ontogeny recapitulates phylogeny" and that makes more sense to me now.[117]

The nineteenth-century German biologist and zoologist Ernst Haeckel is generally credited for the phrase "ontogeny recapitulates phylogeny." The development of an individual organism, the principle goes, expresses the intermediate forms of its ancestors throughout evolution.

Environmental studies customarily treats breath as accretive.[118] Each breath recapitulates the long history of respiration, and photosynthesis, and the wind; this is one, not strictly anatomical, way ontogeny recapitulates phylogeny. In the collection's inaugural poem, "breathin'," with an *n apostrophe* figures an open-ended synthesis:

I like the purity of all things seen
through the accumulation of thrust
forward between the vehicle
container maybe/or "thing" called body
because time seems to be only *it* appears
to look into the green mountain valleys
or through them to the rivers & nutrient creeks
where was never the problem animal is
I still have a name "breathin' it
with a sigh"[119]

"The accumulation of thrust / forward" takes place between the "vehicle / container" "or 'thing' called body" and—and what? The prepositional phrase is incomplete. The poet rushes, maybe obsessively, maybe distractedly, to musings on time, landscapes, and animals. We are left assuming that the accumulation takes place between *body* and *not-body*. One word for this mediation is *breathing*. And indeed, breathing shows up in the penultimate line, at the end of processes of accumulation—first of thrust, then of digressive clauses.

Wah most often uses *to breathe* as a transitive verb; in the above poem, for instance, the speaker breathes his name with a sigh. It's in another poem on naming that Wah's musings on recapitulation most obviously coalesce into a concept of genealogical breathing. The poem opens with a figure of accumulation, "the buildup":

the buildup
how I listen to myself make it
"hold on"
so that the day remains open
the next collision in the light
and catch up to the breath
breathing somewhere
                        the air

as it comes out ahead of me
wah^h,   wah^h[120]

This poem accrues momentum to culminate with a performance, rather than a description, of the poet's act of breathing his name with a sigh. The ending can be read as two lines ("h h / wah wah") or more cogently as a single, winding line ("wah—h, wah—h"). Each suspended *h* recalls the elevation of the shoulders that amplifies sighing. The suspension also evokes superscripts or mathematical exponents. In this sense, each sigh is prolonged. When the notation reappears a few pages later, Wah's name has turned into the very sigh that previously accompanied it:

$$wuh^{h121}$$

From "wah" to "wuh," the tongue, at first slightly flattened and pulled toward the back of the mouth, relaxes. The change in vowel occasions a buccal release. Wah's poetry resides in the tension between holding on and letting go, between catching up to the breath and sighing. The book's title, *Breathin' My Name with a Sigh*, predicates the poet's exhale on the resilience of those who, well before him, bore the name "Wah." The poet's breath draws on a vitality sustained through experiences of displacement, Wah's ancestors having moved from China, Ireland, Scotland, and Scandinavian countries to Saskatchewan, Canada.[122] The intergenerational connection manifested by breath is contingent and provisional; as the preface notes, any change to the book would "[change] the whole thing it is part of."[123] Wah's genealogical breathing hints at an ecology of the particular: it inhibits possible interpretations of the recapitulation of phylogeny by ontogeny as delineating an even field of experience. Moreover, the triumph that we, as readers, might be tempted to project onto a poetics of resilience is deflated by the affectively ambivalent sigh—a sigh that might express exhaustion, exasperation, relief, or mourning. Vitality and morbidity collide in the poet's "breathin'," an accumulation of thrust synthesized by a decelerative sigh.

Breathin' My Name with a Sigh models a respiratory subjectivity: the poet's identity, indeed his very name, emerges through a sigh. Wah also relies on breath to foster modes of relation between the living and their ancestors that are informed by principles of inheritance, dependence, and contingency. Structured by the two processes modeled by Wah, *Breathing Aesthetics* sketches the development of respiratory subjectivities and the development of respiratory politics.

Aerial View

Breathing Aesthetics joins a humanistic corpus on breath that grew noticeably in the demi-decade over which the following chapters were written. The medical humanities' examination of breath, on display in Rebecca Oxley and Andrew Russell's June 2020 issue of *Body and Society*, titled "Interdisciplinary Perspectives on Breath, Body and World," tends to assume an analogy between everyday and scholarly attitudes toward respiration: this life-giving and life-sustaining process is often taken for granted, and it has likewise been overlooked as a topic of research.[124] This premise weaves into every argument a normative, meta-theoretical declaration: that respiration deserves our attention and is a worthy object of inquiry.[125] The impulse to validate the "unusual research concern" that is breath also animates Magdalena Górska's *Breathing Matters: Feminist Intersectional Politics of Struggle* (2016)—but Górska's contribution to feminist science studies goes further, showing what we stand to gain from attuning ourselves to breathing, namely, an appreciation of its function as an "ethical and political force for feminist political struggle."[126] I am indebted to the turns to respiration within the medical humanities and feminist science studies, which have yielded, respectively, a relational model of embodiment and a politics of experience exceeding sexual politics in the strict sense. Yet I refrain from overstating either breathing's idiosyncrasy or its novelty as an object of study. Following the lead of such theorists of the ordinary as Kathleen Stewart and Berlant, I operate on the assumption that intensities that never quite rise to the status of event might reveal just as much about contemporary crisis as events that occupy a properly dramatic register.[127] What is more, the equation between ordinary inattention to breath and a general silence around the topic risks concealing rich histories of respiratory research in scholarly and artistic disciplines. Traditions from psychoanalysis to performance have produced the conditions that enable scholars like Górska to speculate a radical ethics or politics of breath, and it is one aim of *Breathing Aesthetics* to excavate these traditions.

The encounter with breath staged in this book is more formal than those of the medical humanities and feminist science studies. Stefanie Heine attends to the formalization of respiratory sounds and rhythms in the meticulous *Poetics of Breathing: Modern Literature's Syncope* (2021). Heine describes how various twentieth-century writers attuned their practices to breath and, in doing so, reflected on the relation between corporeality, expressivity, and mediality.[128] Whereas Heine, in focusing on breath as a compositional principle or a precondition for writing, expands projectivism beyond the terms and corpus laid out by Olson, I am interested in what art does with and to breathing, specifically in how aesthetic mediation makes breathing available as a resource for living through crisis. In the pamphlet *Breathing: Chaos and Poetry* (2018), Franco "Bifo" Berardi turns to poetry to picture a collective release from such crisis. But across the book, both poetry and respiration lose their meaning: the former comes to designate a tension between chaos and harmony that the author spots everywhere except, it turns out, in poems; the latter is reduced to an attunement to a "vibration of the cosmos" compromised under finance capitalism.[129] So vaguely defined, respiratory poetry is but a promise of transcendence—an autonomous realm that, if we are to trust Berardi, enables us to escape present conditions. The genre- and medium-specific analysis of *Breathing Aesthetics* is more pragmatic. The aesthetics of respiration is no antidote to the crisis of breathing. Or, if it is to be considered an antidote, it should also, per the logic of the *pharmakon*, be considered a poison. Respiratory tactics and strategies do not chart an easy way out of precarity, insofar as breathing makes survival and depletion inextricable—not to mention that depletion may feel like survival, and survival like depletion. "Seen not as an empty virtual space but as particular," Jennifer Scappettone remarks, "air makes for a democracy of harm that has had artists and authors strategizing remedies for generations—remedies that are always necessarily incomplete."[130]

Breathing Aesthetics' closest affiliates—an aspirational statement, to be sure—may be Crawley's *Blackpentecostal Breath: The Aesthetics of Possibility* (2016) and Hsu's *The Smell of Risk: Environmental Disparities and Olfactory Aesthetics* (2020), two monographs that map out respiration's uneven geographies. Like Crawley, I see aesthetic mediation as a process that reveals and makes use of breathing's contradictions, affirming the possibility of minoritarian life from its conditions of impossibility.[131] And like Hsu, I take a comparative approach as I track the management of respiratory morbidity across media, environmental, and cultural contexts.[132]

Five chapters and a coda follow this introduction. The first two chapters form a diptych on breathing subjectivity. Chapter 1, "Breathing against Nature," describes respiration as a mode of spectatorship in the same class as watching and listening. Developed in the 1970s and 1980s, elemental media such as Ana Mendieta's earth-body sculpture and Amy Greenfield's cinema dance invite spectators to process embodiment as epiphenomenal to environments that are both sustaining and depleting. The artists make breathing the site of postpastoral experience, a dysphoric encounter with pastoral ideals of natural vitality and purity. Whereas in the first chapter being shocked or eased into a consciousness of breathing constitutes a disorganizing event, the second chapter, "Aesthetic Self-Medication (Three Regimens)," asks how writers and artists find order amid chaos by channeling their conscious breathing toward a more or less stable sense of self. Surveying the queer life writing and performance of Dodie Bellamy, CAConrad, and Bob Flanagan and Sheree Rose, I argue that therapeutic notations of breathing, even incoherent or disorganized breathing, achieve aesthetic self-medication: they structure the experience of crises ranging from chronic illness to environmental collapse.

The third and fourth chapters diagram respiratory politics. Chapter 3, "Feminist Breathing," further probes therapeutic approaches to respiration by tracing a genealogy of feminist breathing since the 1970s. Deviating from narratives of decline that locate in that decade the end of breathing as a means of feminist socialization and politicization, this chapter demonstrates that Indigenous and Black feminisms have continuously relied on respiratory rituals as tactics or strategies for living through the foreclosure of political presents and futures. Linda Hogan's ceremonial poetry and Toni Cade Bambara's fiction on healing exemplify a feminist breathing that enmeshes restoration and risk to destabilize the wholeness or wellness it affords. The fourth chapter, "Smog Sensing," maps out the ethics and politics of opacity in multimodal works by Renee Gladman, in particular a cycle of speculative novels set in the city-state of Ravicka. In a context where the racial and sexual identity of characters is as inscrutable as the smog-filled city in which they dwell, relations are organized by symptomatic breathing, an interpretive attitude that consists in learning the limits of what is graspable about embodiment and experience. While chapter 3 surveys the political possibilities of synchronized breathing, chapter 4 approaches respiratory asynchrony as a resource in itself.

The fifth chapter, "Death in the Form of Life," turns to the discourses of the nonviolent last breath that circulate in Frederick Wiseman's and Allan King's cinema vérité. I lay out a paradox between, on the one hand, the limited consciousness and responsiveness that typify the good death in the era of life support and palliative care and, on the other, the dying subject imagined by witnesses: a subject who in the event of the last breath is present enough to "leave peacefully," one who returns to the scene of sociality only to subtract themself from it. The fantasy that in the last breath the dying individual encounters finitude on their own terms fulfills a social function, helping survivors to manage their own respiratory contingency—to keep breathing, with loss.

Like all genealogical inquiries into how the present became itself, this book contains the traces of alternative, unrealized presents—presents that, throughout, I seek to activate. Jayne Elizabeth Lewis writes, in a study of literature in the long eighteenth century, that air and "atmosphere cannot be stood outside of, so [they] can never be completely objectified, fixed, or, as a result, intellectually possessed."[133] Lewis is right that air, atmosphere, and breath are elusive objects of inquiry. However, more than two centuries after the period that concerns Lewis, air and breath appear, in at least some ways, to have been seized. Their pollution, weaponization, and monetization have turned them into dispositifs of state control and violence. It's also the case that, under such conditions, breathing has become a minoritarian aesthetic and political vernacular in its own right.

The figures who populate this book have had to come to terms with breathlessness—with what it means and what it does. Breathlessness is a modality of breathing, not its negation. My contention in *Breathing Aesthetics* isn't, then, that breathlessness ought to be eradicated. Not all respiratory interruptions feel like injury or oppression, and it may be elating to have our breath taken away or to encounter someone or something breathtaking. Breathlessness, in short, may be life-giving and life-sustaining. Whereas Achille Mbembe, in the context of the COVID-19 pandemic, calls for a "universal right to breathe" and condemns "everything that fundamentally attacks the respiratory tract, everything that, in the long reign of capitalism, has constrained entire segments of the world population, entire races, to a difficult, panting breath and life of oppression," I do not believe it is logical, or especially productive, to speculate some easy, egalitarian breathing that would solve and exist apart from respiratory constraints.[134] Breath, even defined as "that which is both ungrounded and our common ground" or "that which we hold in common," mediates histories of asphyxiation.[135] What I'm after in *Breathing Aesthetics* is an imaginary that accommodates the fullness of breathing and makes room for a range of *benign respiratory variations*, a term I take up in the coda. In the chapters that follow, I assemble a repertoire of responses to crisis so that we may imagine breathing, indeed breathlessness, as greater than an occupational hazard of contemporary life.

Breathing against Nature

The music video for "Breathing," a single from British singer-songwriter Kate Bush's album *Never for Ever*, opens with a close-up of the artist.[1] She sports big hair, gold eye shadow, and cranberry lipstick: the year is 1980. She lip-syncs to the track:

Breathing
Breathing my mother in
Breathing my beloved in
Breathing, Breathing her nicotine, breathing
Breathing the fall out-in, out-in, out-in, out-in, out-in.

In the video, Bush moves back and forth, drawing and expelling air (figures 1.1 and 1.2).

Sung from the perspective of a fetus frightened by nuclear fallout, "Breathing" echoes antiabortion rhetoric. I listen to Bush's antenatal voice, emblematic of a vulnerability to radiation, and hear Lauren Berlant's well-known claim that "in the process of collapsing the political and the personal into a world of public intimacy, a nation made for adult citizens has been replaced by one imagined for fetuses and children."[2] The fetus in "Breathing" is white—a feature, Mel Y. Chen notes, of ideals of purity and innocence within Western imaginaries of toxicity.[3] Bush's song and video corroborate Rebekah Sheldon's assertion that

Figures 1.1 and 1.2. **Stills from the official music video for Kate Bush's "Breathing" (1980). EMI Records.**

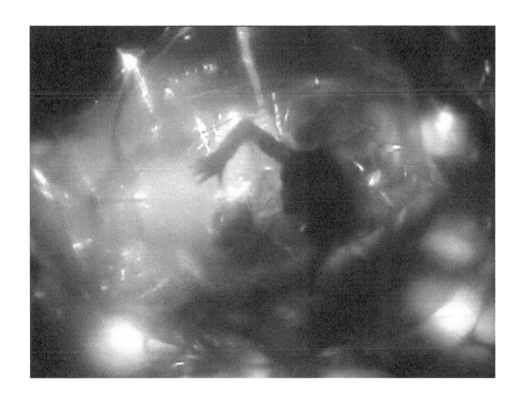

apocalypticism has figured the child, in this case the child-to-be, as a vital resource worthy of protection.[4] In "Breathing," the fetus takes on breath and air's symbolic work as life-giving and life-sustaining resources when those appear irremediably jeopardized:

We've lost our chance
We're the first and the last
After the blast
Chips of Plutonium are twinkling in every lung.

And yet, fetal ventriloquism in "Breathing" serves an antireproductive stance. Being made to breathe in an unbreathable world comes across as coercive. Two lines from the first verse, "I've been out before / But this time it's much safer in," posit the womb as a refuge from the world, but we must note the anachronism. How could the fetus have been out before? Borne by a breathing being, the fetus is inevitably, as Stacy Alaimo would put it, "embedded in, exposed to, and even composed of the very stuff of a rapidly transforming material world."[5] The fetus "goes out" every time the pregnant person breathes in. It may be "much safer in," but nowhere truly counts as inside. In and out don't appear so distinct when a pregnant person inhales nicotine or when radiation passes through their porous skin. In the "Breathing" video, the fetus and the womb are not merely exposed to pollution; they are pollutants. The garment worn by Bush and the large balloon in which she dances are made of plastic, a derivative of petrochemicals. In this gloomy portrayal of gestation, the fetus and the womb constitute metonyms for the industrial pollution that endangers them. *Fetal* is in close proximity to *fatal*. To breathe, first by proxy and then on our own, is to be defined by morbidity—not quite a mortality that delimits biography (we live, then we die) but a morbidity that proves existential and endemic (pre-, peri-, and postnatally, we process death, taking it in and letting it out).

Even in utero, the singer belongs to a respiratory commons held together by a shared if uneven exposure to toxicity. Bush's declaration, "I love my beloved / All and everywhere," anticipates by a quarter century Juliana Spahr's *This Connection of Everyone with Lungs* (2005). In Spahr's ecopoems, of which some stanzas are addressed to the speaker's "beloveds," breathing recapitulates the process through which individuals shape and are in turn shaped by their milieus.[6] Iterative respiration figures the local, national, transnational, and planetary repercussions of the September 11, 2001, attacks and the subsequent wars in Afghanistan and Iraq. "How lovely and how doomed this connection of everyone with lungs," concludes the first of two long poems, evoking respiration's dual operation as sustaining and depleting.[7] In "Breathing," Bush's address eventually morphs into a plea. Near the end of the song, her soprano gets raspier as she and Roy Harper (on backing vocals) intone,

> We are all going to die without
> Leave me something to breathe
> Oh God, please leave us something to breathe
> *What are we going to do without?*
> Life is—.

Breathing and "Breathing" are simultaneously interrupted. We cannot do and will die without something to breathe, tells us a song that ends midbreath.

In the video's final minutes, Bush, no longer confined to the synthetic womb, finds herself in the water and on the land. She and seven other performers experience a nuclear blast. The negative-image effect, in shades of orange and blue, evokes radioactivity. Bush occupies the frame on her own when she utters the song's final line, "Life is—." The artist's image dissolves into a mushroom cloud shown in reverse motion. In a silent epilogue, the performers, dressed in hazmat suits, lounge on the grass. We might be tempted to view the second explosion, the backward one, as a reversal of the first blast. In this reading, the video would be a cautionary tale that returned to a pastoral present of picnics on the grass to warn us against the nuclear threat. But the pastoral before us is a twisted one. Enormous mushrooms exaggerate the mutations and deformations caused by radiation, and the performers' faces are bluish. The performers appear idle as yet another bomb detonates far in the background. Bush, in a leisurely recline, watches the explosion, then slowly turns her face—the only white one in the frame—and gazes near the camera (figures 1.3 and 1.4). Hers is not the facial expression of someone giving spectators a warning. She looks distracted, indifferent. Bored? This epilogue stages what Joseph Masco calls the "nuclear uncanny": the shift in "perceptual space" or sum of "material effects, psychic tension, and sensory confusion" brought about by nuclear warfare.[8] The desensitized performers fail to react to an explosion that is part of everyday life. Whether any one blast is shown in forward or reverse motion, the epilogue suggests, there's no going back to a preatomic era. Radioactive particles are suspended in the air, and we breathe it (out, in, out, in).

Combining total creation with total destruction, nuclear power dominates the imagery of Bush's meditation on the imbrication of life and death. But her name for the condition associated with this imbrication eschews spectacle; it is simply, frighteningly, breathing. How did breathing come to operate, in a 1980 popular song and its accompanying video, as a shorthand for the experience of an

Figures 1.3 and 1.4. Stills from
the official music video for
Kate Bush's "Breathing"
(1980). EMI Records.

environment where life and death don't exist in binary relation? And what role did the pastoral, or a perversion of the pastoral, play in this process? To answer these questions, I turn to the avant-garde practices on which Bush drew. A pop-cultural artifact with wide appeal, the "Breathing" video nevertheless engages experimental traditions in dance and cinema. It was directed by Keith Mac-Millan, whose training combined the visual arts and ballet. MacMillan wasn't solely responsible for the importance of dance and movement to the "Breathing" video; Bush had long collaborated with the choreographer and performer Lindsay Kemp, to whom was dedicated the 1978 song "Moving." This chapter uncovers an avant-garde sensibility at the junction of movement and film. In the latter half of the twentieth century, this sensibility depastoralized breathing, calling into question its status as an eternally and evenly accessible life force.

Two avant-garde artists especially active in the 1970s and 1980s come into focus in this chapter: Ana Mendieta and Amy Greenfield. These artists' works have rarely if ever been shown side by side, but I propose that they are united by their appeal to breathing as a mode of spectatorship in the same class as watching and listening. Through breathing—breathing that is seen, heard, and in turn performed—Mendieta's and Greenfield's spectators process embodiment and experience as environmentally contingent, and environments as historically contingent. Respiratory confrontations with catastrophes past, present, and future amount to an aesthetic experience I term *postpastoral*, one that is haunted by the expiration of the pastoral and its ideals of natural purity and vitality. In these figures' art, as in Bush's "Breathing," soured pastorals cause a dysphoric spectatorial experience that isn't easily assimilable into feel-good ecocritical narratives such as coming to environmental consciousness and becoming environmentally responsible. The main difference between Bush's ruined pastoral and those of Mendieta and Greenfield is iconographic; the latter artists, whose commitments are more explicitly minoritarian, do not have recourse to the symbolic arsenal of sentimental whiteness that characterizes the fetal melancholy of "Breathing."

Whereas the next chapter, the second in a dyad on respiratory models of subject formation, describes aesthetic strategies for intuiting from disordered breathing structures that organize life amid crisis, here I pause to consider the ways art shocks or eases us into a consciousness of breathing in the first place. I employ *consciousness* to refer not to a reified civic or moral position but to something technical: breathing is conscious when it cannot be ignored. Together, chapters 1 and 2 sketch complementary modes of breathing subjectivity: a receptive one, tied to aesthetic experience, and a productive one, tied to artistic creation. The inhale, and the exhale.

Mendieta and Greenfield have elaborated practices that, for the purposes of the present inquiry, I classify as *elemental media*.[9] The artists treat breathing as a medium, a channel through which body and milieu interact. And they make this mediation explicit in intermedia works: earth-body sculptures in Mendieta's case, and cinema dance in Greenfield's.

Born in Havana, Mendieta was sent to the United States through Operation Pedro Pan, a clandestine program that smuggled children out of Cuba at the start of Fidel Castro's regime. Mendieta would not see her mother for five years and her father for eighteen. She and her sister Raquelín alighted first in Florida and then in Iowa, where they were separated and shuttled between foster homes.[10] In 1967 Mendieta enrolled at the University of Iowa, from which she would earn a master of fine arts degree a decade later. At Iowa, she studied with Hans Breder and partook in Fluxus-inspired intermedia workshops.[11] When in 1978 she moved to New York City, Mendieta joined the all-women gallery Artists in Residence (A.I.R.), which welcomed experimental, ephemeral, even unsellable work.[12] At age thirty-six, Mendieta went out the window of the thirty-fourth-floor apartment she shared with her husband, the artist Carl Andre. While her death was ruled a suicide, many believe that Andre pushed her.[13] Mendieta's untimely demise haunts accounts of her life and work. In a superb essay on Mendieta's—and her own—trips to Cuba, Christina A. León writes, "The mystery of Mendieta's death is, for many of us, not a mystery at all. We, those of us who follow her legacy beyond her death, know that the blood poured on any museum which deigns to exhibit Carl Andre carries with it a guilty sentence, even if the law excused murder. We know what happened. The mystery is that business goes about as usual after a massive crime has been committed. The mystery is that a predictable, pathetic, and weak misogyny still rages, and rages all the harder against people of color and of marginalized genders."[14] In retrospect, the proximity of life to death that can be felt across Mendieta's corpus reads as a tragic presage. Mendieta made nearly one hundred films and gathered a massive collection of slides and photographic negatives documenting her ephemeral earth-body sculptures.[15] In her silent films, to which I devote most of my attention in this chapter, Mendieta's body ought to be inferred from her breathing, not the other way around. I glean from this sequence—first breath, then body—a theory of embodiment and experience animated by a morbid vitalism.

Greenfield turned to film after studying dance for a decade at the New England Conservatory, at the Martha Graham Studio, and with Merce Cunningham and Company.[16] She has since made more than forty films: one feature, *Antigone: Rites of Passion* (1990), as well as many shorts, video installations, and even holograms. Greenfield's shorts have tested the possibilities of cinema dance as an intermedium that exceeds the sum of its parts, one that reflects Matt Tierney's assertion that "intermediality is not the joining of this discrete medium with that one but is instead the site where nothing joins and where a thing is neither this nor that nor even fully itself."[17] Cinema dance, Greenfield proclaimed in 1969, ought to stem from the relation between physical energy, camera motion, and principles of nonchronological time in editing.[18] This chapter focuses on an informal elemental cycle within Greenfield's corpus. *Dirt* (1971) may be understood as Greenfield's earth film, *Tides* (1982) as her water film, *Element* (1973), with its use of mud, as a synthesis of the two, and the more recent *Wildfire* (2002) as of course her fire film.[19] If there is, at least as of writing this, no air project in Greenfield's filmography, it is perhaps because the element suffuses much of her work; all four elemental films adopt formal strategies for making the air visible and audible. Breathing, the performers' and our own as spectators, draws attention to itself in encounters with the elements made unsettling by cinematic interference.

Psychoanalytic theories of the gaze best describe the postpastoral and its relation to filmic distortion. I am not referring to the experience of mastery, however illusory, famously theorized by Laura Mulvey as a "determining male gaze [that] projects its fantasy on [a] female figure" who embodies the attribute of *"to-be-looked-at-ness."*[20] I am instead referring to what Todd McGowan, in a reading of Jacques Lacan's *Seminar XI*, defines as an experience of submission. To describe the gaze, Lacan turns to Hans Holbein the Younger's 1533 painting, *The Ambassadors*. The painting, which features two world travelers and the riches they have accumulated, is disrupted by a stain-like figure unrecognizable at first glance. The figure is anamorphic; looking at it downward and from the left reveals a skull. For Lacan, the stain-turned-skull marks the location of the gaze, where spectators lose their critical distance from the painting and become involved in what they see.[21] "Instead of being an experience of imaginary mastery (as it is for traditional Lacanian film theorists)," McGowan explains, the gaze "becomes—at least potentially—the site of a traumatic encounter with the Real, with the utter failure of the spectator's seemingly safe distance and assumed mastery."[22]

Postpastoral experience constitutes one such potentially traumatic encounter, wherein spectators, no longer able to regard themselves as social beings distanced from the nature they observe, confront their objectness, or their exposure to environments that sustain and deplete them. The gaze may issue from an actual face. Bush's flippant stare, for instance, instills in us, its objects, the shame of, perhaps, having hoped that the explosion's reverse motion would erase the facts of nuclear destruction and toxicity.[23] But the gaze need not be activated by an on-screen subject's actual stare; Mendieta's and Greenfield's elemental media themselves cast a gaze. An anamorphism comparable to the one in Lacan's example is at play: Mendieta and Greenfield at times compose pastoral scenes where performers interact harmoniously and pleasurably with nature, but also where floats the faintest sense that something is askew. As the artists sustain our attention, we slowly come to identify what, exactly, has felt off. This encounter with the Real, as McGowan would describe it, isn't entirely visual; it is also, importantly, respiratory. The disruption of the spectators' breathing draws their attention to the ways mise-en-scène and editing turn the pastoral against itself and deflate its ideals. Through postpastoral experience, we may account in more-than-visual terms for the disturbances that McGowan's Lacanian film theory attributes to the gaze. To attune oneself to breath is to be the object of elemental media's gaze; this experience entails, but exceeds, vision.[24]

Postpastoral. Why the neologism? The turn away from nature in humanistic inquiry has coincided with a turn toward ecology. These turns lend themselves to a positivist reading: a simplistic notion of nature as one pole of the nature-culture binary gave way to a more sophisticated understanding of ecosystemic interconnection and interdependence. Along with sophistication came progressivism: the ecology concept distributed the burden of responsibility and care across human and nonhuman beings. The term *postpastoral* deflates the sharp distinction between the natural past and the ecological present to record the ways we are haunted by the pastoral's specter. Mendieta and Greenfield display the investment in interconnection and interdependence typical of ecological art, but they also ask how the pastoral comes to feel bad—a question that ecology, as a shorthand for complexity, doesn't capture. According to Terry Gifford, to whom the term is generally attributed, the postpastoral does not mark a clean break with the pastoral.[25] Neither does it in my view. Our uses of the postpastoral are however not isometric. Whereas Gifford insists that the concept "is not temporal but conceptual and therefore can refer to a work in any time period," I locate my spin in the contemporary era that, in the introduction to this book, I declared a crisis in breathing.[26] Gifford's postpastoral is recuperative or redemptive; it enables artists and audiences to remain in the vicinity of the pastoral, where "a dynamic, self-adjusting accommodation to 'discordant harmonies'" may be achieved.[27] Inversely, the artists included in this chapter overstay their welcome in pastoral settings, depriving spectators of the ease with which they might otherwise occupy a paradigm predicated on harmonies, however discordant.

A few words on that paradigm are in order. The pastoral points to at least three traditions: a first that has documented the lives of shepherds in poetry and drama, a second that has depicted rural life, more generally, in contrast to urban life, and a third that its critics have condemned as a naïve celebration of nature that ignores threats like pollution, deforestation, and erosion.[28] The pastoral's melancholic structure is aptly expressed by poet Lisa Robertson's pithy definition: "Let's pretend you 'had' a land. Then you 'lost' it. Now fondly describe it. That is pastoral."[29] For this chapter's purposes, pastoral designates a paradigm that externalizes nature, or pushes it beyond the reach of the social, to endow it with such qualities as purity and vitality.

The long history of aesthetic and philosophical engagements with nature, as Lawrence Buell recounts it, has until recently been a history of pastoralism.[30] The nineteenth-century transcendentalists Ralph Waldo Emerson and Henry David Thoreau, who located nature outside of the social institutions that in their view corrupted self-growth, may be viewed as the foremost American ambassadors of pastoralism. Their legacy was called into question when landmark studies like Rachel Carson's *Silent Spring* (1962) announced that the pristine nature they had imagined had been spoiled. Carson didn't entirely break ranks with the transcendentalists; *Silent Spring* opens with a fable set in a preindustrial town. In this town, as in pastoral utopia, "all seemed to live in harmony with its surroundings."[31] Until it didn't. The remainder of the fable and the book inventory chemicals that add up to "the pollution of the total environment of mankind [sic]."[32] *Silent Spring* demonstrated the unsustainability of notions of natural purity and vitality at a time when, in the United States and beyond, sustainability imperatives—imperatives that prescribe responsible interactions with the environment to avoid resource depletion and encourage long-term environmental quality—were starting, though slowly and insufficiently, to inform legislation.[33] Carson's fable and the enchanted vision of nature it initially presents are in the service of a pedagogy of disenchantment. As evidence of toxicity piles up page after page, the pastoral reveals its ahistoricity and ideological bankruptcy.

Mendieta's and Greenfield's elemental media, too, orchestrate a certain disenchantment. The artists do not relay abundant facts about environmental decline but instill a dysphoria that clashes with a sensory and affective repertoire dominated by wonder, awe, and bliss. As William Cronon has shown, the rise in the nineteenth century of wilderness, an ideology that preserves the purity and vitality of a natural beyond, concurred with aesthetic theory's sharpened attention to the sublime.[34] The experience of the sublime can combine seemingly incompatible feelings like wonder and horror, insofar as individuals faced with sights that Immanuel Kant describes as "great beyond all comparison" confront not only prodigious beauty but also their own shattering finitude.[35] Whether or not it is pleasant, this experience tends to be cathartic. By contrast, postpastoral experience is noncathartic, meaning, in Sianne Ngai's words, that it offers "no satisfactions of virtue, however oblique, nor any therapeutic or purifying release."[36] The postpastoral names an encounter with the pastoral that is (temporally) anachronistic and (spatially) disorienting. If there is horror in the postpastoral, it is understated, ambient.

To articulate the relation between breath and nature in elemental media, I locate Mendieta's and Greenfield's art in tension with a critical idiom of particular significance in the 1970s and 1980s: elemental feminism. It would be inaccurate to interpret Mendieta's and Greenfield's works as direct responses to elemental feminism. Even situating Mendieta's art near feminism may be contentious, given the artist's reported rejection of a movement that, in her evaluation, was designed to benefit only white middle-class women.[37] I nonetheless move that the discomfort with the pastoral to be inherited from Mendieta's and Greenfield's elemental media is best understood as a discomfort with what is pastoral about elemental feminism. Elemental feminism posits an intimacy between a being or quality (woman, femaleness, the feminine) and the natural world, and it identifies breath as a conduit for this intimacy. In *Pure Lust* (1984), Mary Daly invites women to express "Elemental female lust" by mustering "Elemental powers"—powers, such as the "creative breath of life," that are for the most part airborne.[38] Daly explains, "As inhabitants of the air, Lusty women are breathers/speakers of Radiant Words. Insofar as we are elemental, our speech releases words from the state of contamination. Like sharp wind, it cuts through smog, clarifying, making it possible to breathe freely again. The more we become attuned to Radiant words and give them incarnation (in speech, writing, music and other art forms, as well as in our lives), the more effectively we remove the man-made obstacles to breathing."[39] Daly toggles between literal and figurative contamination: between atmospheric pollutants (smog) and ambient patriarchy (what, in her previous book, *Gyn/Ecology* [1978], she calls "the mind/spirit/body pollution inflicted through patriarchal myths and languages on all levels").[40] She ventures that women, were they to harness a vital breath that is fundamentally theirs, would manage to dispel all contamination. Another feminist philosopher, Luce Irigaray, similarly contends that breath's "feminine divine" carries the potential to restore homeostasis, transforming nature "without ruining it" and synchronizing "the universe's breath, related to the wind, [and] the cosmic breathing."[41] In 1980, Irigaray initiated a cycle of books that would apply an elemental nomenclature to the study of the Western philosophical canon. In her water book, Irigaray diagnoses Friedrich Nietzsche's fear of feminine fluidity, and in her air book, the suppression of the air in Martin Heidegger's metaphysics of presence.[42] The latter text recovers what Irigaray deems Heidegger has taken away from his readers: a rapport with the air, or the ability to live, move, and breathe. While it has launched an evocative critique of patriarchy's atmospheres and moods, elemental feminism has relied on circular reasoning: the solution to not being able to breathe, it implies, is to breathe better. So committed to the belief that a divine, feminine breath could overcome masculine obstructions, Daly and Irigaray stop short of noticing that respiration renders vitality and morbidity inseparable.

Elemental feminism has been contested on grounds that exceed its logical fallacies. Daly and Irigaray have been associated with a certain essentialism—a reduction of *woman* and *female* to unchanging biological traits, or to a (sexual) nature imagined as pure and uncontaminated. Although it would be hard and, I think, pointless to deny Daly's well-documented transphobia, some scholars, myself included, have suggested that Irigaray's philosophy lends itself to interpretations not so tethered to fantasies of binary gender and heterosexuality.[43] Caroline Godart and Danielle Poe note that Irigaray focuses not on women's being but on their becoming. By this logic, the natural is at once inherited and cultivated, a product of material and cultural factors.[44] As I've written elsewhere, what Irigaray sees in the natural is, rather than fixity, a realm of difference that opens the world up to its potentialities.[45] These potentialities approximate what Elizabeth Grosz, a champion of Irigaray, calls "the surprise of sexuality, its liability to unpredictability, to openness, formlessness, boundlessness."[46] Such interpretations of Irigaray's philosophy align with feminist science studies' effort to inhibit the conflation of biology and nature with essentialism. One architect of this effort, Elizabeth Wilson, makes reductionist or deterministic accounts spin until the biological appears not quite unmoored and unconstrained, as with Grosz, but animated by theoretically productive tensions and contradictions.[47] Elemental feminism, I propose, has a built-in mechanism for upsetting its essentialist proclivities, and that mechanism is respiration. Breath, Daly and Irigaray remind us, isn't any one individual's property. By insisting on breath's femaleness or femininity, Daly and Irigaray unwittingly hint at a distributed model of subjectivity. In this model, a person's essence resides in a milieu. It can be processed, but not contained. Respiration's status as a loophole within elemental feminism is revealed by Mendieta's and Greenfield's elemental media, wherein pastoral fantasies of untamable vitality and natural purity run out of breath.

Body after Breath: Ana Mendieta

In 1972, Mendieta took a series of photographs collectively known as *Untitled (Glass on Body Imprints)*. The photos bear some of the earliest traces of Mendieta's attention to the contortions necessary to keep breathing under strain. In film photography, bodies and objects leave an imprint on light-sensitive material, and *Untitled (Glass on Body Imprints)* duplicates this process. For *Untitled (Glass on Face)*, a suite of six photographs included in the series, Mendieta pressed her face onto a square of acrylic glass, creating an additional imprint within the frame. The project gives breathing the density, grain, and warmth that typify respiratory media.[48] In one photograph, Mendieta's left cheek and ear are squished. Condensation located near her mouth draws attention to the passage of air (figure 1.5). In another photograph, Mendieta looks directly into the camera and appears to hold her breath. Her mouth sticks to the glass sheet like a suction cup. Her nostrils are front and center, her chin drawn back. Whether her grimacing signals juvenile humor or pain is up for debate.

Although transparency promises explicit access to Mendieta's face and nude upper torso, glass imprints distort an image of youthful femininity and flatten erotic expression. The photos could be seen, from one vantage point, as evidence of the emergence in the second half of the twentieth century of "the explicit body in representation," Rebecca Schneider's term for a body that bears "markings delineating social hierarchies of privilege and disprivilege."[49] Yet, by zooming in on a "mass of orifices and appendages, details and tactile surfaces," all of which Schneider attaches to "the explicit body," Mendieta calls into question the existence of The Body—a whole, a unitary body, a body that preexists its representation.[50] Mendieta's body must be extrapolated from what the photographs accentuate, such as her mouth, her nostrils, and the steam that settles on the glass as she breathes through the likely discomfort. Mendieta grants spectators only partial access to a body onto which a politics of Cuban American female visibility might be projected. Rather than some immutable body, it is respiration, a nexus of bodily formation and deformation, that leaves an imprint across her corpus. With *Untitled (Glass on Body Imprints)*, Mendieta trains us to watch for difficult or held breath—a training that proves especially relevant to the films she would go on to make in the 1970s. In these films, individuals and milieus ought to be inferred from their entanglement, which breath figures and materializes.

From glass breathing to grass breathing. Shot in Iowa, the silent short film *Grass Breathing* (1974) riffs on *Grass on Woman*, a 1972 performative action captured only with a photo camera. Patches of grass occupy the quasi-totality of the frame; only in the top-right corner can some trees and a shed be intuited. The composition is relatively monochromatic: gradient greens, muted yellows. The film is a puzzle of sorts; it asks us to locate movement in an establishing shot that could initially be mistaken for a still photograph. In the first seconds, the only discernible motion is caused by the wind flowing through the blades of grass. One patch of grass in the top third of the frame starts to rise and fall ever so slightly, as if it were breathing (figure 1.6). As the film goes on, the grass

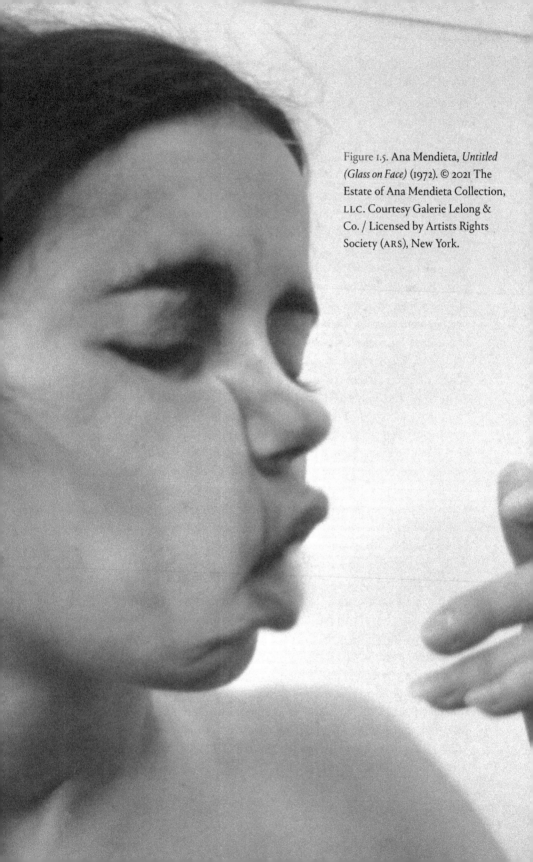

Figure 1.5. Ana Mendieta, *Untitled (Glass on Face)* (1972). © 2021 The Estate of Ana Mendieta Collection, LLC. Courtesy Galerie Lelong & Co. / Licensed by Artists Rights Society (ARS), New York.

Figure 1.6. Still from *Grass Breathing*
(1974), directed by Ana Mendieta.
© 2021 The Estate of Ana Mendieta
Collection, LLC. Courtesy Galerie
Lelong & Co. / Licensed by Artists
Rights Society (ARS), New York.

breathing gets quicker and less regular. Light wrestling and convulsion are visible. As the film nears its conclusion, labored inhalations and exhalations abate. Whose are they? Mendieta's: we know from curatorial notes that she is lying under the patch of grass. But the film doesn't disclose this information. Mendieta remains hidden, such that the breathing could be anyone's. It could be an animal's. A machine's. Or it might be some other movement that happens to approximate breathing. Whatever respiration we attribute to Mendieta is a product of speculation, a derivative of the titular grass breathing.

Grass Breathing reveals bodies as epiphenomenal—phases in respiratory individuations that span milieus. The philosopher Gilbert Simondon has imagined the individual as a corollary of the metastable, nondyadic individual-milieu couple.[51] Whereas Simondon's theory relies on the origin myth of the "pre-individual," an ecstatic entity that overflows into individuation, the movement of the grass in Mendieta's film more closely resembles a choreography, the central concept in Erin Manning's *Always More Than One: Individuation's Dance* (2012).[52] Choreography organizes relations, not bodies. It shifts the "experiential ground" and atmosphere at the same time as it exposes bodies as "more ecological than individual."[53] As I watch *Grass Breathing*, I try to infer Mendieta, an individual, from her breathing (one set of relations), and her breathing from a kind of topographic respiration (another set of relations). Respiration marks a coincidence of movements from which a body can be only minimally and provisionally conjectured. Mendieta's body is, as Steven Connor would put it, an "[effect] of interference."[54]

Grass Breathing inverts the pastoral's visual conventions. Mendieta does not lounge on the grass but lies under it. She does not meet the landscape in a vivifying communion. The artist's intent was to merge her body with the landscape, but this merger, as I see it, isn't a friendly one: she appears to collapse under the weight of the landscape. I notice such an asphyxiating pressure in much of Mendieta's art. In *Burial Pyramid* (1974), a reflection on rebirth, spiritual transformation, and the passage of time she shot the same year as *Grass Breathing*, Mendieta performs an uneasy respiration that recapitulates histories of oppression sanitized by the pastoral. Set in Yagul, Mexico, *Burial Pyramid* is another long take that comprises two acts: the intensification of breathing followed by its abatement. But unlike *Grass Breathing*, *Burial Pyramid* gradually unveils Mendieta's nude body. Her head initially protrudes from piles of rocks and patches of weeds. Thirty seconds or so into the film, the performer's breathing catches our attention. It can no longer be dismissed as the kind of illusory motion we make up when we stare at something still for too long. Mendieta's chest, arms, pelvis, and legs thrust, and rocks trickle down (figure 1.7). Mendi-

Figure 1.7. Still from *Burial Pyramid*
(1974), directed by Ana Mendieta.
© 2021 The Estate of Ana Mendieta
Collection, LLC. Courtesy Galerie
Lelong & Co. / Licensed by Artists
Rights Society (ARS), New York.

eta, whose eyes are closed, seems to be struggling to breathe under the pressure. We may identify Mendieta as the architect of her own suffocation; after all, she arranged for the stones to be placed on her body. In this sense, *Burial Pyramid* exemplifies Jennifer Fay's proposition that the relation between set and world in cinema allegorizes the planet's status as a product of anthropogenic design.[55] At the same time, Mendieta's compromised breathing indexes uneven geographies of asphyxiation under capitalism, colonialism, and imperialism. As Ara Osterweil puts it, Mendieta tries to "find her breath under the weight of time and history."[56] The medium of performance maintains a tension between causing one's suffocation and accentuating an experience of suffocation that exceeds one's control. Performing breathlessness, however willfully, makes Mendieta breathless in ways that may not be entirely manageable.

Mendieta's art is not pure ephemerality, pure flux; Jane Blocker warns us that such a diagnosis would reproduce the stereotype opposing "the trauma, dislocation, and subjugation of Latinity" to a "clear, unproblematic, and fixed" Western white identity.[57] Yet her ephemeral earth-body sculptures refrain from extending histories of land appropriation and transformation.[58] What is more, as Blocker concedes, Mendieta debunks the notion of essence, her treatment of exile evoking "the lifelong process of coming to terms with the estrangement that is the soul of identity."[59] Charles Merewether likens Mendieta's art to Afro-Caribbean mimetic practices that, by reproducing the self, make it other.[60] Another technique for inducing self-difference and self-estrangement is respiration. As she breathes, Mendieta registers the forces that constrain Latina life in exile while meddling with the expectation that the subject attached to this critique should be self-identical, coherent, and legible.

By the end of *Burial Pyramid*, Mendieta is still again, and her breathing is undetectable. We have access to none of the vital signs that the artist exhibits in a related film, *Creek* (1974). In *Creek*, Mendieta lies on her stomach in a shallow creek. Her neck is twisted. Even though we don't see her mouth, nose, or torso, we know she is still breathing because, were she to lose consciousness, her neck would relax and her face would be submerged. Mendieta concludes *Burial Pyramid* in corpse pose. She might be intentionally regularizing her breathing. She might no longer be breathing. The undetectability of the artist's respiration in the film's last seconds makes the extension of life and its extinction remarkably similar. According to José Esteban Muñoz, Mendieta's art renders a self whose deformation and displacement supply "evidence of expired life" while imagining "regeneration."[61] The artist conveys an intense, potentially destructive vitalism that summons "death-in-life."[62] While it was not his intention, Muñoz could not have summed up Mendieta's treatment of respiration any better. As we watch for breath, we process Mendieta's morbid vitalism, a dialectic between regenerated and expired life that recapitulates histories of oppression.

Pedagogy of Debilitation: Amy Greenfield

Mendieta arrived at film via the visual arts, and Greenfield, via dance and performance. Greenfield's cinema dance belongs to an avant-garde tradition that she calls "kinesthetics" and traces back to such figures as Maya Deren and Hilary Harris. These filmmakers and multidisciplinary artists, Greenfield holds, revealed "the structural essence of modern dance in a way possible only on the screen."[63] I attribute this revelation to the magnification of breath by film and video technologies. Kinesthetics authorizes a mode of spectatorship foreclosed in live performance. The stage, even when it extends beyond the proscenium, sets a boundary between performers and spectators. In kinesthetics, by contrast, choreographies that involve dancers and cameras are immersive. The background turns into the foreground, and the foreground into the background; nowhere is offstage. Granted, this fantasy of total immersion has its limitations. Even if the camera is mobile, spectators face a screen the same way they would a stage. However freed from the constraints of theatrical architecture, the movement captured on film is, in the event of projection, reinscribed in a frame.

Acting, Ross Gibson has argued, consists in managing breath to induce an affective reaction.[64] Theories of acting that emphasize respiration owe a debt to Antonin Artaud, according to whom the (stage) actor conjures "*le souffle qui rallume la vie*" (the breath or blow that reignites life) to push embodiment and action to their limit, where representation becomes an organic function or second nature.[65] These theories rest on the assumption that spectators are breathing the same air as performers. Instead of attempting to reproduce this alchemy, the artisans of kinesthetics play to the medium's strengths and enhance breath. The respiratory close-ups of kinesthetics show precisely how dancers interact with a variety of environments—what they take in and let out, what invigorates and exhausts them, when and how their bodies reach their limit.

The origins of Greenfield's cinematic attunement to respiration are evident in two short, black-and-white, 16 mm films by her precursors, Deren and Harris. Deren's *A Study in Choreography for Camera* (1945) features sequences of expansive and recessive gestures filmed in interior and exterior settings. The dancer Talley Beatty uses his entire body to exaggerate the motions of inhalation and exhalation, straightening his torso, then curling up on himself. Harris's *Nine Variations on a Dance Theme* (1966/1967), too, displays the folding and unfolding of its sole performer, in this case Bettie de Jong. But unlike Deren, Harris interrupts breathing's cyclicality. Jump cuts leave gestures partial, unrealized. The vertiginous Dutch angle that captures de Jong's développé suggests unrest and disorientation. Nonchronological editing and shifting perspective make breathing a perilous activity.

Greenfield's elemental short film *Tides*, on which Harris worked as a camera operator, intensifies the respiratory confusion of *Nine Variations*—although the disorder isn't immediately obvious. *Tides* relies on an analogy between breathing and the back-and-forth of the waves. Greenfield's energetic performance is set on a beach. Over the span of twelve minutes, she runs toward tall waves or awaits their arrival, registers their impact, loses her footing, and drifts away—only to start all over. Greenfield holds her breath, the way a swimmer would, before she's submerged. This athletic breathing is reminiscent of the techniques that she and her dance partner Ben Dolphin developed in *Videotape for a Woman and a Man* (1978), shot a few years before *Tides*. In improvisations that combine dancing, jumping, and wrestling, Greenfield and Dolphin's breathing reveals an effort to sustain some momentum. Between episodes of intense activity, the dancers pant loudly, trying to catch their breath. They occasionally fold their bodies forward, letting their shoulders rise and fall spasmodically. At one point, the artists lie in an embrace halfway between postcoital stasis and postcombat capitulation. In *Videotape*, variations in the intensity of breathing signal exertion or rest. Greenfield never relaxes in *Tides*, but she does give the impression that she is experiencing some release by emitting what appear to be cathartic screams of joy. We, the spectators, cannot hear these screams, for the splashing that serves as the film's score isn't synchronized with the image. All we witness is Greenfield's wide-open mouth as she succumbs to the force of the waves. Her movement is rendered in slow motion.

We are ostensibly in pastoral territory. The delight Greenfield exhibits as she encounters a natural setting matches elemental feminism à la Daly or Irigaray. But dismissing Greenfield as an essentialist would ignore the critical valence of her formal engagement with the pastoral. Jennifer Peterson makes a comparable argument about Barbara Hammer, another feminist filmmaker who worked with nudity. Hammer's "portrayal of lesbian sexuality," writes Peterson, "explicitly [linked] erotic desire to elements of nature."[66] Hammer's aesthetics was calibrated to the US cinematic avant-garde of the late 1960s and early 1970s, preoccupied as it was "with bodies in all their unruly messiness," but it would seem somewhat at odds with the "countercinema" informed by feminist academic concepts that would arise later in the 1970s.[67] "Against this changed framework," Peterson sums up, "Hammer's films seemed rooted in politically retrograde notions of feminine essence."[68] It is easy to picture Greenfield on the receiving end of similar accusations. Peterson defends Hammer's cinema by declaring it timelier than its initial reception suggested. Hammer's film *Jane Brakhage* (1974), for instance, eluded the "retrograde conflation of women and nature" by taking an anti-anthropocentric stance and interrogating the naturalization of women's roles as wives, mothers, and muses.[69] My stance on *Tides'* subversion of essentialism is slightly different: Greenfield's film appears out of time, and that is the point. The artist's manipulation of cinematic temporality leads us to register the pastoral as anachronistic.

Tides intervenes in the interplay between on- and off-screen breathing to retract the catharsis it affords. Diegetic breathing, as Davina Quinlivan has shown, possesses a mimetic quality. Spectators tend, intentionally or not, to adjust their breathing to match the respiration of on-screen figures in situations of strain, shock, or relief.[70] Through this respiratory contagion, film earns the definition that Vivian Sobchack, riffing on Maurice Merleau-Ponty, gives it: "an expression of experience by experience," or "life expressing life."[71] The experience of *Tides* is marked by a dissonance between content and form. *Tides* relays a pastoral scene—an encounter with nature's sublimity that generates a catharsis evidenced by Greenfield's beatific smile and open arms (figure 1.8). But the slow motion, the asynchrony of image and sound, and the occasional reverse effect prevent me, as a spectator, from feeling the same release. I'm tempted to imitate Greenfield and exhale with satisfaction when I should instead hold my breath in preparation for submersion. The mixed respiratory signals of *Tides* interfere with proprioception—my awareness of my body's relative position.[72] My panic isn't a reflection of the panic conveyed by an on-screen subject; it is triggered by the formal distortion of the bliss she expresses.[73] The experience of *Tides* activates what Kyla Wazana Tompkins would call a pedagogy of "deformation": my disorientation causes me to unlearn the historical processes through which the pastoral "comes into social coherence."[74]

Tides opens with a red herring in the form of a quotation from the legendary dancer Isadora Duncan: "We do not stand on the beach and inquire of the ocean what was its movement in the past and what will be its movement in the future. We realize that the movement peculiar to its nature is eternal to its nature." In her 1903 manifesto "The Dance of the Future," Duncan locates the source of dance in the elements—in the motion of the waves, the wind, and the earth. Body and soul will be freed, she predicts, as the dancer of the future grows harmoniously with nature.[75] Cinema dance defies Duncan's insistence that dance not be recorded and throws her philosophy into disarray. *Tides'* sharp cuts and loopy chronology meddle with the illusion of eternity given by slow motion. If,

Figure 1.8. Still from *Tides* (1982),
directed by Amy Greenfield.
Eclipse Productions.

as Peterson notes, "an essentialist . . . misunderstands 'nature' as an unchanging, inviolate concept," then Greenfield's editing fulfills an anti-essentialist function by leading us to experience the film's setting as a historical datum.[76] The waves are so tall because *Tides* was shot a few days after the passage of a hurricane on the edge of the Atlantic.[77] Greenfield, then, does invite spectators to consider the movement of the ocean in relation to its past and future. This movement is heightened by a disaster whose frequency and impact have increased as climate crisis has accelerated. In Greenfield's pastoral gone wrong, the mediation of an image of nature as a source of inspiration and replenishment renders it asphyxiating. Proprioceptive disturbances help us to process that there's nothing timeless about the back-and-forth of the waves. With *Tides*, an attunement to breath leads to an alertness to environmental disaster.

Greenfield gives up pastoral pretenses in *Dirt* and *Element*, two short films, the former in color and the latter in black and white, where the performer appears vulnerable to violent forces. In *Dirt*, set to rock and electronic music, Greenfield is dragged through the dirt with increasing brutality. Whereas Greenfield's attacker is only partially shown in *Dirt*, her antagonist is depersonalized in *Element*: it is her surroundings. Greenfield once again appears nude, and here she is covered in mud. Her improvised choreography is similar to that in *Tides*. She rises and falls, over and over. Yet the mood in *Element* is different. More linear than *Tides*, *Element* documents a strenuous combat with the elements that leaves its performer depleted. Even in the absence of panicked editing, it remains hard to discern what is going on at any given point. Stains on the camera lens obfuscate the action in a film where the omnipresence of mud already troubles the separation between performer, costume, and set (figure 1.9). When I watch *Element*, I scan for breath, the irregular inflation and deflation of Greenfield's belly, for it is my best bet at knowing where in the frame I should direct my attention. Then my own breathing, also irregular, becomes impossible to ignore. Respiration operates as an engine of "haptic visuality," Laura U. Marks's term for the film experience, a touch without hands.[78] In watching for Greenfield's breath and attuning themselves to her exhaustion, spectators encounter the natural world as hostile and inhabit the afterlife of the pastoral.

Element both anticipated and extended Henri Lefebvre's 1974 declaration that nature, seemingly "resistant . . . and infinite in its depth," had been "defeated" and was awaiting "its ultimate voidance and destruction."[79] The defeat of nature posited by Lefebvre, Greenfield's shortness of breath suggests, leads to human beings' self-defeat. The performer resembles a creature caught in an oil spill, a disaster, caused by fossil fuel overreliance, that would become even more common in the decades following the film's creation. *Element* constitutes

Figure 1.9. Still from *Element* (1973), directed by Amy Greenfield. Eclipse Productions.

an avant-garde, nonnarrative counterpart to what Amitav Ghosh and others have called "petrofictions," a loose genre that tackles the production, consumption, and effects of petroleum-based energy.[80] Not everyone is equally responsible for environmental destruction in Greenfield's oeuvre. The formal resonance between *Dirt* and *Element*, a pair of films made just two years apart, genders brutality. The combination of these films relays an amended elemental feminism: a critique of destruction as male or masculine that does not submit, as its solution, women's pastoral reacquaintance with natural vitality.

I have described, via *Tides* and *Element*, complementary cinematic strategies for staging postpastoral experience. The former film tampers, at the editing stage, with the invigoration tied to harmonious pastoral encounters, while the latter invites a spectatorial attunement to exhaustion within a brutal and brutalized environment. These films teach us something, but the pedagogy before us isn't one wherein a spectator exposed to environmental catastrophe can be expected to acquire specific insights and become a good environmental citizen willing and able to pose sound actions. Neither *Tides* nor *Element* inculcates what Nicole Seymour describes as "'proper' environmentalist feelings—often, reverence, love, or wonder—[that] educate the public, incite quantifiable environmental activism, or even solve environmental problems."[81] The measure of cinema dance's pedagogy is not action but incapacitation. As a spectator, I must dwell on a discomfort I'm given no opportunity to transcend. In postpastoral experience lies a pedagogy of debility: I unlearn the codes of the pastoral as I lose my breath, breathe out of sequence, or fail to let out a sigh of relief.

Test Case: Combustion

This chapter has sketched a respiratory spectatorship that entails a confrontation with environmental catastrophes and their unevenly distributed repercussions. Having addressed hurricanes and oil spills, I now turn to wildfires. Wildfires related to droughts and heat waves have caused immeasurable damage in the late twentieth and early twenty-first centuries, killing animal beings, eradicating plant life, and jeopardizing air quality. Donna J. Haraway writes of the California wildfires, "Fire in the North American West has a complicated multispecies history; fire is an essential element for ongoing, as well as an agent of double death, the killing of ongoingness. The material semiotics of fire in our times are at stake."[82] This concluding section interrogates the interest in fire and combustion that Greenfield and Mendieta both eventually developed. Doing so returns us to the relation between respiration and combustion at play in Bush's atomic "Breathing." Greenfield's and Mendieta's combustive turns, so to speak, index the acceleration of the historical processes amounting to the crisis in breathing. Combustion's near-instantaneous transformation of oxygen into carbon dioxide pushes unbreathability to its extreme, at which point the exchange between individual and milieu turns into deadly fusion. Combustion marks the apotheosis of a contemporary breathing aesthetics that, by enmeshing what makes life possible with what imperils it, constitutes a record of lived impossibility. Conjuring sublime affects like awe and horror, combustion also functions as a test case of sorts for the noncathartic affective repertoire I have associated with respiratory spectatorship and postpastoral experience.

In *Wildfire*, an elemental film made two full decades after *Tides*, Greenfield's cinema dance analogizes performers to flames. The film opens and closes with clips from *Annabelle Serpentine Dance* (1895), produced and distributed by the Edison Manufacturing Company. In these excerpts, the dancer Annabelle Moore, nicknamed Peerless Annabelle, twirls energetically, her arms drawing a figure-eight pattern. The gesture, amplified by her dress's draped sleeves, exaggerates respiratory motion. Moore appears not as a breather but as breathing itself. Much like *Tides'* citation of Isadora Duncan, the inclusion of *Annabelle Serpentine Dance* in *Wildfire* at once locates Greenfield's art in a genealogy of modern dance and marks a historical shift in the conception of human beings' relation to the natural world. Greenfield enlists Moore's ghost to perform the kind of invigorating breath that no longer seems viable in the contemporary portion of *Wildfire*.

This contemporary portion features four performers: Andrea Beeman, Francine Breen, Bonnie Dunn, and Cynthia DeMoss. The dancers are nude if not for the capes they use to exaggerate each gesture, as does Moore with her sleeves. The indoor set affords a controlled environment where the lighting designer Jason Boyd can deviate from the reliance on natural light in Greenfield's other elemental films. The dancers perform in front of a wall that doubles as a screen onto which footage of flames is projected. They bathe in light that shifts from yellow to orange, red, green, and blue, with the occasional overlap. The transition from yellow to blue gives the impression that the flames are getting hotter. Covered in glitter, the dancers perform a hybrid of modern dance à la Moore and Parisian cabaret. Whether they are dancing to Philip Glass's recursive score is unclear because diegetic sound is muted. Greenfield's editing achieves a boomerang effect by tying together forward and reverse motions. Cuts are frequent. The superimposition of establishing shots and extreme close-ups produces the illusion of a fire seen from multiple perspectives at once, with the dancers engulfed by the very flames they ignite as they curve their bodies (figure 1.10). Moore's return in the film's last seconds is uncanny. Despite the choreographic

Figure 1.10. Still from
Wildfire (2002), directed
by Amy Greenfield.
Eclipse Productions.

and compositional elements shared by *Wildfire*'s archival and contemporary components, the ten or so minutes during which Greenfield's dancers go up in flames stress the anachronism of Moore's free breathing. In Greenfield's choreography, expressive breathing comes to signal oxygen scarcity.

Wildfires make breathing hazardous for inhabitants of neighboring regions, especially those who already suffer from respiratory illnesses.[83] In Greenfield's *Wildfire*, the unavailability of oxygen imposes itself as an ecological issue and a feminist one. One way to decrypt the relation between fire and sexuality would be to liken Greenfield's choreography to what Nigel Clark and Kathryn Yusoff call the expression of "pyrosocial desire." "As a 'queer' reproductive logic that regenerates prodigiously without recourse to sexual or species reproduction," Clark and Yusoff contend, "fire models genealogies that are both exuberant and future-oriented—to offer another kind of reproductive futurism that is not grounded in those logics of patriarchy, family or progeny that remain decidedly intra-species and intra-planetary."[84] *Wildfire*'s homo- and pyrosocial scene aligns with Clark and Yusoff's theorization of (re)production without heterosexuality (and, in this case, without men). The asphyxiating quality of Greenfield's film, however, suggests that Clark and Yusoff may be embellishing the way destruction, once labeled queer, looks or feels like renewal. In expecting queerness to perform an ameliorative function, the authors display a certain pastoralizing tendency, one that clashes with a film where the burning of women doesn't solely register as a matter of intention.[85]

A more convincing way to grasp the relation between fire and sexuality would entail connecting *Wildfire*'s imagery to the sacrificial burning of women accused of witchcraft for surrendering to so-called natural instincts. Here again, Greenfield, who appears at once fascinated by and skeptical of women's intimacy with the natural world, wrestles with some themes dear to elemental feminism.[86] The witch hunts, Silvia Federici has influentially argued, spectacularized the disciplining of female bodies in an attempt by state and church to convert the individual's power into labor power. The medieval body as a source of magical power had to be gendered first and killed second to pave the way for the self-managed and self-regulated body.[87] *Wildfire*'s use of superimposition, which turns some female performers into the very flames that swallow others, compresses the historical process narrated by Federici. As Greenfield's imagery reminds us, climate crisis, a phenomenon that, according to scientific research on rates of pulmonary diseases, makes breathing especially difficult for women, was precipitated by capitalism, a process itself premised on women's alienation from their physical capacities.[88]

In her sprawling *Silueta* series, Mendieta, too, engages, with much ambivalence, the iconography of elemental feminism. In these earth-body sculptures, Mendieta's body is neither partially nor fully concealed; it is spectacularly absent. Humanoid silhouettes evoking chalk outlines on a crime scene are drawn with gunpowder and fireworks. They are designed to be set on fire, a practice that Olga M. Viso links to the Mexican tradition of burning effigies of Judas during Easter Holy Week celebrations.[89] Many of the burning silhouettes are in goddess pose, with their arms forming a right angle and their hands pointed upward. Much attention has been devoted to Mendieta's goddess aesthetics, which according to some critics and spectators betrays an essentialist view of femaleness and femininity.[90] Mendieta developed a marked interest in deities in 1971, in the context of her coursework and field research in Mexico. She pursued this interest by visiting Oaxaca from 1973 to 1978.[91] When in 1978 she relocated to New York City and began to travel to Miami and Cuba, she started to incorporate more Afro-Cuban iconography into her art.[92] As Alaimo notes, female artists exhibiting ecological concerns have had to walk a fine line between dispelling the masculinist affects that surround acts of environmental destruction and reifying or fetishizing a distinctly female natural sensitivity external to the social realm.[93] Debates on whether or not goddess icons are essentialist risk distracting us from the fact that Mendieta's art disputed that an essence could be contained by a figure. Mendieta reportedly had a fraught relation to goddess aesthetics. She eventually became resistant to having her work seen as another iteration of a trend that had become, in Adrian Heathfield's words, "increasingly suffocating and rigid."[94]

Heathfield's reference to suffocation is judicious. Whereas in *Wildfire* Greenfield elaborates a kinesthetics of combustion, Mendieta documented the actual incineration of her earth-body sculptures with Super 8 films and 35 mm slides. In a film like *Silueta de Cohetes (Firework Piece)* (1976), set against a dark mountainous backdrop, the goddess figure goes up in flames mere seconds after appearing on-screen. Made of firework materials and covered in branches and hay, the figure lit up in *Untitled: Silueta Series* (1979) is more vaguely anthropomorphic. As they burn, the materials curve and twist like guts spilling out. Smoke eventually saturates the frame. When the smoke dissipates ten or so seconds later, only ashes remain, making figure and ground undistinguishable. In these short films, Mendieta trades Greenfield's total destruction for controlled, localized burns. What dazzles is not the magnitude of each fire but the sheer abundance of films documenting combustion—an abundance that brings to mind the casualization of violence against both women and the environment. By creating silhouettes that recall the pose she strikes in previous works but exiting the frame before their ignition, Mendieta survives to burn again and again, in absentia.

Thanks to their imperfections, films and slides constitute ideal media for documenting Mendieta's combustible earth-body sculptures. Slides lose some of their clarity when they are converted into photographs. In some films, smoke is so prevalent that the action is hardly decipherable. The flaws and slow decay of the material support duplicate the sculptures' destruction. According to Stephanie Rosenthal, Mendieta's experiments with fire were a long prelude to an unrealized sculpture that would have been made of smoke. The sculpture, which the artist mulled over for several years, "would [have materialized] for a short moment, [changed] shape, [faded] out and [disappeared], leaving a trace on the camera and in the memory."[95] Smoke, Mendieta imagined, would not have been the outcome of an artwork's destruction by combustion; it would have been the artwork. The evanescent project would have offered a paradigmatic example of the postpastoral. Mendieta's brief atmospheric disturbance would have made the air a locus of (artistic) production and destruction, and it would have continued, long after vanishing, to haunt the spectators' relation to their milieus and their own bodies.

Aesthetic Self-Medication (Three Regimens)

Breathing is often implicit. We don't necessarily notice it, let alone think about its life-giving and life-sustaining functions. Not minding our breathing has its benefits. Insofar as it goes unnoticed, breathing supports a tacit structure of experience that equips us with a sense of ownership over our sensations, thoughts, and actions. This is what Jacques Derrida and others term "autoaffection," and what Drew Leder terms "self-effacing transitivity."[1] As an exchange between bodies and milieus that enables experience but stays muted or hidden, such that our sensations, thoughts, and actions feel like ours, nonconscious breathing is an even better example of autoaffection—or auto-*hetero*-affection, as it is sometimes labeled—than Derrida's analogs of choice: hearing ourselves and (via Jean-Luc Nancy) touching ourselves.[2] Didier Anzieu's psychoanalytic theory of the "skin-ego" similarly posits that nonconscious respiration, more precisely the nonconscious respiration and perspiration of our skin, guarantees our somatic integrity or holds us.[3]

According to another psychoanalyst, Michael Balint, the way we come to see ourselves as vulnerable to our environments mimics the way we become conscious of our breathing. The emergence of primary objects—that is, children's transition from an "undifferentiated environment" of "interpenetrating mix-up" to cathexes toward caregivers—approximates the process through which the air we breathe imposes itself as an object: we notice the sustenance it provides when it is not readily available.[4] In health-related or environmental crises, or in situations of exertion or shock, becoming conscious of our breathing confronts us with the possibly panic-inducing fact that respiration has already been going on, indifferent to our awareness of it. As breathers, we take in particles that are nourishing and toxic—often beyond discernment. When being conscious of our breathing implies being conscious of our vulnerability or exposure to risk, we must perform breathing as a gesture that no longer feels natural. It seems forced. Off-pitch.

Yet we would be wrong to infer that a consciousness of breathing is never desirable. Breath's entry into the realm of consciousness can register as a disorganizing event, surely, but also as an occasion for self-management. Meditation explicitly encourages a consciousness of breathing. Mindful breathing cultivates a sensitivity to surrounding energy in hopes of producing an alignment between self, body, and milieu. It capitalizes on the fact that breathing, as L. O. Aranye Fradenburg puts it, "tells us that we are and are not captains of our fate."[5] A comprehensive overview of the scientific literature on yogic breathing published in the *Journal of Ayurveda and Integrative Medicine* in 2019 reports that pranayama practices have been found to influence neurocognitive abilities, autonomic and pulmonary functions, and biochemical and metabolic activities.[6] Clinical studies have shown the effects of yogic breathing in modulating cardiovascular variables among patients with hypertension and cardiac arrhythmias, relieving symptoms of bronchial asthma, reducing the symptoms and enhancing the antioxidant status of patients undergoing radiotherapy and chemotherapy for cancer, improving the mood of individuals withdrawing from cigarette smoking, and managing anxiety and stress in students.[7] The advantages of slow, regular respiration demonstrated by pranayama practices shouldn't distract us from the occasional allure of breathlessness, a mode of breathing rather than its negation. Sex may be breathless. An aesthetic encounter may be breathtaking. Suspense may lead subjects to hold their breath. As an outcome of crises across scales, in mindfulness exercises, or in nonfatal instances of breathlessness, conscious respiration brings up the question of how to secure some sense that we are in control of our bodies and able to intervene in our environments despite our openness or through our receptivity.[8]

This chapter extends the inquiry, begun in chapter 1, into the relation between aesthetic mediation and the emergence of respiratory subjectivities specific to the late twentieth and early twenty-first centuries. In the preceding chapter, I described a mode of respiratory spectatorship through which we unlearn the pastoral's treatment of nature as an unspoiled life force. By interfering with breathing, avant-garde elemental media stress the contingency of embodiment and experience on milieus that at once sustain and deplete us. To be a subject of breathing, as these elemental media make palpable, is to be of a world where life and death do not exist in binary relation. Whereas the art surveyed in chapter 1 shocks or eases spectators into a consciousness of breathing, thereby inducing a breach in autoaffection, the artistic practices to which I turn in this chapter come into play once such a breach has occurred and individuals cannot, or can no longer, ignore their breathing. Here I investigate scenes where breathing has imposed itself as an object in the Balintian sense and artists must learn to live with this disturbance by developing new practices of attention and modes of writing.

I tell a three-part story about the ways breathing as an ordinary or exceptional effect of crisis gets entangled with breathing as an aesthetic tactic or strategy. To do so, I assemble an archive of broadly experimental and broadly queer life writing published between the 1990s and the 2010s. *Broadly queer* isn't just an imperfect generic term for a group of writers and artists who identify as queer, nonbinary, and belonging to sexual subcultures (though it is also that). Broadly queer writing locates subject formation in desire. In such writing, breathing is a tool for managing libidinal energies—for dealing with a messiness of desire that, in crisis situations, becomes harder to disavow. The life writing featured here catalogs and obtains its form from breathing as a repetition, deliberate or not. By inducing breathing as an aesthetic form, or by transcribing and dramatizing the patterns and rhythms of breathing, Dodie Bellamy, CAConrad, and Bob Flanagan and Sheree Rose aspire to minimally coherent self-encounters amid loss. Self-encounters are coherent when they match the existing narratives of desire and attachment that make up these individuals' identities. If so much of the evidence compiled in this chapter is biographical, it is because I account for the impact of each artist's experiences on their artistic production and vice versa. Just as an artist's breathing can shape a respiratory aesthetics, a respiratory aesthetics can help to manage an artist's breathing. The artistic notation of breathing for therapeutic purposes corresponds to what I term *aesthetic self-medication*.

Some of the crisis breathing described in this chapter falls under the rubric of disability. Flanagan, for instance, lived with, and died of, cystic fibrosis (CF). And Bellamy has at least written about environmental illness in the first person.[9] But as I mentioned in the introduction, I do not presume that only individuals who disclose disability live with it. Here again, an ecology of the particular, which I have defined as an account of breathing that considers the broad impact of environmental harm without generalizing the experiences of people with respiratory disorders, proves a valuable methodological principle.

The practices of aesthetic self-medication I examine do not imply that disability and debility are one and the same, or that the latter has (heuristically, historically) supplanted the former. By making breathing a locus of artistic and therapeutic intervention, these practices render disability and debility as different kinds of mediation—different configurations of the relation between individuals and milieus. Practices of aesthetic self-medication are not reducible to the medically sanctioned cures that, according to Alison Kafer, align with a pathological model of disability regardless of their desirability.[10] Bellamy and Conrad's embrace of alternative medicine entails a rejection of medical pathology. Instead of pinning their dysphoria on internal causes, they seek to identify and rectify the environmental and structural conditions that foster it. Still, Flanagan and Rose borrow from medical codes and procedures, including the doctor-patient dynamic and the symptomatology template. Their "medical performances," as Petra Kuppers calls them, rearrange without rejecting a medical system of reference.[11] Medicine for them is, rather than the domain that Nirmala Erevelles claims is antipodal to "actual embodied experience," a sensory and sensual realm for negotiating self-presence and personality.[12]

I recognize a certain risk in calling something a crisis in breathing and locating it in the vicinity of disability: the risk of subsuming disability ordinaries into a state of emergency. My point isn't that disability equals crisis, but, as Marta Russell and Ravi Malhotra also propose, that persons with disabilities disproportionately bear the weight of capitalism and the environmental collapse it has engendered. The economic system induces crises to exclude persons with disabilities from the workforce and, in the absence of a welfare state, from the realm of security and protection.[13] Crises are manufactured, but their effects are real, and it's the objective of an ecology of the particular to map out their uneven distribution.

Crisis here has to do with overlapping meanings of the term *life*: life as an existential and historical condition; life as a socially and technologically mediated, organic phenomenon; and life as biography. Bellamy faces "a crisis of urban bombardment," or a crisis of overstimulation in corporatized San Francisco.[14] Conrad writes in reaction to a crisis with existential, artistic, and ecological dimensions. They aim to escape a "brutality" epitomized by the capitalist, homophobic, and transphobic regimes that mechanize embodiment.[15] Flanagan and Rose, in his own journals and in their solo and collaborative works, write and perform through—and, in her case, in the wake of—a crisis pertaining to the intensification of CF symptoms.[16] The unaffordability of medical treatments forced Flanagan into a crisis state. At the time of Flanagan's death, he and Rose could no longer afford to live. They had accumulated debt and had been struggling to obtain adequate financial compensation for their performances and installations. In footage of a show, Flanagan tells a visitor that Medi-Cal doesn't cover lung transplants and that doctors at the Stanford Medical Center consider his lungs too scarred for experimental treatment.[17] Flanagan: "Life is my full-time job, and the pay stinks."[18]

What unites Bellamy, Conrad, and Flanagan and Rose is a condition of psychic disorganization marked by loss. Bellamy has lost her bearings in a fast-transforming city. Conrad laments the loss of their partner Earth and the loss of *the* earth. Flanagan, too, is in mourning. What he misses isn't the imaginary, nondisabled self to be rehabilitated that Kafer associates with nostalgic narratives of disability.[19] He instead mourns a particular genre of, or set of affective expectations toward, pain. In Bellamy's, Conrad's, and Flanagan and Rose's works, loss is symptomatized by, and provisionally remedied through, breathing.

Provisionally being a key word.

This chapter's argument is not that self-expression through writing solves problematic breathing—although, as we shall see, New Age's specter is never very far whenever writing, breathing, and the therapeutic are in close association. On what basis, then, should a text be included in the archive of aesthetic self-medication? The life writing I examine extends beyond the Enlightenment tradition of autobiography to include prose and verse that provide nonfictional accounts of experience, meaning accounts that are rooted in lived reality, not necessarily truthful ones.[20] These accounts take various shapes, from commentaries on daily meditations to poems based on peculiar rituals, to comically pathetic journal entries. Life writing that casts breathing as a symptom of and antidote to crises is best described as a mode that combines the two meanings of Michel Foucault's "*souci de soi*": first, care of the self, which is how the title of the third volume of *The History of Sexuality* is officially translated; and second, anxiety about the self. Foucault's *souci de soi* designates a medical perception of the world that solidified at the end of the twentieth century. We exhibit this *souci* by scanning our milieus for aspects beneficial or detrimental to our health.[21] But breathing is not an either-or situation. We, as breathers, dwell in environments that at once heal and injure us, and from which we can never entirely abstract ourselves. When we say that life writing is not just personal, we typically mean that some memoirs owe their wide appeal to the so-called universality of the experiences they relay. By rendering the self as a source of anxiety and a beneficiary of care—in short, as an entity whose integrity cannot be taken for granted—breathing accentuates the relational dimension of subjectivity and authorship and thereby destabilizes the category of the personal without appealing to a criterion of universality.

Bellamy, Conrad, and Flanagan learn to live and write with conscious breathing as a performance technique. Performance, a formation closely linked to 1960s radicalism, stages corporeal positions and gestures, such that patterns of stillness and movement become techniques.[22] Performance artists have used breathing to dramatize the interplay between abandonment and control—between their exposure to risk or receptivity to stimuli in a live setting and their control as initiators of an artistic act.[23] Although only Flanagan and Rose are known primarily as performance artists, Bellamy and Conrad borrow the codes of performance, specifically athleticism, duration, and endurance, in their meditations and rituals.[24] Athleticism, as Jennifer Doyle uses the term, refers to artistic, recreational, and sport-related practices of the self that constitute physical exploits.[25] When such exploits necessitate stamina and sustained focus, performances tend to be durational, meaning that their form and signification hinge on their (long) duration.[26] Performances count as endurance art when, as Martin O'Brien writes, they offer "a way of persisting through an experience of sufferance or difficulty."[27] In Bellamy's, Conrad's, and Flanagan and Rose's works, text isn't the antithesis of performance or ritual; text arises from deliberate techniques or improvised gestures.

I focus on experimental life writing because it highlights a performative dimension of aesthetic self-medication that remains elusive in popular memoirs of crisis breathing. Granted, Tim Brookes's *Catching My Breath: An Asthmatic Explores His Illness* (1994), among other such popular memoirs, contains the germ of an experimental sensibility. In an attempt to discover the causes of his asthma, Brookes elaborates a whodunit. He designates "possible culprits" in both his body and his milieu, in addition to flagging "unanswered questions."[28] *Breathing for a Living* (2003), Laura Rothenberg's memoir about living with CF, similarly plays with styles and genres. In email exchanges peppered through the book and in a chapter devoted to "What Others Wrote about [Rothenberg's Lung] Transplant," friends, relatives, medical workers, and educators contribute narratives and poems about Rothenberg's medical condition, particularly her labored breathing.[29] Paul Kalanithi's phenomenally popular cancer memoir, *When Breath Becomes Air* (2016), also presents breathing as a site where multiple voices meet. In the epilogue, Lucy Kalanithi recounts that the day her husband died, his "breaths became faltering and irregular" until he "released one last, deep, final breath."[30] Variations in styles and genres (in Brookes's and Rothenberg's books) and shifts of points of view (in Rothenberg's and Kalanithi's books) underscore the relational character of breathing in an effort to distribute the weight of health crises. While Brookes, Rothenberg, and Kalanithi lay out narratively compelling life stories punctuated by instances of experimentation,

Bellamy, Conrad, and Flanagan and Rose repeat and chronicle breathing until it generates forms potent enough to organize their relation to themselves and their environments. In its entirety rather than in a limited number of passages, Bellamy's, Conrad's, and Flanagan and Rose's writing presents itself as aesthetic self-medication—the therapeutic process itself rather than merely an account of that process.

The next sections detail three regimens of aesthetic self-medication. I focus on Bellamy, Conrad, and Flanagan and Rose—in this order—to move from planned to improvised modes of breathing and writing. This sequence sketches a formalism of breathing that, even when it succumbs to pressures, such as illness, that are beyond an author's control, continues to afford a minimally coherent structure for moving through loss.

First Regimen: Dodie Bellamy's Banal Sutras

Bellamy's book *The TV Sutras* (2014) is a diptych. The first portion contains seventy-eight sutras, which the author, drawing on the Hindu *Vayu Purana*, defines as follows: "Of minimal syllabary, unambiguous, pithy, comprehensive, nonredundant, and without flaw."[31] Bellamy's sutras are television-generated sound bites of self-help that are "'inspired' in the spiritual sense, meaning [that they are] dictated or revealed."[32] The sutras are also inspired in the sense that they come to Bellamy through the act of breathing. The book's second section is a lengthy essay that guides us unsystematically through the sutras. Leaping from poetry—or something like poetry—to prose, *The TV Sutras*, as a whole, is best understood as a high-concept project.[33]

In "The Source of the Transmission," a brief protocol that precedes the sutras, Bellamy lays out conditions for receptivity and intuition amid a "crisis of urban bombardment."[34] We're introduced to this crisis through the "loud insistent EEHHH EEHHH EEHHH EEHHH EEHHH" of a car alarm that Bellamy hears from her apartment.[35] "There's no escaping it," she reckons; "I either have to meditate through it or give up."[36] She chooses meditation:

> In receiving the *TV Sutras*, I attuned myself to messages that are broadcast into the living room of my San Francisco apartment. My method: I do a half-hour yoga set while watching the DVD *Peaceful Weight Loss through Yoga*. Then I turn off the DVD player and TV, sit cross-legged on the floor, facing the television, and meditate for twenty minutes. I breathe in, wait, breathe out, wait, breathe in, wait . . . try to accept whatever arises, internally or externally. I do not close my eyes because closed eyes equal

duality, I've been told, while open eyes equal oneness. When my mind wanders, I say to myself "thinking," and refocus on my breath. When I finish meditating, I crawl off my cushion and turn the TV back on. Words and images emerge. There's a flash of recognition and my hand scribbles furiously: I transcribe the first words that strike me, then briefly I describe the scene from which the TV sutra arose. I take a breath, scoot against the wall and quickly write my commentary. Sometimes my interpretation surprises me. Sometimes I disagree with it. But I write down whatever comes. I do not attempt irony, cleverness or perfection— or art. The *TV Sutras* are totally in-the-moment sincere, even if that sincerity makes me cringe afterwards.[37]

Bellamy's meditation protocol brings to mind New Age self-help manuals and how-to guides. The practices and beliefs known as New Age refer to the personalization of mostly Eastern religion and spirituality, which in a Western context was catalyzed by 1960s counterculture.[38] The writers and artists included in this chapter all borrow from New Age's repertoire of breathing practices: Bellamy adopts yoga and meditation, Conrad pagan rituals, and Flanagan and Rose bodywork. Although some readers may be eager to consider Conrad's New Age tendencies peripheral to their ecopoetics, indeed to distinguish a noble environmentalist project from a potentially derided interest in crystals and spells, their poetry asks us to sit with the uneasy affinity between environmentalism and New Age. Both doctrines point to holistic worldviews and promote a harmonious interaction between body and milieu. For Bellamy, New Age designates an antiart. When she writes that she "[does] not attempt . . . art," she means that she doesn't purport to elevate New Age–speak to the rank of Serious Literature.

And yet, it's difficult to grasp *The TV Sutras* as anything other than an artistic gesture. The sutras and their companion essay are packaged into a book that displays the seal of approval of Ugly Duckling Presse, a collective esteemed for its poetry, essays, and hybrid writing. In *The TV Sutras*, Bellamy remixes, but does not give up, her avant-garde habits and aspirations. The project is animated by at least two tensions: one between Bellamy's receptivity to revelation and her control as the initiator of an artistic act, the other between New Age's in-the-moment sincerity and avant-garde sophistication. It is the movement between these poles that gives Bellamy's process of composing with breathing its therapeutic value.

Bellamy's writing practice entails mindful breathing and television watching. While they demand focus—on breath, on the television—the sutras register stimuli indiscriminately. In Sutra 25, Bellamy's exposure to stimulation results in a scene that I, as a reader, struggle to map out:

Put good in, put good out.

Orange juice commercial.

COMMENTARY

Be aware of your influences, of what you can take in. We consume on all levels of our being. Be conscious in your choices. Life is a process of exchange. We are never alone in this, but a beat in a much larger pattern. Inhalation/exhalation. Stay with the breath. We are a conduit of exits as well as entrances.[39]

The last sentence recalls a fortune cookie maxim that got lost in translation. The commentary doesn't state that we are at once exits and entrances—for the air we breathe or the energy we host. It states that we are a *conduit* of exits and entrances. Instead of delimiting a circuit, exits and entrances circulate through it. The phrase "Put good in, put good out" functions simultaneously as a slogan in an orange juice commercial and a mantra for "Inhalation/exhalation." In the haze of meditation—Bellamy is still high when she picks up her journal—breathing and television watching contaminate each other.[40] Bellamy describes her practice thus: "Not observation, absorption."[41]

Bellamy's phenomenology of breathing, wherein inside and outside are interchangeable, spatializes her definition of New Narrative as a movement that "[problematizes] and [confuses] the division between intra- and extra-diegetic."[42] Bellamy has been a key figure in New Narrative, a movement that sprang from Robert Glück and Bruce Boone's workshops and reading group meetings at San Francisco's Small Press Traffic in the late 1970s and early 1980s. Whereas "CULTURED," the long essay included in *The TV Sutras*, showcases New Narrative's blend of fiction and autobiography, the actual sutras clash with the movement's prioritization of long-form prose. The ambition of this prose, as Kaplan Page Harris points out, is to "forge connections across disjunctive or paratactic units of meaning."[43] The sutras mark a formal shift while preserving the spirit of New Narrative. Bellamy's meditative practice retains the core qualities of New Narrative sex writing: an embodied composition process, an embrace of being in relation, an openness to stimulation, and a commitment to explicitness.[44] If sex writing, broadly conceived, records what happens to us and to our bodies when we open ourselves up, encounter each other, and negotiate the borders of pain and pleasure, injury and healing, then *The TV Sutras* fits the bill. The sutras might be, and intentionally so, Bellamy's least hot work of sex writing.

Bellamy's late partner Kevin Killian makes a cameo in "CULTURED" that exemplifies New Narrative's amalgamation of text and metatext. Bellamy reports that New Narrative, in Killian's estimation, reclaimed what was considered vulgar in poetry.[45] In the context of New Narrative, what was considered vulgar in poetry more or less meant what the Language poets deemed vulgar: writing that refers to a materiality located beyond the text, and authors who present themselves as the speakers of their texts.[46] What Harris calls "characteristic New Narrative abjection" is clearly on display in *The TV Sutras*.[47] It just goes by a new name: New Age.[48] Bellamy ponders, "New Narrative Dodie versus New Age Dodie. Can one ever stop embarrassing the other? Dare I reclaim what's considered vulgar in spirituality?"[49]

In a passage structured by the inhales and exhales of meditation, Bellamy reveals what is so vulgar about New Age: "*In breath out breath* I have always wanted to write the best book ever *in breath* as if there were shame in being plain and just getting the ideas out there *out breath* do I still need to be part of an avant-garde *in breath out breath* no longer am I sure what is surface, what is depth."[50] Being plain means embracing porosity as a source of wisdom.[51] It means taking seriously the usefulness of breathing in and out to achieving some balance. It means accepting that there may be no enlightenment possible beyond a naïvely optimistic declaration like this one: "Counting breaths will lead you to accomplishing your goals."[52] It means forgoing irony and abstaining from neutralizing New Age flights of fancy with snark or pop-culture references. Bellamy: "If Kevin were doing the *TV Sutras* he'd include the names of the movies or TV shows, and the stars who are speaking. He'd reveal that Chevy Chase spoke Sutra 73, Woody Allen spoke Sutra 78, silent Sutra 6 is mimed by Winona Ryder, Cary Grant is the dad in Sutra 15, Farrah Fawcett wears the prison dress in Sutra 58, the obnoxious wife in Sutra 29 is Cameron Diaz, Rock Hudson is the disillusioned soldier in Sutra 41. Most of the details I've forgotten."[53] That Winona Ryder is the ghost behind Sutra 6, which instructs us to "take in the glory of each breath, its preciousness," makes for amusing trivia.[54] But because Bellamy didn't write the sutras the way Killian would have written them, I, as a reader, am not aware of such information as I encounter most of the vignettes, which feature figures simply introduced as "Woman," "Man," "Girl," or "Boy." In contrast to more self-serious New Age works, the sutras are funny, but not I'm-smarter-than-you funny. I'm nodding here to Bellamy's own parodic motto for New Narrative "at its worst": "I have sex and I'm smarter than you."[55] An updated motto for the plain sutras could be, "I meditate because I'm not smarter than you."

Whereas New Narrative has traditionally focused on an exclusive literary scene—"in the heyday of New Narrative, everyone wanted to be written about," says Bellamy—the sutras aim for accessibility and banality.[56] "Banal," Bellamy reports, is how Killian describes the sutras.[57] She agrees with Killian's diagnosis, but insists that the banality of the sutras represents their greatest asset. With Bellamy, banality designates embodied meaning that is relatable and transferable: "Behind all those rainbows, unicorns, feel-good slogans, deprivations and rituals, behind the closed doors of the temple, there's a meaning machine in libidinal overdrive."[58] She speculates, "Perhaps it's not the trappings but meaning itself that's banal. . . . In both English and French, banal came from this idea of the commons. Isn't that the promise—or the hope of the *TV Sutras*, that meaning is a sort of commons, available to everyone?"[59] New Age is vulgar, then, insofar as it vulgarizes information. It generates nuggets of wisdom that are easily understood, memorized, and applied. Even the crisis that Bellamy experiences is relatively banal, especially contrasted with the crises on which she touches in her other works, from HIV/AIDS to environmental illness, to the acute homelessness caused by the San Francisco tech boom.[60] The crisis of urban bombardment in *The TV Sutras* constitutes a canvas onto which readers can, to a certain extent, project their own life crises. The sutras say as much about Bellamy as they do about the stimuli she receives in her apartment and about New Age's pool of banal meaning. Bellamy tells David Buuck that "with a bit of knowledge anybody can write some fucking book that Shambhala will publish."[61] Her admittedly cynical remark points to a crucial aspect of her composition process: the cultivation of an impersonal disposition that turns her into the kind of "receptor" or "wisdom-generating machine" that "anyone [else could] become."[62]

The reception or absorption that Bellamy cultivates recalls Ralph Waldo Emerson's "Over-soul," a type of inspiration that Sharon Cameron calls impersonal, for the individual it saturates can have no proprietary relation to it.[63] Cameron argues that personality and impersonality do not stand in binary relation, such that the rubric of impersonality enables us to reencounter persons and personalities without presuming that there exists something fundamentally distinct about them.[64] The Over-soul, in Emerson's description, is an agent that breathes forces into individuals who then become agentive thinkers and actors: the Over-soul amounts to genius "when it breathes through [an individual's] intellect," virtue "when it breathes through his [*sic*] will," and love "when it flows through his [*sic*] affection."[65] Bellamy's objective isn't to ignite her genius, a notion at odds with her commitment to plainness. However, her impersonal combination of breathing and writing enables her to produce a book that bears her personal signature, her very own twist on New Narrative.

Bellamy's aesthetic self-medication begins with the formalization of meditative breathing into sutras and culminates in the commons of banal meaning.

The TV Sutras channels the co-constitution of personality and impersonality to therapeutic ends. On the one hand, New Age posits an impersonal subject: a subject inspired or overtaken by ambient energies. On the other hand, New Age fetishizes personality, as evidenced by the omnipresence of empowering mantras and aphorisms that urge us to be ourselves or raise our voices.[66] The promise of meditative breathing, one in which Bellamy ultimately chooses to believe (even if it's embarrassing, even if it feels like abjection, even if she expresses residual cynicism), is to make openness and control compatible. The repetitive nature of the *TV Sutras* project enables Bellamy to reencounter herself as someone who isn't irremediably disorganized by a crisis of urban bombardment. Stimulation can be coextensive with inspiration.

Second Regimen: CAConrad's Ecodeviant Rituals

"There are no poets writing in quiet caves," writes Conrad, "because every poet is a human being as misshapen as any other being."[67] Conrad takes a breathing-attuned writing practice out of an apartment like Bellamy's and into a variety of private and public spaces. In doing so, they elaborate an experiential poetics that registers the impact of encounters with human and nonhuman beings. Conrad's awareness of the risks of living amid pollution and violence rushes them into a consciousness of breathing. They manage the risks of breathing by devising, in the pagan idiom of *ecodeviance*, rituals for finding solace in vertigo, danger, and even a proximity to death. Confrontations with alterity, some tender and some brutal, yield therapeutic effects. Conrad's rituals provide self-medication at the same time as they pervert the very idea of a self, transgressing distinctions between poet and world, usable matter and waste, and the living and the dead.

Together, *A Beautiful Marsupial Afternoon: New (Soma)tics* (2012), *Ecodeviance: (Soma)tics for the Future Wilderness* (2014), and *While Standing in Line for Death* (2017) compile more than seventy (soma)tic rituals, each of which is followed by a varying number of poems, themselves of varying form and length. Conrad's rituals are performances that intensify experience or, in the terms laid out in chapter 1, proprioception. In rituals, Conrad writes, "the many facets of what is around me wherever I am can come together through a sharper lens."[68] Of all the figures included in *Breathing Aesthetics*, Conrad, who inhales new surroundings to exhale new poems, is best aligned with the mid-twentieth-century projectivist tradition of breath poetics I touched on in the introduction.[69] Conrad details the rituals in protocols, some of which are in the imperative mood while others, closer to reports but nevertheless replicable, are in the declarative mood.

The rituals are just as inventive and just as moving as the poems they yield. The juxtaposition of rituals and poems encourages an impossible recognition game. I look for traces of the rituals in the poems, only to realize that there's no obvious thematic correspondence between the two. For example, title notwithstanding, there's very little yellow in "we're on the brink of UTTER befuddlement yellow hankie style," a poem that Conrad wrote "after eating only yellow foods for a day while under the influence of a yellow condom tucked into [their] left sock."[70] Although respiration activates composition, the poems do not constitute notations of breathing in the strict sense. Conrad notes anything that catches their attention within the sensory and perceptual field expanded by a ritual.

Conrad's books of (soma)tics mark a shift in their life and career. After visiting the industrial Pennsylvania town where they had grown up, Conrad realized that they had been treating poetry writing as a one-worker factory.[71] They imagined (soma)tic rituals as an alternative to the assembly line, one that would remedy "the worst [problem] with the factory": "lack of being present."[72] The phenomenological presence and temporal "extreme present" to which Conrad aspires synthesize transcendence and immanence: the author's spelling of (soma)tic protects between two parentheses the soma (divine) in somatic (tissue or nervous system).[73] Whereas in The TV Sutras Bellamy wants to "become a machine," Conrad aims to sidestep mechanization by never writing more than a few poems before moving on to a new ritual.[74] Conrad summarizes, "I cannot stress enough how much this mechanistic world, as it becomes more and more efficient, resulting in ever increasing brutality, has required me to FIND MY BODY to FIND MY PLANET in order to find my poetry."[75] Let us note the accumulation of infinitives. Coordinates that might help Conrad find their body might also help them find their planet and their poetry—all in one breath.

Therein lies a paradox: Conrad's rituals are a nonmechanistic, and thus less brutal, means of confronting the brutality that the poet associates with mechanization and its environmental repercussions. Conrad considers themself an "extension" of "the beauty of a patch of unspoiled sand, all that croaks from the mud," but also of "garbage, shit, pesticides, bombed and smoldering cities, microchips, cyber, astral and biological pollution."[76] They see themself as contingent on a planet that, while sustaining them, harbors violence by normalizing transphobia, homophobia, misogyny, and racism. In a (soma)tic ritual titled "DOUBLE-shelter" and another one titled "I LOVED EARTH YEARS AGO," Conrad outlines rituals in memory of their late partner, an environmental and HIV/AIDS activist who went by the name Earth.[77] Although the police ruled Earth's death a suicide, Conrad maintains that he was gay-bashed and set on fire.[78] In Belinda Schmid and David Cranstoun Welch's documentary on this event, one of Earth's brothers suggests that he died from either the burns or the fumes.[79] Whether Earth's porous skin was burned or his airways were obstructed, his death cannot be untangled from his breathing. According to Conrad, only the poems included in their third major collection of (soma)tics, *While Standing in Line for Death*, enabled them "to overcome [their] depression from [their] boyfriend Earth's murder."[80] More straightforward than previous works, the rituals and poems included in *While Standing in Line for Death* clearly thematize Earth's murder. One untitled poem from the "Mount Monadnock Transmissions" series begins, "the men who killed you / justify your abbreviated breath."[81] Another one from the same section goes,

your rapists were the last
to taste you in this world
their breath and
terror down
your neck
keeps me
up at night.[82]

In a somatic called "POETRY is DIRT as DEATH is DIRT," conscious breathing creates a momentum for capturing brutalities of all kinds:

Go to your local graveyard, spend some time searching for a spot to sit. Be where no one will bother you, you're busy, you're here to write poetry, not to be pestered with small talk! When you have found your place sit on the ground. Take time to look closely at ALL OBJECTS at your feet, in the trees, etc. Find 3 objects, one of them on the ground, or at least touching the ground: your feet, a grave marker, tree trunk or roots, etc. The other 2 off the ground in a tree, a building, but make them things that are stationary so you can stay focused on them. Draw a triangle connecting these 3 objects. Focus hard on the contents of your triangle, keeping in mind that the ground object you have chosen connects to the dead.

Imagine your triangle in different forms of light, weather, and seasons. Imagine someone you love in the triangle dying. Imagine yourself inside it dying. Gather notes in this process, take notes, as many notes as you can about how you feel and what you feel. Then PAUSE from these notes to focus again on your triangle, THEN write QUICKLY AND WITHOUT THINKING for as much as you can manage. Often it's these spontaneous notes that dislodge important information for us. DO NOT HESITATE to write the most brutal things that come to mind, HESITATE at nothing for that matter. *Take some deep breaths* and think about death by murder, war, cancer, suicide, accidents, knives, fire, *drowning,* crushing, decapitation, torture, plagues, animal attacks, dehydration, guns, stones, tanks, bombs, genocide, strokes, explosions, electrocutions, guillotine, firing squads, parasites, *suffocation,* flash floods, tornadoes, earthquakes, cyanide, poison, capital punishment, falling, stampedes, *strangulation,* freezing, baseball bats, overdose, plane crashes, fist fights, *choking,* etc., imagine every possible form of death. Take notes on your feelings for death at this point, DO NOT HESITATE.[83]

Deep breaths appear only once in this ritual, but they fulfill a pivotal role. They turn an attunement to a particular milieu—a graveyard—into a confrontation with "every possible form of death," including mass extinction. Forms of death like drowning, suffocation, strangulation, and choking imply the inability to breathe. As the ritual shifts from the measured pace of observing and drawing to the fast pace of note taking, and finally to the extreme present of deep breathing, respiration remains on Conrad's mind. Poetic insight into the function of breathing in "POETRY is DIRT as DEATH is DIRT" shows up not in "I'm TOO Lazy for this World," the poem that comes after the ritual, but in "QUALM CUTTING AND ASSEMBLAGE," the one that precedes it. The lengthy poem concludes,

our bones
our muscles
get rising
to one
and
two
breaths
the common
lung this
world a
mouth into
a mouth
breathing
back
and
forth
so

then
so
then
mouth
sings to
mouth
so then
mouth
sings to
mouth
so then
all night
so then
a day
then a
day so[84]

The poem's combination of enjambment and parataxis both breaks apart the respiratory process it documents and complicates recitation: When to pause? The poem even ends midbreath, with an incomplete causal conditional. Breathing, which here approximates the mouth-to-mouth of kissing or cardiopulmonary resuscitation, is a heuristic of incompleteness. It's an embodied "What else?" that figures and materializes the interconnection and interdependence of organisms within a "common / lung." Conrad's figure of the common lung recalls Juliana Spahr's *This Connection of Everyone with Lungs* (2005), which I also mentioned in chapter 1. As Lauren Berlant writes, Spahr generates "a holding environment that articulates the commons in common but reshapes it too: . . . verses move across mesosphere, stratosphere, islands, cities, rooms, hands, cells."[85] "Holding environment" is D. W. Winnicott's term for the mother's provision of a comfortable and sound environment for the baby.[86] Polluted and weaponized, breathing and air constitute hazardous holding environments. Neither Conrad's nor Spahr's common lung guards the held against risk.

Yet many of Conrad's (soma)tics are amusing, even outright funny. Rituals present opportunities for ecodeviance, a queer practice that finds excitement amid what gets rejected from categories of the normal and the civilized. At once defiant and playful, Conrad takes pleasure in recycling waste products like bodily discharge for creative purposes. To replicate the ritual "WHITE HELIUM," a relaxation protocol that takes place over the course of four days, you would need a balloon, gum, and "snot or blood or semen or pussy juice or earwax or piss or vomit or shit or spit or sweat or whatever excretion you have available."[87] Ecodeviance aligns with theories wherein breathing distributes erogeneity onto the entire body, and in some cases beyond it. These theories range from Aristotle's belief that pneuma is the life-giving heat produced by semen in its contact with the menses to Wilhelm Reich's orgone therapy, a precursor of New Age, developed in the 1930s, that uses respiration to occasion an emotional release comparable to the orgasm.[88] In line with Conrad's project of normative and civilizational unlearning, Ellen Willis contends that Reich's notion of a basic erotic unity shattered by genital repression not only explains neurosis but justifies sexual liberation as a movement that undoes the submissive attitudes imposed by patriarchal civilization.[89] Conrad uses breathing to eroticize their milieu and reencounter themself and their gender identity under new terms.[90] In a ritual designed for a (soma)tic poetry workshop held in New York City in 2008, deep breaths of fresh air and the smell of rosemary generate conditions for imagining embodiment otherwise:

> Before sniffing the rosemary take some notes about your gender, or write about your feelings and ideas about gender in general. Take those initial notes to break open space in yourself for gender. Then take a few deep breaths of fresh air, then squeeze the leaves of the rosemary to release the oils and take a nice DEEP BREATH. Now, imagine yourself a different gender. What do you feel when you imagine this? What are your hands like? Your feet? How are you walking as this Other? What name would you like to have as this Other? Take another DEEP breath of your rosemary and say that name out loud to yourself. Really let INSIDE this Other you.[91]

In this ritual, breathing makes possible a confrontation with gender alterity. Breathing is embodied transgression; it opens experience up to surprise.

Queer theory's forays into ecology and wildness, too, stage a tension between the morbid and invigorating aspects of an intimacy with what civilization rejects or damages. Catriona Sandilands identifies affinities between practices of grieving the ungrievable in the context of HIV/AIDS and in the context of ecological degradation—affinities that could not be clearer in Conrad's mourning of both Earth, an HIV/AIDS activist, and the earth.[92] In a dissonant register, one that endows nature with a feral quality, Jack Halberstam advocates the relevance of the wild. With the wild, Halberstam imports into an ecological framework José Esteban Muñoz's definition of queerness as "the rejection of a here and now and an insistence on potentiality or concrete possibility for another world."[93] In Halberstam's view, the wild sparks "unpredictability, breakdown, disorder, and shifting forms of signification."[94] Conrad makes a claim compara-ble to Halberstam's: that through poetry we may return to the "seismic levels of wildness" of a world that precedes "the hypnotic beep of machines, of war, . . . the banal need for power, and things."[95] At the cost of reproducing the colonial fantasy that supports the ontologization of nature's queerness and its location in a preindustrial past, Conrad relays, via wildness, a desire for less regimented ways of relating to themself and others.[96]

Conrad's aesthetic self-medication regimen shares some features with Bella-my's. Both cultivate impersonality, which for Conrad takes the form of a radi-cal confrontation with the productive and destructive elements of the milieus they occupy. The two weave writing practices into a certain ritualization of breathing. Bellamy doesn't believe that her sutras count as art because anyone could have composed them, whereas Conrad insists that their writing is poetry and affirms that "anyone can be a poet"; those are two sides of a coin.[97] Where Conrad's books of (soma)tics most strikingly depart from *The TV Sutras* is in the higher degree of improvisation and risk demanded by an ever-renewed reper-toire of rituals. Conrad sets up a challenge for themself: to continue to breathe in a context where respiration entails metabolizing a dying earth and commem-orating Earth's death. For Conrad, brutality ought not to be avoided, and death ought not to be deferred. Brutality and death saturate every breath in wounded ecologies. Conrad cannot isolate pleasure from pain in their confrontations with alterity, but what they can do is formalize these confrontations. Rituals and poems make loss feel less like paralysis and more like a process.

Third Regimen: Bob Flanagan and Sheree Rose's Sick Journals and Performances

The regimens of aesthetic self-medication I've sketched thus far—Bellamy's protocols for banal sutras and Conrad's ecodeviant rituals—have remained in the vicinity of meditation. Even though Conrad's rituals call for regular adjust-ments to shifting and at times risky conditions, both writers are ultimately able to structure their experience into sutras or poems. This chapter's third and last regimen proves essential when crisis breathing exceeds intentional efforts of regularization and ritualization, imposing its own rhythm on living and writ-ing. To outline this regimen, I relate the evolution of Flanagan and Rose's life and art.

Breathing is seldom the first thing critics and art enthusiasts mention when they discuss Flanagan and Rose. Statements with and about shock value are more common—statements like Rosemarie Garland-Thomson's oft-cited descriptor for Flanagan: the artist "famous for pounding a nail through his penis in one of his performances."[98] Flanagan was a masochist. He and Rose met in 1980 at a Halloween party. She was dressed as Jayne Mansfield, he as a character from *Night of the Living Dead*—two dead figures. Shortly after their meet-cute, Flanagan and Rose began to live in a full-time slave/mistress relationship. He submitted to her by cooking, cleaning the house, running errands, and forfeiting dominance over their sex life. For Rose, who before meeting Flanagan had transitioned from stay-at-home wife and mother to icon of Los Angeles's 1970s underground punk scene, the BDSM lifestyle offered a feminist riff on heterosexual domesticity.[99] Flanagan idealized himself as Supermasochist, an ironic superhero who bore pain better than phonies "who [could] take anything *they* [told] you to do," as he quipped in his song "Smart-Ass Masochist."[100]

Masochist was not the only label Flanagan claimed; *sick* proved equally important. Flanagan had CF, a disorder marked by an abnormal production of mucus that clogs the lungs. The lack of oxygen causes depletion in the blood and the brain, such that people who suffer from this hereditary disorder ultimately drown in their secretions. Flanagan and Rose titled one of their shows *Bob Flanagan's Sick*. Kirby Dick later borrowed the term for the 1997 documentary *Sick: The Life and Death of Bob Flanagan, Supermasochist*, which relies heavily on footage shot by Rose. The word *sick* suggests physical illness as well as deviance and perversion.[101] *Visiting Hours*, a museum piece presented at the Santa Monica Museum of Art in 1992 and at the New Museum in New York City in 1994, explicitly conflated CF and sadomasochism (SM). The piece included a room modeled on a medical clinic and a wall made of 1,400 alphabet blocks spelling "B-O-B," "S-M," and "C-F." Through a system of ropes and pulleys, Rose sporadically lifted Flanagan, his ankles strapped into a harness, above the hospital bed on which he otherwise sat all day.[102] The act gave Flanagan a spatially but not affectively uplifting break from his stasis. The convoluted scene both amplified his suffering and foregrounded the strength and dedication of Rose's support. Like their endurance performances, the elevation in *Visiting Hours* required controlled breathing on the part of both artists. Lifting a body necessitates strength, and hanging upside down, a dizzying act, necessitates calm and stamina. Flanagan and Rose had to train themselves to breathe the way athletes would. Controlled breathing was how Flanagan conveyed a receptivity that turned him into the all-powerful Supermasochist, and it was how Rose conveyed a control that turned her into a hyperattuned magician's assistant. In breathing, contractual submission and domination easily flow into one another. Flanagan: "I am ultimately (this is what every masochist hates to hear, or admit) in full control."[103]

Scholars in performance and disability studies have written extensively about Flanagan and Rose's slave/mistress relationship and extreme performance practice. Garland-Thomson explains that Flanagan's performances exemplify "disability autobiography," a genre of visual and narrative self-presentation that intervenes in "the social construction of disability identity."[104] Renate Lorenz and Kuppers separately observe that Flanagan publicizes the pain in SM and the pain of sickness as interconnected but not interchangeable.[105] Dwelling on the convergence of disability and erotic fantasy, Robert McRuer argues that Flanagan and Rose's work is transgressive precisely because it flirts with the "co-optation" of disability.[106] Linda S. Kauffman, for her part, claims that Flanagan's didactic, step-by-step exposition of the reorganization of human senses by technology in pieces like *The Visible Man* and *Autopsy* makes him a "live model of the posthuman."[107] This scholarship tends to simplify Flanagan and Rose's life and work by making torture and suffering politically straightforward and thus less threatening to spectators. McRuer, for instance, reads in Flanagan's extreme vulnerability a "message" or solved riddle about living with disability: "In a moment of danger and noncompliance, . . . 'some future person' or collectivity might detect in that sick message the seemingly incomprehensible way to survive, and survive well, at the margins of time, space, and representation (they might, in fact, detect that surviving well can paradoxically mean surviving sick)."[108] If we bracket Kauffman, who provides a technogenetic account of embodiment, the scholars above share an interest in the ways Flanagan resignifies and reclaims his disabled body. Casting Flanagan's body as the one to be resignified and reclaimed erases Rose's feminist politics. Moreover, critics have largely overlooked the transformation of Flanagan and Rose's life and work once the positions of Supermasochist and Mistress Rose became unsustainable. I understand their later work as the result of a shift in respiratory aesthetics—a shift away from the mix of controlled breathing and ecstatic breathlessness of BDSM performance and toward the labored breathing of CF in lived experience and its memorialization.

Flanagan's solo journals telegraph first his coming of age as a masochistic performer and then his coming to terms with a diminished ability to control his breathing. Two of Flanagan's journals have been published. The other documents I label journals are sustained writing practices in notebooks and on loose leaves of paper that can be found, generally incomplete, across Flanagan and Rose's two archival collections, hosted by separate institutions.[109] One massive journal, from the late 1970s, just before Flanagan and Rose met, shows us a pre-Supermasochist Flanagan who had yet to develop techniques of controlled breathing through performance.[110] Another project, undertaken in the mid-1980s, is an epistolary journal: a series of dated letters addressed to Rose. These letters catalog the temporary relief from shallow breathing offered by medical treatments and a tattooing session that feels like inhaling "pure oxygen."[111] Like all volumes published by Hanuman Books, Flanagan's first published diary, *Fuck Journal* (1987), comes in the shape of a tiny prayer manual. The journal records, in all caps, Flanagan and Rose's sex life throughout the year 1986. Entries blend tales of erotic asphyxiation with Flanagan's realization that he's otherwise increasingly "NOT BREATHING WELL," and decreasingly willing to submit to Rose.[112] Another unpublished journal written the same year constitutes a depressive counterpart to the high-octane *Fuck Journal*. The April 7 entry, which moves from prose to verse, concludes,

> I'm still here
> And I wish I wasn't. Sick of this life.
> Everyday is another kind of loss.[113]

The loss that Flanagan reports in his journals, registered in the 1970s but helplessly disorganizing by the 1990s, is the loss of masochism. In a piece titled "S," published in the magazine *Frame/Work* along with photos by Rose, Flanagan tracks the minutiae of his breathing to narrate this loss:

> You'll notice I have the letter "S" carved into the right side of my chest. It might seem strange and kind of silly for a grown man to risk infection and permanent scarring (not to mention the pain) and allow someone to carve an "S" into his flesh like this, but I'm serious about it. I have an "S" on my chest and I feel sentimental about it. It was put there by Sheree, my soul mate, sex partner, and sidekick for the past twelve years. It's her signature. "S" for SHEREE, and mine too: "S" for SLAVE; which is what I am, or what I have always aspired to be, except that now I'm not so sure. This "S," which used to be the symbol of STRENGTH and STAMINA, has started fading. . . .
> There's an "S" on my chest and that's what it stands for: SICK. . . .
> These days, when we have sex, or when I have sex by myself—or forget sex—when I'm just climbing up the stairs, or doing anything that produces a physical strain of some sort, I get severely short of breath and have to stop everything, gasping like a fish, while I suck air through my nose and then exhale slowly through clenched teeth, making this swooshing sound with my mouth, like I'm telling everyone to—"Shhhhh"—be quiet, but I'm just trying to save my breath.[114]

Flanagan's labored breathing speaks for him. Breathing here opposes physical exertion, including the exertion of actual speech, in the absence of strength and stamina. "Underdog," a piece that is not attached to any specific project, amplifies breathing's negation: "'No' is the first word out of my mouth, it's part of my breathing now, no . . . no . . . no . . ."[115] Flanagan here performs what François-Bernard Michel, writing about asthma in French literature, describes as disabled language's refusal of air.[116] Michel writes of advanced asthmatics, "Pour exister, ils n'ont plus que leur symptôme" (To keep living, they possess little more than their symptom).[117] Likewise, Flanagan's existence becomes structured by asphyxia, which, in Michel's nomenclature, is a miming of death by life.[118]

The Pain Journal (2000), Flanagan's second published journal and last work, is his most explicit and substantial postscript to his and Rose's BDSM life and work. Flanagan wrote The Pain Journal between December 27, 1994, and December 16, 1995. The entries chronicle the everydayness of a pain that no longer catalyzes pleasure and gratification. Intentional, episodic pain gives way to unintentional, chronic pain. Flanagan never had the luxury of nonconscious breathing. He never tried to become aware of his breathing. Instead, in his performances with Rose, he tried to cultivate an awareness of breathing that differed from the one tied to CF. This cultivation isn't possible in The Pain Journal, where CF determines the terms by which he's made aware of his breathing. At that point, Flanagan starts "[hating his and Rose's performance] work," finds it "pathetic," is "embarrassed" by it.[119] The spectacular shock of the couple's BDSM performances dissipates. What remains is "difficulty," Doyle's term for art that combines intimacy, exposure, and explicitness.[120]

In his March 19, 1995, entry, Flanagan situates his masochistic identity in the past: "Thought I'd escape writing tonight, but found myself mulling over why it is I don't like pain anymore. I have this performance to do on April 1st, and I'm shying away from doing or having SM stuff done to me because pain and the thought of pain mostly just irritates and annoys me rather than turns me on. But I miss my masochistic self. I hate this person I've become. And what about my reputation?"[121] Further into the Journal, on November 8, 1995, Flanagan describes the fading of masochism as a betrayal, a stratagem that did not operate as long as needed. "I set it up so that pain was supposed to be so good, something to endure and to conquer," he deplores. "Anything short of that feels like failure."[122] According to the Cystic Fibrosis Foundation, the predicted life expectancy for people with CF born between 2015 and 2019 is around forty-six years.[123] When Flanagan wrote the Journal, the average life span was closer to twenty-nine or thirty years. "At 42," he observes, "I'm one of the anomalies."[124]

The speaker of the poem "Dead Air" resents having to save his breath—or survive—to appease his audience and his addressee (Rose, in all likelihood). The poem's title, which refers to an interruption of the video signal during a television broadcast, entangles a failure to entertain with a breath that heralds death:

> That's all that's there
> but what do you care?
> I'm wasting my breath
> waiting for death
> choking on my own phlegm,
> saving it all for them
> the audience and you."[125]

The rhyme scheme (AA DD CC D) is so simple as to recall nursery rhymes. The movement from "wasting" to "waiting" and "breath" to "death" is predictable; if we were to fill in the blanks, we would likely come up with the same words. "Dead Air" accomplishes little by way of figuration. The poetic toolbox is as depleted as the poet who holds it. For Flanagan, surviving feels like failure because it means outliving masochism and hence falling short of deriving a sense of self-control from the experience of pain.

Although Flanagan feels alienated from his and Rose's BDSM performance work in *The Pain Journal*, the book itself unfolds as an endurance performance. Before meeting Flanagan, Rose had studied psychology at California State University, Northridge, where she had become familiar with therapeutic techniques associated with New Age. A personal journal from the fall of 1977 details her discovery of hypnosis and self-hypnosis, which she deems "a valuable learning tool."[126] She recalls serving as a subject in a demonstration of neo-Reichian techniques. Around the same time, she became involved with Radix, a body therapy collective.[127] When Rose and Flanagan met in the early 1980s, she introduced him to bodywork, and he introduced her to BDSM play. The therapeutic and theatrical techniques they taught one another influenced *The Pain Journal*. In order to pursue his project despite suffering, Flanagan had to remain disciplined, follow "the rules," and "be a good boy."[128] Whereas Flanagan and Rose's BDSM performances employed knives, nails, and ball gags, his journal writing was contingent on such aids as masks, respirators, and oxygen pumps.[129]

Flanagan's writing in *The Pain Journal* is loopy and ongoing. His inability to catch his breath translates into lengthy sentences like this one:

> Excuse me while I put ear plugs in cause Sheree's asleep and breathing heavy
> and that really bugs me cause I want her up and talking to me and watch-

ing tv with me now that it's one in the morning and I'm awake and *The Picture of Dorian Gray* is on tv after she came down and woke me up after I left her upstairs sleeping on the couch after her long day long drive home from Irvine—but never mind that—I was pissed that she wasn't watching a tv show about murder in our own Rampart district and then some dumb movie about a terminator substitute teacher blowing kids away while she snored away and I had a bunch of things I wanted to tell her but it wasn't only that she was asleep, I was depressed and out of breath and could barely talk anyway, but I stormed away with my stupid fashion pack drug pump slung over my shoulder like a huffy bitch, short of breath and with a headache like a penned up rodeo horse trying to kick its way out of my head—everyone who's critical of my nastiness: put a plastic bag on your head all day and every couple of hours slam your head into the coffee table and press your thumbs into your eye sockets until your eyeballs squish like bloody grapes and then tell me what a great mood you're in.[130]

The sequence of conjunctions—"and . . . and . . . and"—offers no respite. Flanagan doesn't hierarchize his claims. His long sentence is filled with digressions, some of which we're belatedly asked to disregard. "Morning" is misspelled, but Flanagan doesn't pause to make corrections. Rose's noisy breathing, addressed at the beginning of the sentence, is only a distant memory by the time we get to the end and Flanagan's own difficult breathing has taken over. He's short of breath, out of breath, and a huffy bitch. Here and throughout *The Pain Journal*, Flanagan's writing succumbs to the respiratory repertoire of CF—to wheezing, coughing, being out of breath, and breathing that feels like drowning.

I wouldn't go so far as to say that documenting difficult breathing affords Flanagan the kind of control that Bellamy and Conrad enjoy as a result of their rituals. Nevertheless, Flanagan's practice of writing with difficult breathing is therapeutic. It bears proxy libidinal structures, including boredom and humor, which make his defenselessness less disorganizing in the absence of masochism. Bored is how Flanagan feels as he translates into journal entries the humdrum of not breathing, yet not dying. Across the entries included in *The Pain Journal*, Flanagan repeats that his "chest hurts," that he "can't breathe," and that he's "wheezing" and "coughing."[131] He's "not depressed, but not happy. Just alive. Just living. Barely breathing."[132] "Again," he sums up, "I'm boring myself."[133] Nowhere is Flanagan's weariness of his recursive symptomatology clearer than in his July 21, 1995, entry:

I don't know what to write in here anymore. The same old story every night. Headache blah blah blah hospital blah blah blah can't breathe blah

blah blah dying blah blah blah tv blah blah blah Sheree blah blah blah Mom and Dad blah Tim blah stupid brother John blah blah letters to write blah blah blah camp blah my penis blah blah list keeping and blah blahs a poor substitute for real writing blah blah blah blah blah not enough pain killers blah blah but if the breathing's bad enough on Monday Riker might up the pain meds because what have we got to lose blah blah blah blood in my phlegm blah blah blah vital signs not so blah blah vital no change no up no down blah blah lost in the blah blah and the pain med but the pain's still here and there's no rush anymore blah blah blah whah whah why won't this nurse clean out my phlegm basin huh blah huh this is so awful I don't deserve to live blah.[134]

Flanagan's "same old story" is overwritten. Onomatopoeias substitute for markers of relation and punctuation. "Whah" evokes an infantile cry, and "huh" sighing or wheezing. Generic sound words that perform difficult breathing convey Flanagan's boredom in the face of recalcitrant symptoms.

In his July 14, 1995, entry, Flanagan casts himself as a boring type: "[Sheree and I are] supposed to be fucking, but she's snoring and I'm boring. Snoring and Boring. Thank you Ladies and Germs."[135] Flanagan and Rose were supposed to remain Mistress Rose and Supermasochist, but now they are Snoring and Boring. A nonconscious habit and an affective state here congeal as types that bring to mind clowns or characters on a children's TV show. Fashioning himself as a type, not unlike Bellamy's and Conrad's therapeutic cultivation of impersonality, organizes Flanagan; it sets expectations about gestures and behaviors. By calling himself Boring, rather than simply boring, Flanagan is in a sense saying, "My shtick is that I complain a lot about not being able to breathe." Perhaps Flanagan "can't stand the boredom," but boredom coextends with a set of expectations that ensure his continuity as a subject.[136]

The boring repetition—with little difference—of Flanagan's labored breathing does not lead anywhere, but it holds the mood. I derive this formulation from Adam Phillips's notion of boredom as "that state of suspended anticipation in which things are started and nothing begins, the mood of diffuse restlessness which contains that most absurd and paradoxical wish, the wish for a desire."[137] Boredom, for Phillips, makes tolerable the experience of waiting for something without knowing what it could be.[138] As a "blank condensation of psychic life," boredom "[holds] the mood," keeping alive, at one remove, the possibility of desire.[139] Phillips's allusion to holding refers to Winnicott's "holding environment." Boredom is not an end in itself. It is a transitional prehesitation, a stage that comes before the mental conflict or "asthma"—Winnicott's term!—of letting feelings develop.[140] Flanagan's boredom defers an asthma-like experience of psychic disorganization by holding (on to) CF's respiratory patterns and rhythms.[141] Flanagan's transition from extreme performance to boring writing isn't so surprising in light of Doyle's argument that once we set aside concerns of repression and censorship, we may perceive in sexually explicit art "the quotidian cycles of desire, . . . antiheroic portraits of anxiety, pleasure, rage, and boredom."[142] From BDSM performances emerged a boredom that in *The Pain Journal* Flanagan harnesses as a survival mechanism, one that gets him "from one place to the other," from one day to the next.[143] Boredom recasts crisis as a new normal, a new business as usual that ironically turns chronic pain into medication by postponing a loss of personal identity. In the manuscript of his ambitious "Book of Medicines," Flanagan recalls writing in 1979, as he was new to slave/mistress relationships, "I'm excited again just thinking about it. But I have to slow down now. I've got to stretch this out for a long time. I'm going to make it a life-style, and not just a mood."[144] A mood, boredom, returns when excitement as lifestyle becomes too onerous. This shift reveals variations in attachments within the category that Kafer calls "crip time": a temporal regime occupied by persons with disabilities and indexed by such notions as chronicity, relapse, remission, and prognosis.[145] Late in Flanagan's life and career, the drawn-out temporality of sustained cathexis makes way for the dragged-out temporality of deferred cathexes.[146]

Writing *The Pain Journal* might have been boring for Flanagan, but I don't find the experience of reading his jittery prose strictly boring. When I read, I alternate between the boredom of going over the symptomatology of CF for the nth time and the shock of witnessing persistent suffering. I also alternate between the desire to rush to the end of the book and the impulse to slow down in a pathetic bid to postpone Flanagan's inevitable death. These contradictory feelings amount to what Sianne Ngai calls "stuplimity," an affective structure that begins with the dysphoria of shock and boredom and "[culminates] in something like the 'open feeling' of 'resisting being'—an indeterminate affective state that lacks the punctuating 'point' of an individuated emotion."[147] To illustrate stuplimity, Ngai considers, among other (modernist) works, Samuel Beckett's *Stirrings Still*. Her account of Beckett's final prose work resonates uncannily with *The Pain Journal*: "The theme of survival and endurance in the wake of a traumatic loss is conveyed here through a drastic slowdown of language, a rhetorical enactment of its fatigue—in which the duration of relatively simple actions is uncomfortably prolonged through a proliferation of precise inexactitudes."[148] We encounter Flanagan's painful breathing through the repetition of precise inexactitudes, from sound words to erratic syntax. The more

Flanagan's language collapses into labored breathing, the more indistinguishable the breathing and writing components of his ultimate performance appear. Whereas in *The TV Sutras* this indistinguishability ensues from a deliberate composition technique, in *The Pain Journal* it points to Flanagan's inability, at a certain point, to write prose that isn't taken over by his labored breathing.

As hinted by a phrase like "Thank you, Ladies and Germs" that plays with the format of standup comedy, boredom doesn't cancel out the vibrant humor that typifies Flanagan's work alone and with Rose. Flanagan borrows the phrase "Ladies and Germs" from the late comedian Milton Berle, who would say to his audience, "Good evening, ladies and germs. I mean ladies and gentlemen. I call you ladies and gentlemen, but you know what you really are."[149] Flanagan's comedy relies on musicality. In the documentary *Sick*, Flanagan prefaces a song that borrows the tune of *Mary Poppins*'s "Supercalifragilisticexpialidocious" with a warning: "I know that any Disney people here, they'll probably tell me to cease and desist, and believe me, I will . . . but not yet. In my own time." Coughing intermittently, he then intones,

> Supermasochist Bob has cystic fibrosis
> He should've died young, but he was too precocious
> How much longer he will live is anyone's prognosis
> Supermasochist Bob has cystic fibrosis
> I'm dili-dili, I'm gonna die
> I'm dili-dili, I'm gonna die.

Even if the *Journal* doesn't contain actual songs, Flanagan pays close attention to moments when prose turns into a melody. For instance, in the June 1, 1995, entry, his symptomatology turns to air (labored breathing) at the same time as it turns into an air (a melody) from *The Sound of Music*: "Feel awful. Neck ache. Headache. Sore eyes. Chest pain. Difficulty breathing. These are a few of my favorite things."[150] In musical theater, transitions from colloquial speech to conventional musical numbers mark moments of dramatic tension or exacerbated emotion. Think of the "I want" song, which early in a show clarifies the protagonist's motivations, or the "eleven o'clock" number, which just before the finale raises the stakes of the play.[151] By contrast, musical structure in *The Pain Journal* diffuses tension. It distracts. It allows the masochism evacuated from a pain that plainly hurts to return.

Interpretation is key to Leo Bersani's theory of sexuality as structurally masochistic: sex acquires the form of sexuality when we "interpretively [remember]" the self-dissolution we experience in sex as a sign and a promise of something potentially pleasurable.[152] Similarly, when Flanagan no longer derives pleasure from pain alone, he finds himself adrenalized by the "clever writing" and "magical writing" that he deciphers in his manuscript on pain.[153] Whether they are boring or comedic, Flanagan's therapeutic self-encounters rely on his artistic production. They hinge on Flanagan's ability to interpret symptoms arranged into a hum, a melody, or even a joke as evidence of his persistence as a subject. Flanagan stopped writing only three weeks before he died, on January 4, 1996.

Ever since Flanagan's death, Rose has been aware of her breathing in intentionally and unintentionally triggered situations of exertion that have doubled as occasions for memorialization. Rose recounts a hiking trip to the Himalayas, where at a high altitude she "felt so close to [Flanagan] because of the physical thing [she] was feeling with the breathing."[154] She adds, "And that, of course, made me cry all the more because I never realized how difficult it was for him."[155] It's hard to imagine that Rose never realized how difficult it was for Flanagan to breathe. She had to be sharply attuned to his symptoms in order for the pair to engage in BDSM. But Rose's encounters with breathing following Flanagan's passing have likely intensified this attunement. She has sought to preserve this awareness in everyday and artistic performances. Yoga, which she has been practicing in Los Angeles and with the Satchidananda Ashram in Yogaville, Virginia, has given her the opportunity to meditate on "the breath of life, and the idea that you are only allowed so many breaths." She says, "I think about Bob a lot during yoga because he could never deep breathe. He never had a comfortable breath."[156] In an outtake from the interview just quoted, Rose adds that even watching her granddaughter breathe reminds her "that Bob could never take a decent breath."[157]

In *Corpse Pose* and *Gurney of Nails*, two staged performances, Rose occupies the position of the fakir that would have been Flanagan's in their BDSM performances. She lies on a table or a bed of nails and remains stoic for approximately forty-five minutes as collaborators paint her body or pour hot wax onto her. For these performances, she "consciously [tries] to make [her] breath as narrow, as skinny as [she] can, and barely breathe at all."[158] Rose's aesthetic production of breathing, in yoga and in performances, puts her in a position similar to Conrad's: both memorialize loved ones by generating specific respiratory conditions. Rose works with breathing to reencounter herself in proximity to Bob, or as Bob.

For Rose, as for Conrad, breathing does not have to be depressing just because it coincides with mourning. What better way to remember Flanagan than with some twisted humor? In 1996, shortly after Flanagan died, Rose was invited to Tokyo to present relics of some of the couple's collaborations. She decided instead to create a new installation: *Boballoon*, a twenty-foot inflatable depiction of Flanagan, complete with erect penis, piercings, ball gag, and strait-jacket. Rose's choice to memorialize with an inflatable structure a person whose lungs were filled with phlegm isn't as ironic as it appears. With *Boballoon*, Rose inflated Flanagan in the most literal sense, but even as she immortalized him, she made sure not to subtract one of his defining characteristics: his inability to breathe well. If *Boballoon* breathed properly, if it let out the air it let in, it would deflate.

Respiratory Subjectivity (a Précis)

With Flanagan's *Pain Journal* and Rose's memorialization of her late partner's labored breathing, we arrive at a version of respiratory self-encounter that affords something like coherence even when breathing remains incoherent. Rose can, up to a point, exercise the kind of controlled breathing demanded by Bellamy's and Conrad's protocols and rituals. But breathing becomes an autonomous force in Flanagan's late-career writing. Breathing, even of the disorganizing variety, tends toward a structure. Fortifying this structure, as do Bellamy, Conrad, and Flanagan and Rose in different forms and genres of life writing, fulfills a therapeutic function amid crisis. The trajectory of aesthetic self-medication doesn't reveal much about the health benefits of regular or deep breaths. It instead teaches us that aestheticization enables certain subjects to sustain a respiration made irregular or shallow by toxicity, violence, or illness.

The first two chapters of *Breathing Aesthetics* have considered the role of aesthetic mediation in producing models of contemporary breathing subjectivity. In such models, breathing is a shorthand for a condition marked by the inextricability of vitality and morbidity. These chapters have charted the receptive mode of breathing subjectivity (as a spectatorial formation) as well as its productive mode (as a corollary of artistic creation, or what artists make with and of their breathing). To show that this subjectivity is fashioned by an uneven distribution of resources and risks, I've begun to map out ecologies of the particular. Within such ecologies, breathing is revealed as, in one case, a conduit through which imperialism, colonialism, and sexism are felt and negotiated, and in the other, a site where the line between disability and debility is redrawn in real time. A denomination like *the breather*, then, is self-contradictory: there is no monolithic respiratory subject. Put simply, we are all breathing beings, but none of the same kind. The next two chapters ponder the politics made both necessary and possible by breathing, that which is shared but differently experienced.

Feminist gatherings of the late 1960s and early 1970s are remembered, in part, for the talking. Consciousness-raising (CR), which Kathie Sarachild called "one of the prime educational, organizing programs of the women's liberation movement," wove a political pedagogy into monologues on personal experiences.[1] With CR, women gave themselves the means to hone their political voices.[2] Proponents of CR maintained that sharing experiences would lead women to acquire knowledge about, and fight against, a patriarchal system of domination.[3] Sarachild predicted that the CR meeting would spill over into "a mass movement of women [and] put an end to the barriers of segregation and discrimination based on sex."[4] In the optimistic conclusion to *Ms. Magazine*'s "Guide to Consciousness Raising," too, small-scale transformations balloon into large-scale ones: "After the group has grown and changed together, the individual will have grown and changed, too. We will never be quite the same again. And neither will the world."[5] The weapon of CR was talk—and lots of it.

Yet, historical accounts of women's gatherings bring out, more than the content of individual stories, the mood that issued from their circulation: how it felt to be in the room, to take it all in, to let it all out. Women who shared personal experiences with honesty transformed the host's home into what Pamela Allen called "Free Space."[6] Alix Kates Shulman remembered CR, some twenty years after its heyday, for "the passion, excitement, and high energy," the "rapturous feelings of discovery, newness, awakening, even rebirth."[7] Nora Ephron similarly wrote that CR, when she first tried it, set "off a kind of emotional rush, almost a high"; "There were tears. There were what seemed like flashes of insight."[8] Estelle B. Freedman aimed to capture CR's thrill when in the late 1980s she applied the model to her feminist studies course. A student's comment cited by Freedman—"I now understand why feminist consciousness-raising groups in the 1970s were so effective in generating women's energies"—posits the transmission of vitality as the most accurate metric for CR's value.[9] In the CR meeting and the CR-inspired classroom, women, pushed beyond themselves, could find their excitement and rage stimulating rather than alienating.

In Luce Guilbeault, Nicole Brossard, and Margaret Wescott's documentary *Some American Feminists* (1977), shot between 1975 and 1976, Kate Millett offers breathing as a figure for a "tremendously euphoric time" during which women discovered and expressed themselves. When the magic of a program like CR operated, the ecstatic breathlessness of breakthroughs cohabited with the delightful inhalation and exhalation of recognition and support. Under ideal conditions, breathing within CR approximated the kind of respiration that, on the other side of the Atlantic, philosophers working in French identified as feminist praxis: from the *"bouffée d'amour"* (deep breath or burst of love) that female lovers feel in their throats and brachial plexuses to the "fluid density which leaves space for every growth," a "matter that, not yet divided in itself, permits sharing."[10] Dressed in loose white clothes and sitting in a lotus position fit for meditation—though, funny enough, a lit cigarette is resting on a nearby ashtray—Millett amplifies her breathing by raising and lowering her chest and arms. She then declares, "This is a whole class of people oppressed for millennia suddenly, you know, breathing air!" A beatific smile appears on her face.

In the mid- to late 1970s, the mood shifted.[11] Unable to sustain the radical activism for which she had been known, Shulamith Firestone encountered the world as a series of "airless spaces." The title of her autobiographical short story collection, *Airless Spaces* (1998), refers to the sites, including the mental hospitals, where she ended up after the publication of her monograph *The Dialectic of Sex: The Case for Feminist Revolution* (1970).[12] Holding *Airless Spaces*, writes Sianne Ngai, feels "like holding a representation of the lost history . . . of a feminist activist and intellectual."[13] Throughout *Airless Spaces*, Firestone appears to be, in Kathi Weeks's words, "no longer an agent, or by this point even a subject, of feminist history."[14] "So crushed by the burdens of the present," she cannot bear the label of feminist, let alone imagine feminist futurity.[15] The notion of airlessness, as Firestone uses it, blurs the line between the literal and the figurative. In the story "I Remember Valerie," for instance, Firestone foregrounds respiratory dysfunctions like "larynx trouble" and "bronchial pneumonia" to describe Valerie Solanas, another figure relegated to the margins of feminism after the publication of a groundbreaking text—the *SCUM Manifesto* (1967).[16] In 1968, Solanas, convinced that Andy Warhol and Olympia Press owner Maurice Girodias were conspiring to steal her work, infamously shot Warhol and art critic Mario Amaya before turning herself in to the police. She was diagnosed with paranoid schizophrenia and given a three-year prison sentence with psychiatric treatment. Solanas would die of pneumonia two decades later. Firestone and Solanas had a hard time putting up with organized feminism, but the airlessness they experienced outside of its confines proved even more debilitating.

The trajectory of feminist breathing telegraphed by these accounts is a tale of deflation. In the latter half of the seventies, the tale goes, breathing in and out of the spaces of feminist socialization and politicization ceased to be cathartic. Vigorous breathing gave way to exhausted, frustrated breathing. Yet Firestone's *Airless Spaces* marks the end of the story of feminist breathing only if we ignore minoritarian feminist traditions wherein respiratory practices supply tactics and strategies for weathering depletion. We would be wrong to accept that feminist breathing didn't survive what Jane Elliott terms feminism's "declension," or that feminist breathing, if it has endured at all, has done so as an anachronistic artifact of the Second Wave's political highs.[17] What might best be called feminist breathing since the 1970s instead structures the experience of political lows.

This chapter resumes the examination of therapeutic articulations of breathing begun in the previous one while inaugurating a new dyad on respiratory politics. This chapter and the next ask how breathing and its uneven commons have inspired contingent models of social and political life. Here I center Indigenous and Black feminisms, exemplified by the poetry of Linda Hogan (Chickasaw) and Toni Cade Bambara's novel *The Salt Eaters* (1980). The world as Hogan and Bambara view it isn't a capacity into which feminist praxis can easily be extended. Nor is it an arena that, by transforming itself, even gradually, maintains the promise of a large-scale, feminist social shift. Feminist breathing, as it emerges in texts that activate a ceremony and stage a healing, designates a set of rituals for living through the foreclosure of political presents and futures. In this genealogy, feminists train themselves to keep inhaling without the certainty that there will be a world to welcome their exhalation.

The breathing tactics and strategies that exist in literature by women of color are not intended to revive the blend of ecstasy and self-presence that typified CR. On the contrary, some of the earliest traces of respiratory rhetorics in feminist-of-color texts expose the labor performed by women of color to sustain the nonconfrontational spaces conducive to the excitement and relief of their white counterparts. In a piece written in 1980, Cherríe Moraga, a Chicana author and activist, describes "another meeting" where matters of race and racism unsettle CR's official breathing script: "I watch the white women shrink before my eyes, losing their fluidity of argument, of confidence, pause awkwardly at the word 'race,' the word 'color.' The pauses keeping the voices breathless, the bodies taut, erect—unable to breathe deeply, to laugh, to moan in despair, to cry in regret. I cannot continue to use my body to be walked over to make a connection. Feeling every joint in my body tense this morning, used."[18] The bodies of all women present in this scene—those of white women and those of women of color—are presumably taut, erect, but for different reasons. The white women's shrinking concurs with the felt awkwardness of formulating feminism as a struggle that encompasses the distinct realities of women of color. On the other hand, Moraga's own body feels tense because, as hinted by the title of the anthology she edited with Gloria Anzaldúa, *This Bridge Called My Back* (1981), women of color act as bridges as they carry the weight of a world in which white women can recognize themselves without being confronted with alterity. White women lose their composure and eloquence when they can no longer task women of color with producing continuity in a feminist project that doesn't acknowledge the singularity of the latter's experiences. As Moraga makes clear, the ability to experience cathartic breathing—to breathe deeply and to laugh, moan, and cry, all of which compress and extend the airways— was a matter of privilege among CR participants, a matter often contingent on the concealment of the breathing needs of women of color.

Early 1980s debates over hierarchies within and access to feminist spaces also played out in the open air, at festivals that took place outside of the primarily urban or suburban settings of CR meetings. Bernice Johnson Reagon, an African American composer and scholar, delivered at the 1981 West Coast Women's Music Festival an address in which breathing physicalized the inequalities that persisted even in spaces designed to yield coalition rather than consensus. According to Reagon, a festival could lead women to perform coalitional work, for such work "is not done in your home. . . . And it is some of the most dangerous work you can do."[19] Building coalitions pushed women beyond their bodies' limits, but this ecstasy differed from the excitement of rebirth within Free Space. Coalitional work made women feel a heightened sense of risk, as if they were about to die. Reagon formulated coalitional work as showing up for difficult breathing. California's Yosemite National Park, where Reagon spoke, exacerbated the discomfort from which coalitions arose. The site's high altitude made breathing hard:

There is a lesson in bringing people together where they can't get enough oxygen, then having them try to figure out what they're going to do when they can't think properly. I'm serious about that. There probably are some people here who can breathe, because you were born in high altitudes and you have big lung cavities. But when you bring people in who have not had the environmental conditioning, you got one group of people who are in a strain—and the group of people who are feeling fine are trying to figure out why you're staggering around, and that's what this workshop is about this morning.[20]

Breathing, as Reagon politicizes it, registers with unusual intensity the vital and frustrating aspects of being in relation that coalitional feminism keeps entwined. Reagon distinguishes between two camps based on the smoothness or strenuousness of their breathing. Women of color appear to compose one of these camps, and white women the other. Women of color, who through coalitional work have been conditioned to breathe limited air, appear to be the more skillful breathers, confused by the staggering of their white counterparts. At the same time, and paradoxically, Moraga might say that white women are at an advantage under such conditions, for they haven't already been exhausted by coalitional work. Easy and difficult breathers cannot always be identified prior to their encounter. Coalitional work is challenging because parties don't know in advance how they'll react when confronted with unfamiliar experiences. According to Reagon, it is once assembled that these parties should interrogate their own breathing and help alleviate the strain put on the breathing of others. Feminism, as she imagines it, should use as its ground zero what Stacy Alaimo calls "the uneven distribution of risk," specifically the risk of being open and vulnerable to others and the world that comes with breathing but that certain bodies disproportionally absorb.[21]

Moraga and Reagon turn to breathing to reshuffle the dynamics of political assembly. Hogan and Bambara, for their part, turn to it to establish the conditions that make assembly possible in the first place. The psychoanalytic theories of respiration covered in chapter 2 posit that individuals tend to notice breathing and air when those no longer fulfill their life-giving and life-sustaining functions. That breathing calls attention to itself when a glitch appears in the ongoing exchange between individuals and milieus is as much a phenomenological statement as a historical and cultural one. It is when breathing imposes itself as a locus of colonial violence, patriarchal oppression, and ecological degradation that Hogan and Bambara ponder its use in creating and mending communal ties. These writers generate minoritarian forms and discursive contexts to accommodate a breath that signals healing and injury—often at once. Hogan and Bambara work with breathing, that is, to summon vigor and thrust while refuting the notion that wellness and wholeness would neutralize vulnerability. The next sections follow feminist breathing across feminist-of-color traditions to sketch an anatomy of feminist persistence after the 1970s.

Accommodating Breath: Linda Hogan

Included in Hogan's career-spanning anthology *Dark. Sweet. New and Selected Poems* (2012), the poem "V. Who Will Speak?" asks, "Who will make houses of air / with their words?"[22] The poet's question is rhetorical: if anyone's words will make the world more breathable, it will be those of Native women. Hogan's ceremonial poetry, which emblematizes the political and spiritual project of Chickasaw ecofeminism, poses the problem of breath's accommodation, where *accommodation* means both shelter and arrangement or understanding.[23] Her poems induce a breath that functions as a Native commons—a loose structure that provides hospitality amid settler colonialism and helps its dwellers to develop a less alienated relation to their own breathing.[24] This breath-turned-commons isn't transcendent; it is produced through Native women's attunement to a broken world, a world whose resources are depleted, whose atmospheres are saturated with toxins and toxicants. To articulate a genealogy of feminist breathing premised on the management of vulnerabilities requires that we grasp how breathing, at the same time as it registers injury, repairs fractures within and between communities.

Writing is no less concrete than other modes of intervention. In *Dwellings: A Spiritual History of the Living World* (1995), Hogan describes her writing as "the first part of the ceremony, [her] part in it."[25] The ceremony, variants of which are performed by many Indigenous peoples and nations, recapitulates histories across scales. In Hogan's words, the ceremony contains "not just our own prayers and stories of what brought us to it, but also . . . the unspoken records of histories, the mythic past, and all the other lives connected to ours, our families, nations, and other creatures."[26] Paula Gunn Allen, a writer of Laguna, Sioux, and Lebanese descent, notes that the ceremony welds such art forms as chant, dance, drumming, and incantation, generating a "formal structure . . . as holistic as the universe it purports to reflect and respond to."[27] The Michi Saagiig Nishnaabeg scholar and writer Leanne Betasamosake Simpson adds that ceremonies are systems of accountability and responsibility.[28] In this worldview, writing doesn't represent value and belief systems; it overflows into their enactment. Writing is politics. Hogan's work demands that we unlearn the idea that respiratory scores or notations exist on the page, and respiratory rituals off the page. Hogan's poetry presents itself as ceremonial—an integral feature of a process of atmospheric transformation rather than a prompt for a ritual that would begin where a given poem ended.

Breath animates Hogan's elemental ontology. In her poem "Gentling the Human," respiratory and atmospheric phenomena define the human. One stanza begins, "And the human is clouds, / lung, mist, and heart," and another, "A human is breath, / current and tide."[29] The verb *to be*, as it appears in both stanzas, may be read as cumulative: a human is the sum of certain organs, a product of certain conditions. The verb also indicates a synecdochical relation, with individual body parts and the movement of gaseous and liquid particles standing in for the human as a whole. "A human is breath": the line sublimates the paradigmatic human, making it aeriform.

The breath constitutive of all that exists figures as female in Hogan's poetry. Let us consider the opening of the two-part poem "Old Ocean, She":

At the place of *She of Whom We Cannot Speak*,
near ocean,
she breathes
from rocks and waters,
the great breath
long-lived,
here before the human
breath[30]

The great breath infuses various beings and elements across the poem's first five stanzas. The second stanza, a swift couplet, reads, "So many lives here / breathe at this place of serpent dreaming."[31] In the third stanza, it is "the membrane / between worlds" that breathes—until, that is, a new subject, an unspecified, singing "we," takes over:

we cross into a new song
breathing
like tides coming and going.[32]

Following an allusion to the "breathing land" in the fourth stanza, the poet switches into storytelling mode in the fifth stanza to summarize breath's trajectory thus far:

Remember, it was all laid down
at the very beginning,

the first song,
the breath.
It's the way they say we were stars
passed through time,
slid between the walls of a universe
to be born as a human child taking
her first breath,
and still, many years later,
breathing.[33]

The stanza ends with a female child's first breath and the ongoing breathing that ensues. The poem moves from a vital, female breath to a child's breathing, made possible by the childbearer's ability to breathe for two.

Native women's breathing is not, for Hogan, merely autopoietic; it generates the conditions for other people's survival. The Caribbean Canadian poet M. NourbeSe Philip borrows the term "circular breathing" from jazz, where it labels a technique used by wind instrument players to produce a continuous tone, to designate the "prepositional relationship with breath" linking mother and child:[34]

We all begin life in water
We all begin life because someone once breathed for us
Until we breathe for ourselves
Someone breathes for us
Everyone has had someone— a woman— breathe for them
Until that first ga(s)p
For air.[35]

"While 'I breathe,'" Philip adds, "is semantically complete, its completion would not be possible without that original, prepositional act of breathing for."[36] To breathe prepositionally is to accommodate someone else's breathing. The mother's "expression of radical hospitality" aptly describes Hogan's houses of air.[37] The female breaths of creation and reproduction conjured by Hogan's poetry recast in physiological and atmospheric terms Chickasaw matrilineality and matriarchy.[38] As Paula Gunn Allen indicates, motherhood acquires a capacious meaning in societies where clan membership depends on matrilineal descent: "Of course, your mother is not only that woman whose womb formed and released you—the term refers in every individual case to an entire generation of women whose psychic, and consequently physical, 'shape' made the psychic existence of the following generation possible. But naming your own mother (or her equivalent) enables people to place you precisely within the universal web of your life, in each of its dimensions: cultural, spiritual, personal, and historical."[39] In her account of the "sacred hoop," a paradigm wherein "life is a circle, and everything has its place," Allen explains that Indigenous societies are for the most part gynocratic, positioning "Woman" as "creatrix and shaper of existence."[40] Breath in Hogan's poetry traffics between two modes of reproduction: creation and birth.

The reproductive breath is far from an inexhaustible resource. It is in the same breath that Native women confront planetary destruction and generate houses of air. The tension between debilitative and regenerative respiration is on display in "Morning's Dance." The poem shows Hogan's penchant for metonymy by blurring the line between the poet's act of breathing in an environment and this environment's own breathing, or what is referred to as "land of heartbeats / land breathing."[41] The poet's voice is at one with a milieu both nourishing and toxic:

> Sweet pollution,
> the trees in morning,
> black locust,
> red willow,
> trees the wind moves
> move this life,
> my voice in the leaves.[42]

"The Other Side," an extension of sorts of "Morning's Dance," returns to the figure of the tree to imagine apocalyptic breathing. The concluding stanza reads,

> Even the moon can't stop to rest,
> and the broken branch is innocent
> of its own death
> as it goes on breathing
> what's in the air these days,
> radiating soft new leaves,
> telling a story about the other side of creation.[43]

In "Morning's Dance," the land's breathing takes place amid sweet pollution. The trees are "in morning": every new day is a reminder that the earth is dying and ought to be mourned. In "The Other Side," the broken branch of a tree contaminated by radioactive waste goes on breathing. And through the carbon cycle, it does so prepositionally, facilitating the breathing of other organisms.

Hogan forgoes the fantasy of a pristine, unadulterated environment. Betty Louise Bell (Cherokee) points out that Hogan grasps "ordinary lives, the lives of Native Americans, [as] fragmented and forever effected [*sic*] by extraordinary losses"; the survival of Native people thereby lies in "adaptations to loss that discover continuity and affirm life."[44] Hogan opposes the purism that Alexis Shotwell views as a "de-collectivizing, de-mobilizing, paradoxical politics of despair."[45] "To be against purity," Shotwell claims, "is . . . not to be for pollution, harm, sickness, or premature death. It is to be against the rhetorical or conceptual attempt to delineate and delimit the world into something separable, disentangled, and homogenous."[46] The poem "Dark. Sweet. The Full Eclipse" suggests that it is possible to partake "in the splendid planetary breathing."[47] This breathing does not owe its splendor to the way it might transcend pollution. Planetary breathing is splendid, and frighteningly so, because it persists through pollution. Respiration persists, yes, but it is increasingly labored, erratic.

Hogan holds that Native women display a heightened sensitivity to the planet's deterioration. In *The Woman Who Watches the World: A Native Memoir* (2001), she recounts, "When pain took up residence in my body, I spent years learning it, speaking with it, befriending it, dreaming and seeking out the medicines and plants that might heal it, trying to coax it away with charms."[48] She eventually adopted earth, water, light, and air as her doctors. "It wasn't healing I found or a life free from pain," she specifies, "but a kind of love and kinship with a similarly broken world."[49] Hogan illustrates this condition with an allegory centered on a clay figure or bruja she once bought and had shipped. When the clay woman arrived, "she wasn't whole."[50] Her legs were broken. Soon "she began to fall apart in other ways": her nose fell off, then one of her hands. "Yes," Hogan sums up, "the woman who watches over us is as broken as the land, as hurt as the flesh people. She is a true representation of the world she flies above. Something between us and earth has broken."[51]

Native women's breath is accommodating—it nurtures Native people, repairs relations—only insofar as it remains in sync with, or accommodates to, a hostile world. This breath therefore holds in tension the different meanings of *plasticity*. Catherine Malabou lays out the term's three main significations: the capacity to receive form, the power to give form, and the "deflagration or explosion of every form." "The notion of plasticity," Malabou summarizes, "is thus situated at both extremes of the creation and destruction of form."[52] Malabou insists that the destruction of form is not fatal: "Plasticity must then be understood as *a form's ability to be deformed without dissolving and thereby to persist throughout its various mutations*, to resist modification, and to be always liable to emerge anew in its initial state."[53] Even "destructive plasticity," a type of plasticity wherein a form's original state cannot be recovered, heralds a productive transformation.[54] Damage entails loss, but what is lost, Malabou insists, can reconfigure itself into something new. Zakiyyah Iman Jackson offers a crucial corrective to Malabou's model of plasticity. In slavery and its aftermath, Jackson argues, plasticization has operated as a mode of anti-Blackness.[55] Jackson explains, "My conceptualization of plasticity neither posits that human form can become 'any kind of form' nor affirms such a potential; rather, it concerns the way potential can be turned against itself by bonds of power."[56] The treatment of certain bodies as endlessly transformable is a form of violence. To cast all loss as ultimately generative means erasing, and at worst ratifying, such violence. The friction between Malabou's and Jackson's models of plasticity reflects the animating paradox of Hogan's feminist breathing. Hogan celebrates the life-giving and life-sustaining properties of Native women's breath without romanticizing their attunement to a world scarred by colonial violence and environmental collapse.

Risk Training: Toni Cade Bambara

Hogan's poetry provides some insight into the indissociability of creation and destruction in respiratory expressions of radical hospitality amid crisis. Bambara's *The Salt Eaters* shows that the measure of feminist breathing's success after the 1970s isn't political triumph but the capacity to withstand political failure. In Bambara's novel, Minnie Ransom, the fabled healer of Claybourne, Georgia, announces, "I'm available to any and every adventure of the human breath."[57] This phrase—an adventure of the breath—is an ideal descriptor for a book that relays its characters' efforts to keep breathing through the inflation and deflation of social and political movements.

Bambara has captured the political *ethea* of the early, mid-, and late 1970s; the short story collections *Gorilla, My Love* and *The Sea Birds Are Still Alive* and the novel *The Salt Eaters* were published in 1972, 1977, and 1980.[58] Susan Willis sees in Bambara the foremost archivist of the legacy of "the spirit of black activism generated during the sixties."[59] Gloria T. Hull goes so far as to say that *The Salt Eaters* "accomplishes even better for the [early] 1980s what *Native Son* did for the 1940s, *Invisible Man* for the 1950s, or *Song of Solomon* for the 1970s: it fixes our present and challenges the way to the future."[60] In the preface to her anthology *The Black Woman*, Bambara famously assessed that the 1960s movement had been characterized by "a turning away from the larger society and a turning toward each other."[61] Thirteen years later, Claudia Tate questioned Bambara on the status of the "revolutionary fervor of the [1960s]."[62] Bambara was quick to diagnose a general decline in political ardor in the 1970s and early 1980s. But instead of blaming this decline on a "refocusing of the self" after the 1960s, she maintained that this self had been in need of care, for it is, "after all, the main instrument for self, group, and social transformation."[63] Ideally, as we learn in *The Salt Eaters*, the seventies would have mended the injuries suffered during the thunderous 1960s. The 1970s would have "[drained] the poison, [repaired] damaged tissues, [retrained] the heartworks, [and realigned] the spine."[64] But they didn't: the "heart/brain/gut muscles atrophied anyhow."[65]

Susan Willis writes that *The Salt Eaters* takes place "inside of Velma Henry's numbed consciousness."[66] Here *numbed consciousness* carries two meanings. It refers, first, to the trance that Velma reaches during a healing ritual that activates her unconscious, and second, to a numbed political consciousness. When the healing starts, Velma's breathing is disorganized: "Wasn't even sure whether it was time to breathe in or breathe out. Everything was off, out of whack, the relentless logic she'd lived by sprung."[67] She is puzzled not because the world around her is unfamiliar but because it's too familiar: it hasn't been sufficiently transformed by the revolutionary activism of the 1960s and early 1970s. Spanning the entire novel despite its relative brevity, the healing is punctuated by spun-out, impressionistic flashbacks that showcase the viewpoints of Claybourne's inhabitants and visitors. Bambara's editor, none other than Toni Morrison, observes that the novel's "intricate . . . and almost cunning . . . structure" might leave less attentive readers behind.[68] And yet, it is "out of a [problem-solving] impulse" that Bambara turned to the novel form: "What would it take," she asked, "to bridge the gap, to merge those . . . frames of reference, to fuse . . . camps?"[69] Bambara believed that the novel of healing would hold characters and readers together.[70] A "Pan-Africanist-socialist-feminist," she created a racially heterogenous "traveling troupe of seven women known as Sister of the Yam, Sister of the Plantain, Sister of the Rice, Sister of the Corn" to "argue the bridging of several camps: artists and activists, materialists and spiritualists, old and young, and of course the communities of color."[71] While "the short story is a piece of work," Bambara surmised, "the novel is a way of life."[72] *The Salt Eaters* describes a respiratory ritual from start to finish in a way Hogan's poems do not. The two writers, however, share an investment in the relation between aesthetic and social forms. Hogan's ceremonial poetry presents itself as one component of a holistic breathing ritual that provides hospitality amid settler colonialism. Similarly, the performative force of Bambara's description of the healing is meant to exceed the novel's pages. The novel of healing constitutes a metabreathing room: a capacity that brings together characters and readers across races, faiths, and generations, even the politically alienated.[73]

Derek Alwes points out that Bambara codes isolation as deadly.[74] To attempt suicide, Velma slits her wrists and sticks her head into a gas oven, therefore weaponizing her own breathing against herself. The fantasy that prevails in this episode does pertain to being "sealed—sound, taste, air, nothing seeping in"—and to being "unavailable at last, sealed in and the noise of the world, the garbage, locked out."[75] This said, Alwes's assertion that the healing envisaged as an antidote to isolation entails scrapping "personal liberty" and appropriating a ready-made collective identity misses the full scale of the ritual's effects.[76] Not only is Velma transformed by the healing but so is her community. For example, the healing alters the breathing of Nadeen, a patient of the infirmary who finds herself unable to witness the ritual passively. Absorbed by the healing, she "[breathes] shallowly," "oblivious to the sharp intake of breath, the gasps, the stirrings around her as others [begin] to take notice."[77] This immersive experience, Nadeen deduces, confirms that she's witnessing "the real thing," as opposed to something like "revival healing," which is "just not it."[78]

When it comes to Velma in particular, the healing accomplishes first and foremost crisis management: it enables her to relearn how to breathe. Velma at first "[inhales] in gasps, and [exhales] shudderingly."[79] She then starts "breathing in and out in almost a regular rhythm" but remains distracted, "wondering if it [is] worth it, submitting herself to this ordeal."[80] Her distracted musings eventually give in to a kind of hypnosis kick-started by her attunement to breathing:

Rumor was these sessions never lasted more than ten or fifteen minutes anyway. It wouldn't kill her to go along with the thing. Wouldn't kill her. She almost laughed. She might have died. *I might have died.* It was an incredible thought now. She sat there holding on to *that* thought, waiting for Minnie Ransom to quit playing to the gallery and get on with it. Sat there, every cell flooded with the light of that idea, with the rhythm of her own breathing, with the sensation of having not died at all at any time, not on the attic stairs, not at the kitchen drawer, not in the ambulance, not on the operating table, not in that other place where the mud mothers were painting the walls of the cave and calling to her, not in the sheets she thrashed out in strangling her legs, her rib cage, fighting off the woman with snakes in her hair, the crowds that moved in and out of each other around the bed trying to tell her about the difference between snakes and serpents, the difference between eating salt as an antidote to snakebite and turning into salt, succumbing to the serpent.[81]

In this instance of free-indirect speech, Velma holds on to a thought and feels impatient—until she properly concentrates on the rhythmicity of her breathing. At that point, she experiences a sensory overload that runs through almost every one of the novel's subsequent pages. Being "in the zone" or having reached a "flow state," Velma is at once acutely open or vulnerable and optimally able to marshal the energy supplied by Minnie and the auxiliary healers.[82] The healing makes potent the bodily cost of political activism and events past and future at the same time as it works to alleviate injuries. According to her notes on her writing process, Bambara considered "In the Last Quarter" as a potential title for her novel: "[This title] is to remind myself of the period I'm 'reading,' to remind myself to script flashforwards as well as flashbacks, to remind myself that powerful events of the 1980s and 1990s (nuclear explosions, comet splashdowns, asteroid collisions) resonate in the present."[83] Past and future pull the present in opposite directions, thereby curtailing or expanding the possibilities it offers.

The healing reaches its pinnacle in a passage that mirrors the beginning of the ritual. This new passage, too, is set in motion by Velma's heightened attention to breathing—Minnie's warm breath, in the present case. And this passage also conveys sensory overload:

> Day of Restoration, Velma muttered, feeling the warm breath of Minnie Ransom on her, lending her something to work the bellows of her lungs with. To keep on dancing like the sassy singer said. Dancing on toward the busy streets alive with winti, coyote and cunnie rabbit and turtle and caribou as if heading for the Ark in the new tidal wave, racing in the direction of resurrection as should be and she had a choice running running in the streets naming things—cunnie rabbit called impala called little deer called trickster called brother called change—naming things amidst the rush and dash of tires, feet, damp dresses swishing by, the Spirits of Blessing way outrunning disaster, outrunning jinns, shetnoi, soubaka, succubi, innocuii, incubi, nefarii, the demons midwifed, suckled and fathered by the one in ten Mama warned about who come to earth for the express purpose of making trouble for the other nine. Demons running the streets defying Earth Mother and Heavenly Father and defiling the universe in a stampede rush, rending, tearing creature ideas jumping through billboards and screw-thy-neighbor paperbacks, the modern grimoires of the passing age.[84]

The feeling of Minnie's breath on Velma enables the latter to imagine performing various actions: dancing, racing, running (or in fact "running running"), rushing, rending, and naming. The beliefs that undergird the healing make appearances throughout this mix of creolized and nonreferential languages.[85]

Jinns is a term for intelligent spirits in Arabian and Muslim mythologies. *Innocuii* and *nefarii*, versions of *innocuous* and *nefarious*, are not connected to any particular set of practices or beliefs, but they evoke the healing's status as a double-edged sword (a status to which I return later in the section). Conveying an energy and a cadence, these words exemplify the "abstract expressiveness" of Afrodiasporic practices.[86] Bambara's language also recalls the Pentecostal practice of speaking in tongues, which, as Ashon Crawley notes, mobilizes breath to perform an "incomprehensible blackness" and to orient Black people, together, toward life.[87] The excerpt above is, of course, a far cry from a straightforward summary of the healing. It's unclear what such a summary would even look like. At every turn, *The Salt Eaters* eschews teleological narrative, inasmuch as the "Day of Restoration" to which Velma alludes cannot be grasped in eschatological terms. Nor can Restoration be understood as a paradigm that promises bodily and spiritual integrity—the kind of paradigm that Mary Daly accuses of concealing "the real nature of the breakdown it pretends to mend."[88] Breathing practices reorganize Velma and foster connections with the individuals who surround her. And breathing, as a material for mending and quilting, crafts or repairs vectors of (self-)relation that remain fleeting and fragile.

To be reeducated into politics, Velma needs to do more than relearn how to breathe, on her own and with others. Velma must also enact a figurative breath and orient herself toward political futurity despite the world's resistance to her actions. The distinction "between eating salt as an antidote to snakebite and turning into salt," mentioned at the beginning of the healing, indexes the imperative to affirm a political present and future after the fiery 1960s and early 1970s. Turning into salt is what happens to Lot's wife, a figure first mentioned in Genesis 19, when, instead of fleeing the city of Sodom as God is about to destroy it, she chooses to look back. Lot's wife is calcified for defying a prohibition against longing for a doomed way of life. Martin Harries argues that her defiance anchors twentieth- and twenty-first-century models of destructive spectatorship—models that stress "the potentially self-destructive nature of retrospection, as if looking backward posed dangers to the self, as if to look backward were in itself a form of masochism."[89] Velma, perhaps indeed masochistically, has a hard time letting go of the bad feelings brought about by political shortcomings. Although Bambara does not caution against taking some time to feel the impact of political losses, she explains in her writing notes that "without a belief in the capacity for transformation one can become ossified."[90] Eating salt alludes to the novel's communal project. Velma's godmother, Sophie Heywood (nicknamed M'Dear), posits that "you never really know a person until you've eaten salt together."[91] *The Salt Eaters* underscores not only the sweetness of being in relation—what Avery F. Gordon calls the "sensuality" of life inside and outside of social movements—but also the bitterness, the sourness, the more or less savory aspects of it all.[92] Applying salt, for its part, points to a remedy, a method for decontaminating wounds, though not without pain. Salt can be found in every pantry, but it doesn't come with a posology. And as Daddy Dolphy, Sophie's partner, explains, salt "helps neutralize the venom," but "to neutralize the serpent's another matter."[93] It's one thing to keep breathing in a toxic world—a world plagued by ambient sexism and racism, spoiled by the threat of a nuclear disaster and the reality of chemical spills. It's another thing to make the world more breathable.

The Salt Eaters was published one year after the Three Mile Island nuclear meltdown, in Dauphin County, Pennsylvania. Hailed as the worst commercial nuclear accident in US history, it released radioactive gasses into the atmosphere. The novel, Ann Folwell Stanford writes, "rests on the assumption that the world is sick and that in order to survive, human beings must be about the business of healing it through social, political, cultural, and spiritual channels."[94] Jan, a friend of Velma, contends that Black feminist action should address toxic inequality.[95] Jan asks a comrade, "You think there's no connection between the power plant and Transchemical and the power configurations in this city and the quality of life in this city, region, country, world?"[96] Like Hogan's poetry, *The Salt Eaters* entangles productive and destructive energies. The nuclear dramatizes a dynamic at play in the tension between lethal and restorative breaths. Bambara's characters strive for fusion rather than fission, burning up rather than burning out—but in the heat of the moment, it can be hard to distinguish between these poles. Bambara: "Plutonium's both organic and carcinogenic."[97] This confusion is especially palpable in the novel's ending, so powerfully summarized by Jessica Hurley: "The final event is one yet multiple: it is an accident at the plant, an atom bomb dropping, the destruction of the earth by the gods, the energy released by Velma's healing, an environmental disaster."[98]

The Salt Eaters presents the healing as a precarious and hazardous cure against political impotence. The novel opens with Minnie Ransom's question to Velma Henry: "Are you sure, sweetheart, that you want to be well?"[99] Minnie's question recurs, slightly tweaked, throughout the novel: "Can you afford to be whole?" Minnie, for instance, asks Velma.[100] "As I said," Minnie clarifies, "folks come in here moaning and carrying on and *say* they want to be healed. But like the wisdom warns, 'Doan letcha mouf gitcha in what ya backbone caint stand.'"[101] She further warns, "Just so's you're sure, sweetheart, and ready to be healed, cause wholeness is no trifling matter. A lot of weight when you're well."[102] Minnie goes back to the interrogative mood toward the end of the novel: "Choose your cure, sweetheart. Decide what you want to do with wholeness. . . . What will you do when you are well?"[103] A healer's cautiousness about being well and being whole might appear odd. It is not. "Cure," Eli Clare writes, is "slippery": "Cure saves lives; cure manipulates lives; cure prioritizes some lives over others; cure makes profits; cure justifies violence; cure promises resolution to body-mind loss."[104] Staying unwell, however masochistic it might be, would in a way exempt Velma from active political struggle and its dangers. If being well and being whole imply not just having relearned how to breathe but also having to breathe feminist vitality into the world, then the success of the healing exposes Velma to the risk of getting hurt and being disappointed again.

Willis criticizes Bambara's reluctance to spell out an agenda for political transformation: "For all its yearning and insight, the novel fails to culminate in revolution, fails even to suggest how social change might be produced."[105] True, to a point. *The Salt Eaters* does not build up to a revolutionary crescendo. However, the novel communicates a vision for reestablishing conditions wherein activists can once again bear the thought of revolution. The novel, like the healing it recounts, prepares for what Stanford describes as "the difficult world-healing work ahead."[106] Feminist breathing, as Bambara renders it, is communal training—a prep course for a return to activism. And activism is struggle. In the name of making the world more breathable, feminist breathing ultimately destabilizes the provisional wellness and wholeness it affords.

Durational Breath, Durable Breath

In *This Bridge Called My Back*, an endurance performance staged at the Art Gallery of Ontario in 2017, Madelyne Beckles made of her body a bridge.[107] She spent the performance on a pedestal at the center of a spacious museum gallery. She was on all fours, her palms and knees acting as pillars, her feet and legs as stabilizing cables. She was nude. The soundtrack was a looped recording on which Beckles read excerpts from Moraga and Anzaldúa's collection with a deep, raspy voice. Between each spoken segment played Dionne Warwick's 1963 song "Don't Make Me Over," the chorus of which goes,

> Accept me for what I am
> Accept me for the things that I do
> Accept me for what I am
> Accept me for the things that I do.[108]

Over two hours, Beckles tried to hold her pose, but her body got shakier. She altered the angle of her shoulders, the position of her knees. Her body, just like a bridge meant to bear climatological fluctuations, was not inert but flexible. She occasionally resorted to what in yoga is colloquially called a child's pose. Even then she could be walked over. *This Bridge Called My Back*, the performance, thematized *This Bridge Called My Back*, the anthology. Beckles, a Black woman, physicalized Moraga and Anzaldúa's analogy between back and bridge. Her postural adjustments recalled the strain of feminist-of-color and coalitional advocacy. They reminded spectators of just how hard it had been for someone like Moraga to remain focused in racially stratified feminist spaces.

An endurance performance relays, perhaps better than any medium, the operation of feminist breathing after the 1970s. As I mentioned in chapter 2, the endurance artist persists "through an experience of sufferance or difficulty."[109] As *This Bridge Called My Back* unfolded, Beckles's belly went up and down with decreasing regularity and increasing theatricality. But she kept breathing. Beckles's respiration, that is, was ongoing even in the event of its disruption. Her breathing presented evidence of her persistence at the same time as it made manifest the labor of showing up, taking a stance, and maintaining a position. The performance didn't progress toward a climactic ending. Beckles breathed and stood as still as possible for a set duration. However contained, the performance evoked a more ambitious time scale. Beckles's sustained breath showed her willingness to keep alive, in the present, the feminism of color theorized in Moraga and Anzaldúa's anthology. With her durational breath, she might have sought to conjure a "durable breath."[110] It's no coincidence that Hogan, Bambara, and Beckles all locate feminism in intergenerational kinship. A durable breath is one that concerns itself with reproduction—familial, political, or both.

Feminist breathing is what Dian Million (Tanana Athabascan) calls a "felt theory": it draws attention to the pedagogy within, and sociopolitical repercussions of, processes otherwise relegated to the ordinary.[111] Specifically, feminist breathing, as a set of tactics and strategies for moving through depletion, critiques its conditions of emergence. We might say that all Indigenous or Black breathing condemns settler atmospherics or particulate racism.[112] What makes this critique feminist is its reticulation, or its extension into intergenerational female kinship. Beckles's endurance performance is one version of the respiratory summoning of intergenerational feminist kinship. Alexis Pauline Gumbs's citational experiments, some of which include elements of performance, are another. In the context of her *Black Feminist Breathing Chorus* project, Gumbs developed an online compendium of meditations and collages honoring notable Black feminist figures.[113] One meditation revisits Bambara's reflection on fiction and its potential to bring about revolutionary change.[114] Gumbs utters, over and over, a statement by Bambara: "The most effective way to do it is to do it." The repetition, much like the healing in *The Salt Eaters*, induces a trance. And here also, the promise of therapeutic benefits is contingent on a breathing practice. In her *Black Feminist Breathing Chorus* as well as in a trilogy of books developing a theoretical poetics, breath figures and physicalizes a feminist lineage that includes parental relations—Gumbs has coedited a collection on "revolutionary mothering"—but points to a broader set of inherited commitments: theoretical, political, and aesthetic.[115]

Reparative reading and reparative breathing are alike, and not just homophonically. As Eve Kosofsky Sedgwick reminds us in her essay on paranoid and reparative critiques, it's from the depressive position that we can use our resources to assemble or repair the "part-objects" we have defensively carved out of the world around us into "something like a whole—though . . . *not necessarily like any preexisting whole*."[116] In Hogan's poetry, Native women's affinity with a broken earth typifies the depressive position. So does Black women's political debilitation in Bambara's fiction. These writers ritualize breathing to make participants feel as though they were part of a whole, or as though they were whole, even if this feeling is fleeting, and even if it entails a renewed exposure to risk. Sedgwick's concluding sentence fittingly describes feminist breathing's unfolding under conditions that hinder it: "What we can best learn from such practices are, perhaps, the many ways selves and communities succeed in extracting sustenance from the objects of a culture—even of a culture whose avowed desire has often been not to sustain them."[117] Hogan's and Bambara's breath is reparative—and it is a call for reparations: theirs is a feminist breathing that articulates survival while tallying the cost of doing so within hostile environments.

Smog has long been an attribute of urban life. The term, short for *smoke* and *fog*, was first used in the late nineteenth century and popularized in the early twentieth century.[1] The phenomenon precedes the designation; in a sweeping study, Peter Brimblecombe finds records of air pollution episodes in ancient Egypt, Greece, and Rome, although he attributes the emergence of industrial pollution as a problem to be managed politically to a sharp increase in coal use in thirteenth-century Britain.[2] There exist two types of smog. The first, sulfurous smog, denotes a high concentration of sulfur oxides as a result of the combustion of fossil fuels like coal. Factors such as dampness and suspended air particles aggravate sulfurous smog, whose most famous manifestation is certainly the "pea souper," the soot-drenched fog so characteristic of nineteenth-century London. The second variety, photochemical smog, occurs when the nitric oxide and nitrogen dioxide emitted by gasoline and other fossil fuels are exposed to ultraviolet radiation and undergo a series of reactions with hydrocarbons to produce ozone, nitric acid, aldehydes, peroxyacyl nitrates, and other secondary pollutants.[3] These chemicals can oxidize compounds that do not normally oxidize, and small traces suffice to affect the respiratory tract and damage plant life. The immediate effect of photochemical oxidation, visible almost daily in Los Angeles, Mexico City, and Beijing, is a low cloud in shades of brown, orange, and yellow.

Although it isn't new, smog, especially the photochemical kind, has been something of an emblem of urban pollution in the late twentieth and early twenty-first centuries. Smog shifts perspective and perception, altering the ways we orient ourselves in metropoles. Skylines are partially or totally obstructed, and hazy buildings and landmarks blend into the atmosphere. In an essay on "smog sensing," Jussi Parikka brings up the visuality of limited visibility when he defines smog as a "chemical screen media" and an "urban screen."[4] "The screen is not a background," Parikka says, "but an environment that wraps you inside its toxic cloud."[5] Smog sensors are measurement technologies that produce quantitative data about pollution levels. In so-called smart cities—cities where political problems are met with computational solutions—smog sensing represents one of many ongoing forms of monitoring intended to optimize urban planning.[6] Under the guise of making objective data available to sustainability initiatives, collaborations between cities and corporations support the bio- and necropolitical project of exposing populations deemed disposable to greater environmental risk. Parikka's implicit proposal to make data collection and visualization open and transparent merely reforms the smart city. But a more radical, and more promising, project runs through his description of embodiment and experience amid smog. In his essay, bodies emerge as smog sensors and breathing as smog sensing; both provide qualitative information about air pollution. We register the chemical screen media that is smog, Parikka writes, "with our bodies[,] with every breath."[7] The project that lies dormant in such a statement, one that I activate in this chapter, consists in mapping urban life through practices of smog sensing that don't involve, at least not exclusively, mechanical (and thus not-actually-sentient) sensors. Parikka's account of breathing as smog sensing and smog as chemical screen media redistributes sensory input: smog sensing entails taking in—smelling, choking on, experiencing oxidation from—a visual screen that restricts visibility, one that is omnipresent, enveloping, total. If digital sensors purporting to eliminate smog through optimal planning in fact reinforce inequalities and hierarchies of exposure, then to regard bodies as smog sensors authorizes a minoritarian mapping of urban sociality.

I decipher such a cartography in Renee Gladman's experiments in the literary and visual arts. Gladman has been labeled an experimental prose writer and a "visual poet"; one biographical note describes her as "an artist and writer preoccupied with lines, crossings, thresholds, geographies, and syntaxes as they play out in the interstices of poetry and fiction."[8] Her multimedia and multigenre examination of queer sexuality has generally been interpreted as evidence of the enduring legacy of New Narrative, a movement I brought up in chapter 2. Gladman's name also surfaces frequently in discussions on the constitution of a contemporary Black avant-garde canon.[9] Her most ambitious project to date is an open-ended suite of short, dense novels set in the city-state of Ravicka. Published in 2010, *Event Factory* inaugurated the Ravicka cycle as well as Dorothy, a publishing project led by Danielle Dutton and Martin Riker and dedicated to works by women that exist in the vicinity of fiction. As one of two inceptive titles—Dorothy releases but one pair of books yearly—*Event Factory* modeled the aesthetic and structural adventurousness that would come to distinguish one of the most respected and influential small presses in the United States.[10]

Much like Parikka's descriptions, Gladman's experiments perform a sensory and perceptual confusion that, at the risk of metaphorizing a neurological condition, I would call synesthetic. The sky has a patina or texture, and descriptors pertaining to color and to sound are interchangeable. Breathing, walking, writing, and drawing appear coextensive, such that writing alters atmospheres and breathing produces lines. Gladman's oeuvre, particularly the Ravicka novels and some parallel projects ranging from literary fiction and nonfiction to drawing, imagines social and political life from the vantage point of ordinary smog sensing. In *Event Factory*, an unnamed linguist and ethnographer lands in Ravicka to investigate a crisis prompted by a mysterious cataclysm. "From the sky there was no sign of Ravicka," the narrator and protagonist remarks; "Yet, I arrived; I met many people. The city was large, yellow, and tender."[11] She notes that the air is filled with smoke, but later proposes an amendment: "Honestly, there was no smoke. I meant 'silence,' but silence is not something that moves visibly from one place to another."[12] The word *smoke* fills in for a mysterious crisis that, we learn only in the second volume, *The Ravickians* (2011), has to do with "structures becoming ash" in the wake of a large fire, an "attack from above."[13] While a traditional plot summary of the Ravicka novels would be futile—the very meaning of event being up for debate—I should specify that the volumes following *Event Factory* relinquish the outsider's perspective to adopt points of view closer to various Ravickian dwellers. *The Ravickians* is organized around a speech delivered by the novelist Luswage Amini. The third and fourth volumes, *Ana Patova Crosses a Bridge* (2013) and *Houses of Ravicka* (2017), for their part, center characters who actively experiment with methods of recording and indexing the city's transformations. As new Ravicka books surface, the *novel* designation seems increasingly elastic. We return to Ravicka less to see what will happen than to occupy its atmosphere.

I cannot think of a word other than smog to describe a yellowish smoke-that-isn't-quite-smoke occasioned by combustion on a disastrous scale. Gladman's characters do not use this term, as though smog, the phenomenon, obfuscated its designation. Disoriented, characters depend on their breathing to find their way around. Through breathing, characters intuit the shape of the crisis affecting them and negotiate the personal and impersonal intimacies of contact and care. Their smog sensing happens in the flow of life; it's in the service of acclimating to an atmospheric shift, or reuniting with an old friend, or trying to communicate with a stranger. Advanced data collecting and processing technologies are nowhere to be found in Ravicka. "But, to me," Gladman specifies in an interview, "this isn't a refusal of technology. . . . The body itself is a complicated technology there."[14] While there is a utopian tenor to Gladman's project of reimagining urban life, the author's lo-fi approach does not bracket off the problems afflicting dwellers in today's metropoles. Ravicka's breathers register the kind of "atmospheric differentiation," to borrow Hsuan L. Hsu's term once more, that the privatized monitoring of smart cities would both reproduce and conceal.[15]

The Ravicka series is one manifestation of a broader, cross-media aesthetics of smog sensing. This isn't to say that Gladman has intended to contribute to this aesthetics; I have not come across such a programmatic claim by any writer, filmmaker, or artist. Yet Gladman's characters routinely approach breath as a technology for navigating saturated atmospheres. From one Ravicka novel to the next, smog doesn't dissipate, and breath continues to impose itself as an object of attention and speculation. More than a setting that characters occupy and an activity that they perform whatever else they may be doing, smog and breath constitute preponderant tropes in a corpus, Gladman's, that works through problems of contemporary existence.

The aesthetics of smog sensing is especially noticeable within architecture and design. The now-popular terms *breathing architecture* and *meteorological architecture* point to biomimetic design that reproduces the properties of respiring organisms to respond to environmental conditions, including air pollution.[16] Doris Sung's "living," "sensitive" architecture, for instance, is situated halfway between installation art and ecological media intervention.[17] Sung's design prototype *Tracheolis*—named after the trachea, a respiratory organ; aeolian, related to the wind; and polis, an ideal city—comprises stacked-up concrete chambers that cool down the air circulating through them. The model imitates the tracheal system of grasshoppers, which breathe through spiracle holes in their sides. *Breathing Skins*, a related project by the engineer Tobias Becker, corresponds to a double wall filled with "pneumatic muscles," or balloons that expand and constrict in accordance with internal and external conditions.[18] While the primary aim of *Tracheolis* and *Breathing Skins* is to lower indoor temperature without using nonrenewable energies that accelerate climate crisis, other design technologies are expressly meant to clear the air. In 2011, the chemical company Alcoa unveiled a "smart façade" that "eats smog."[19] The titanium dioxide surface "scrubs" the air of pollutants by releasing spongy free radicals.[20] Breathing, as a descriptor for an architecture that registers and reacts to atmospheric conditions, connotes openness and commonness. And indeed, waste-reducing construction materials and techniques promise greater harmony between the built and natural environments. Projects like the ones I've listed, however, tend to be developed in the context of beautification initiatives that, in the name of urban renewal, further privatize public life. The smart façade may be the smart city's aesthetic coverup. With both, smartness designates an ideal of real-time environmental responsiveness. The façade gives this ideal a form whose organicity or pseudo-organicity naturalizes processes of privatization tied to the deliberate adoption of exclusionary urban policies. In Gladman's world, architecture is detached from a paradigm of human management wherein destructive modes of planning and building ought to be solved by technical and technological research toward modes deemed restorative. Gladman's writing and drawing, as I show later in this chapter, devise a breathing architecture whose adaptability and communality are more than a façade.

Beyond architecture and design, the aesthetics of smog sensing is manifest in screen cultures. A heteroclite genealogy of the cinema of smog sensing takes us from Michelangelo Antonioni's *Red Desert* (1964), wherein the frame is filled with the smoke emitted by a petrochemical plant in industrial northern Italy; to John Carpenter's *The Fog* (1980), a horror tale in which thick fog marks the return of the repressed violence of colonization; to Todd Haynes's *Safe* (1995), a Southern California–set drama of hypersensitivity to urban pollution. If, as Parikka posits, smog is a chemical screen media, then the projection or television screen entails a doubling: the cinema of smog sensing is a chemical two-screen media. Accordingly, the films above use the projection or television screen not just to depict the characters' experience of smog sensing but to allegorize it. The screen becomes a symbol of smog as visual experience.

Smog often fulfills a symbolic role across the literature of smog sensing. In Victorian fiction, the pea souper alternately symbolizes the dangers of city life (William Delisle Hay's "The Doom of the Great City" [1880]), the complexity of a system such as the law (Charles Dickens's *Bleak House* [1852–53]), and a psychological state like clouded judgment (Henry James's *The Portrait of a Lady* [1880–81]).[21] The latter case is worth dwelling on: smog is one of the milieus where the novel has proven itself a technology for the disclosure of psychological interiority.[22] A certain psychologism also prevails in the more recent horror and satirical fiction of smog sensing. Populated by deadly creatures, the titular mist in Stephen King's novella *The Mist* (1980, adapted into a film in 2007 and a television series in 2017) thematizes paranoia. And the "airborne toxic event" of Don DeLillo's *White Noise* (1985)—an event described as a change in weather—confronts characters with the absurdity of their mortal existence.[23]

But in the Ravicka cycle's most notable antecedent, Samuel R. Delany's *Dhalgren* (1973), smog doesn't grant us access to characters' interiority. Irreducible to human psychology, smog's unknowability remains largely, well, unknowable. Much like the narrator of *Event Factory*, *Dhalgren*'s protagonist, Kid (alternatively called Kidd and the kid), arrives in a city—in this case the Midwestern metropole of Bellona—in the wake of a disaster. As a draft of the promotional materials indicates, what "only months ago . . . was a great city" has turned into a "disaster zone," "a haven for the lost, the degenerate, the insane."[24] Riots erupt either because "a house collapsed," or because "somebody got killed," or because "a plane crashed"—"nobody has the story really straight."[25] Technology is out of order. Chronology is arbitrary; one issue of the local newspaper is dated July 14, 2022, and the next July 7, 1837.[26] Buildings burn down, build themselves back up, and burn down again. Most strikingly, the air is saturated with smoke: "The smoke hides the sky's variety, stains consciousness, covers the holocaust with something safe and insubstantial. It protects from greater flame. It indicates fire, but obscures the source. This is not a useful city. Very little here approaches any eidolon of the beautiful."[27] Any information Kid gathers about Bellona is mediated by the smoke. Kid must breathe vigorously to sense something beyond the ambient chaos to which he has acclimated: "No lights in any near buildings; but down those waterfront streets, beyond the veils of smoke—was that fire? Already used to the smell, he had to breathe deeply to notice it. The sky was all haze. Buildings jabbed into it and disappeared."[28]

Gladman has remarked on the parallels between Bellona and Ravicka. When questioned by the editors of the literary magazine *HAUS RED* about her nod to *Dhalgren* in *Event Factory*'s acknowledgments, she explained, "What drew me to *Dhalgren* those many years ago . . . was a desire for novels about cities, where the cities took on the qualities of a character or at the very least a presence or force in the story. Not just a place where things happened but an atmosphere, the city itself a question or questioning about subjectivity and time, etc. . . . I haven't re-read it since, so I've lost many of the details, but I do think the fact that Ravicka has that yellow ('crepuscular') air has something to do with Delany."[29] The characters who roam Bellona and Ravicka can tell by the combustion residues clouding the air that they are in the midst of a socioecological crisis. It is for the same reason—combustion residues clouding the air—that most characters cannot see through the crisis and find out its source, its meaning. In Bellona as well as in Ravicka, characters develop makeshift techniques of smog sensing, treating interrupted, accelerated, or otherwise labored breathing as symptoms of crisis that provide limited information about bodies and milieus. The practice of smog sensing provokes in Delany's and Gladman's novels an encounter with the limits of knowability, one that deflates the smart city's data fetish.

In much of the literature of smog sensing, variations in the intensity of breathing index a disturbance of the sensorium that itself indexes a disturbance in urban living. Gladman goes further, turning to respiratory symptoms to conjecture parameters for city life. When it defines smog as "community-wide polluted air," the *Encyclopedia Britannica* reduces community to a demographic or spatial benchmark by which air pollution is measured.[30] The Ravicka novels shuffle the terms of this definition, describing how community emerges from characters' efforts to deal with polluted air. What Tim Choy calls "the tactility of the atmosphere" is exacerbated.[31] Under such conditions, Dora Zhang's definition of the atmosphere as "the spatialization of relationality" is flipped: structures of relation appear epiphenomenal to the process of breathing a milieu in and out.[32] The remainder of this chapter sketches such structures of relation and articulates the ethics and politics that become available when breathing imposes itself as a device, perhaps the only device, for making sense of the smog-filled city. Throughout, I consider breathing an instrument of what Kathleen Stewart calls "atmospheric attunement": a descriptive and interpretive disposition that follows the "qualities, rhythms, forces, relations, and movements" amounting to "the activity of sensual world-making."[33] "Attending to atmospheric attunements," as Stewart explains and this chapter demonstrates, "means . . . chronicling how incommensurate elements hang together in a scene that bodies labor to be in or to get through."[34]

In chapter 3, I identified a politics of synchronized breathing in the ceremonies and healing rituals of Indigenous and Black feminist literature. The ritualization of breathing, I proposed, organizes collective survival in contexts where revolutionary promises are unfulfilled and emancipatory futures appear indefinitely postponed, if not foreclosed altogether. I introduced my two main case studies—Linda Hogan's poetry and Toni Cade Bambara's novel *The Salt Eaters*—by way of feminist-of-color accounts of coalitional politics by Bernice Johnson Reagon and Cherríe Moraga. In these accounts, distinct breathing styles are indicative of the uneven labor of staying in relation. In the present chapter, the second in a dyad on respiratory politics, I remain within the scene of respiratory asynchrony, regarding it as a resource in itself, rather than a problem that ought to be remedied in order for collective life to proceed. Gladman, I offer, models symptomatic breathing, a practice that consists in coming to terms with the inevitable partiality and potential inaccuracy of interpretive acts seeking to extrapolate experience from respiratory expression. Translations across languages and media—between English and Ravic, between writing and drawing—produce interpretive glitches in the midst of which the only viable ethical and political project is one premised not on sameness (group membership is contingent on a shared experience of the world) but on opacity (coalition stems from the acknowledgment that there is something inaccessible and incommensurable about experience).

We, the readers, are given very little information about the identities of the characters who populate the Ravicka books. Some ethnic and linguistic differences are mentioned—that is it. I nevertheless consider Gladman's books novels of queerness and Blackness. This designation is irreducible to Gladman's own identification as a queer Black woman. Gladman's writing, I suggest, generates an atmospherics of queerness of Blackness. These identitarian markers resist containment by discrete bodies, arising instead as products of exchange and mediation. Queer theory supplies tools for conceiving of queerness as a force that exceeds any one individual's identification. In the field-shaping *Tendencies* (1993), Eve Kosofsky Sedgwick famously declares that "there are important senses in which 'queer' can only signify *when attached to the first person*"—but the first person is no stabilizing agent; "Queer," she writes earlier in the book, "is a continuing moment, movement, motive—recurrent, eddying, *troublant*."[35] In another prominent text, Lee Edelman's *No Future: Queer Theory and the Death Drive* (2004), queerness names a confrontation with the unintelligibility of identity: "The queerness of which I speak would deliberately sever us from ourselves, from the assurance, that is, of *knowing* ourselves and hence *knowing* our 'good.'"[36] (Edelman's polemic hints at a certain theory of opacity; I return to it, via his writing on the symptom, later in this chapter.) The Ravicka series conjures queerness by upending normative structures of relation (the family, heterosexuality, chronology, the public/private divide) and urging characters to improvise new forms of kinship—that is, whether or not they view such improvisation as antinormative, and whether or not they uphold antinormativity as an ideal.[37] In Gladman's novels, breathing takes on sex's role as an exemplar of, as Edelman and Lauren Berlant would put it, the "encounter with the estrangement and intimacy of being in relation."[38]

While influential formulations of queerness in impersonal or more-than-personal terms make an atmospherics of queerness an intuitive notion, the same logic doesn't quite apply to Blackness. When queer-of-color critics, and specifically Black queer critics, use sociological types—Cathy J. Cohen's punk, bulldagger, and welfare queen; Roderick A. Ferguson's transgender man and sissy—to examine the surveillance and policing of sexuality along race and class lines, they do so partly to rectify what E. Patrick Johnson calls queer theory's "homogenizing tendencies."[39] That race stabilizes queerness's fluidity is not queer-of-color critique's contention; it is an implication of reading queer-of-color critique as merely a rejoinder to queer theory. The Ravicka cycle cautions us against such a reading by preventing us from viewing Blackness as somehow more graspable than queerness. I would not say that Blackness is fundamentally atmospheric; mine isn't an ontological argument. My point is instead that Gladman situates Blackness in an atmospherics, making it so particulate that it runs the risk of being departicularized and unrecognizable, in which instance the ethics and politics of opacity reveal their necessity. The principle of opacity represents one tactic or strategy for managing a contradiction with which the Ravicka series's characters and readers must contend: that decrypting what various characters' breathing tells us about their experience of crisis requires an appeal to the very categories of racial and sexual identity that this crisis's foremost manifestation, smog, withholds or conceals. The atmospherics of Blackness warrants further probing. The next section articulates Blackness's relation to the particulate and the aerial in the contemporary city life that the Ravicka novels reinvent.

An Atmospherics of Blackness

Where is Ravicka? The poet and critic David Buuck, whose path has often crossed Gladman's, traces the latter's writing back to the San Francisco of the 1990s and early 2000s. "The Mission during this time," Buuck remembers, "was a vibrant and dynamic matrix of people and encounters, a place of daily contact between diverse groups (inter-racial, cross-cultural, inter-class, inter-generational), where a bohemian ethos (if often pseudo- and/or invisibly well-funded) still reigned, despite the looming gentrification brought on by the influx of hipsters and dot-com money."[40] Without ever writing "San Francisco stories," Gladman has captured the last days of a San Francisco bohemia threatened by the corporate assault on people of color and working-class people.[41] Some parallels exist between San Francisco and Ravicka. The San Francisco Bay Area's notorious fog and Ravicka's smog both limit visibility; the former is a benign product of condensation, and the latter a malign product of combustion. And in San Francisco as well as in Ravicka, a catastrophic event—in one case gentrification, and in the other an enigmatic cataclysm—has made the city unrecognizable to its longtime dwellers. Fog isn't the sole example of atmospheric saturation in the Bay Area. In September 2020, as strong winds transported ash from wildfires in Northern California and the Sierra Nevada, the sky took on an unusually rusty hue. The atmosphere itself took the appearance of a bright orange warning sign about climate crisis. It was a sign that, like Parikka's urban screen, enveloped dwellers, one that they breathed in and out. Widely circulated images of midday tenebrosity seemed to have come straight out of the pages of *Dhalgren* or the Ravicka novels, where chronology and cyclicality are out of joint.

Yet it is in New York City that Gladman found the inspiration for Ravicka's geography of obstructed action, wherein contacts and encounters cannot be taken for granted and must be cultivated. In an interview conducted by Joshua Marie Wilkinson around the release of *Event Factory*, Gladman explains,

> San Francisco was a city where I ran into friends and acquaintances as I walked along the streets, and New York was a city where I ran into buildings. The shift in my work, I think, related to the possibility of connection; it seemed to have diminished once I moved east. My narrators now searching for a way in. Searching for events. Where before the city was the site of intense action that exhausted my narrators, here the city stood in the way of action. My attention turned to structure and the grid. The verticality of buildings, trains, busses, and the crowd that does not know you. I think you can see this most in the two unpublished novellas I wrote between 2003 and 2006, where the city-state Ravicka came into existence. I wanted to think on city living without having to think specifically of New York City living so I found this new place.[42]

Gladman's description of New York City closely resembles her description of Sespia, the setting of the detective novella *Morelia* (2019). *Morelia* is not officially part of the Ravicka cycle, but Sespia and Ravicka are in many ways alike. Sespia is "an unstable city" that "smells sad like pollution but is beautiful in how variously vertical it is," a city where steam "[rises] from the ground as the air is depleted."[43] The narrator muses, "Wherever I go will be new, as this is my first time here. A funny looking city, with half-articulated bridges and water wells."[44]

Gladman's writing captures key aspects of life in San Francisco and New York, but Ravicka is no analog for any one city. Apprehended primarily through experiences of difficult breathing, Ravicka evokes the many urban centers where asphyxiation is deployed in the service of the bio- and necropolitics of anti-Blackness. The Ravicka novels may constitute prophetic statements about the emergence of "I can't breathe" and "we can't breathe" as protest refrains in the years following the 2010 release of *Event Factory*. But as prescient as they are, Gladman's books capture histories of atmospheric violence and environmental racism that stretch far beyond such events as the recorded police murders of Eric Garner, George Floyd, and Elijah McClain and the COVID-19 pandemic. These histories include, for instance, the popularization of spirometry as a pseudoscientific alibi for slavery as well as the rise of allergy and asthma in the majority-Black neighborhoods of segregated cities.[45] Just as, according to many critics, *Dhalgren*'s smoke emanates from the Watts Rebellion that took place in Los Angeles in 1965, I detect in Ravicka's smog residues from the toxins, toxicants, and allergens to which Black people have long been disproportionately exposed.[46]

In Lindsey Dillon and Julie Sze's nomenclature, events like the killing of Garner exemplify the circulation of racism, specifically anti-Blackness, as "particulate matter."[47] Dillon and Sze "interpret the phrase 'I can't breathe' as condensing the histories of persistent patterns of pollution and police violence, both of which have denied breath and healthy breathing spaces to low-income communities of color. In this sense, the inability to breathe can be understood as both a metaphor and material reality of racism, which constrains not just life choices and opportunities, but the environmental conditions of life itself."[48] It is one thing to say, as do Dillon and Sze, that anti-Blackness is particulate, or that it reproduces itself by clouding atmospheres and seizing respiratory systems. It would be another to say that Blackness is, as a result, particulate, for such a statement would run the risk of reducing Blackness to an effect of anti-Blackness, race to racism.

J. Kameron Carter and Sarah Jane Cervenak have argued not that Blackness per se is atmospheric but that an anti-Black world predicates itself on the vaporization of Blackness: "The ether of blackness is, indeed, the condition of possibility of this world, the mythic ground that intoxicates and fortifies whiteness, that which is held and expelled."[49] Cervenak separately remarks that "blackness is said to endanger air's mythic purity, threatening a set of enclosures ranging from white fences to white heterosexual families."[50] The Ravicka series captures something of Blackness's "ether" as Carter and Cervenak define it, but here the diffusiveness of identity does more than register the force of anti-Blackness. Gladman's atmospherics of Blackness occasions a (self-)estrangement that in turn instills in characters and readers alike habits of relation informed by a principle of opacity.

Gladman models (self-)estrangement in a vignette from the nonfiction prose collection *Calamities* (2016) that detaches identity from character or person.

The author juxtaposes such identarian markers as "Black," "African American," and "Eastern European" to dislocate each one from its referent: "I can't get anyone to understand how black people are another kind of Eastern European, especially not the Eastern Europeans. I can't get black people to want to be anything other than black people, which, as a black person, is incredibly inspiring, but on the other hand delays the thinking that black people are like Eastern Europeans, which could be of use when observing the state of things inside a book. . . . How undermining of all that is the case were I to proclaim in my bios, 'Renee Gladman is an Eastern-European African American.'"[51] The formulation "another kind" hints at resemblance rather than equivalence. "Eastern European" induces difference in, or aerates, the meaning of "Black" and "African American," and vice versa. Diffracted through *Calamities*, novels set in a vaguely Eastern European–sounding location, Ravicka, transmit something of the condition of Black life in contemporary US cities while opening it up to what else it might be or mean. In this sense, the Ravicka cycle constitutes a purposely lo-fi, hazy counterpart to Afrofuturism, an aesthetics that pictures Blackness anew in a speculated future of technocultural innovation.[52] Let us remember a line from an interview with Gladman I cited earlier: "I wanted to think on city living without having to think specifically of New York City living *so I found this new place*."[53] In this new place, characters, even as they navigate geographies of inequality, are freed from the pressures of self-identicality. We cannot access their experience by relying strictly on what we know of life in San Francisco or New York. The smog-filled Ravicka institutes a reset: what we learn about Gladman's characters, we do by way of their breathing.

Breathing Architectures

This section considers city life from the vantage point of respiration. I travel across Gladman's corpus to sketch its breathing architectures. Those are living spaces that adapt to physical and atmospheric fluctuations, mediating geographies of obstructed action. In Gladman's universe, architecture names a process that combines breathing, walking, writing, and drawing. In a conversation with Amina Cain, Gladman describes "the city" as "a three-dimensional embodiment of writing, a world propelled by sentences."[54] The titular character in the Ravicka novel *Ana Patova Crosses a Bridge* says that "things architectured other things."[55] "My thinking of architecture," she adds, "resulted from my thinking of the line, how the line made narrative regardless of whatever else it was making, and narrative presented enclosures for your questions about living, and living, for the most part, required space."[56] This line has many referents. It is a line of text, one that carries a narrative. It is the continuous line of cursive writing, which creates shapes and delimits surfaces. It is also the invisible line that connects individuals who breathe together; in *Houses of Ravicka*, one character recounts, "I wanted lines to extend from my throat, the back end of a long-held note, multiple lines escaping me, and moving outward, along circuits of people's spent breath."[57] Architecture, Patova sums up, "contained fictions but it breathed and remembered us and held out the possibility of future architecture, where, even though our buildings were in motion and the terrain was constantly reshaping itself, we were part of a conversation."[58] Zigzagging between discourse markers that signal contrast or contradiction ("but," "even though"), Gladman's writing builds a breathing architecture that archives past experiences while keeping open the possibility of future ones.

A breathing architecture is an architecture of the negative space. *Ana Patova Crosses a Bridge*, Gladman writes in an essay, draws our attention to "the spaces . . . between buildings and bodies, between books and bodies, between one body and another, and on a more abstract level between what it means to write and what it means to live, to have experience."[59] In *Prose Architectures* (2017), Gladman continues to experiment with the line, turning to drawing to visualize "some interiors, some energies of [her] prose."[60] She completed *Prose Architectures*, an art book compiling more or less abstract urban plans drawn without perspectival techniques, in the negative space between Ravicka novels, and the drawings themselves occupy liminal zones. The drawings approximate air flows, water systems, or light trails. When I scan the prose architectures and let myself daydream—after all, they might be viewed as thinner, more delicate counterparts to Rorschach's inkblots—I discern political assemblies, performance spaces, and dance notations (figures 4.1–4.3).

The Ravicka series's most arresting example of breathing architecture appears in *Houses of Ravicka*. In the novel's first half, our new narrator is Jakobi, head of the Office of the Comptroller and author of the amusingly titled *Regulating the Book of Regulations*. Jakobi travels across Ravicka to capture "geoscogs"—"measurements that keep track of a building's subtle changes and movements over time"—of two elusive houses, numbers 32 and 96.[61] More impressionistic, the novel's second act features a phenomenological account of life inside one such house. This is a breathing house, one that expands, recedes, and migrates. The account sublimates architecture and enmeshes breathing, writing, and living: "Living was like writing a long, immersive essay: inside something fluid and labyrinthine, where light shined in at odd angles, even during the new moon. Sleeping was a terrifying pause in writing. Walking was writing. Each room held an essay you wrote as you breathed and the subject of the essay

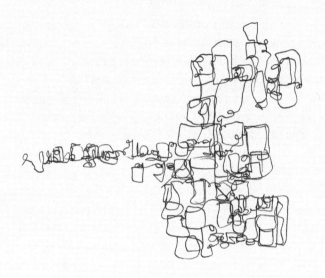

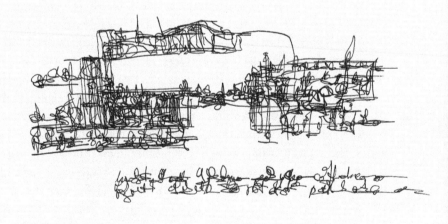

Figures 4.1–4.3. (*Opposite, top*) Renee Gladman, *Prose Architectures 154*, 2013; (*opposite, bottom*) Renee Gladman, *Prose Architectures 9*, 2013; (*below*) Renee Gladman, *Prose Architectures 125*, 2013. Ink on paper, each 9 × 12 inches. Courtesy of the artist and Wave Books.

usually had nothing to do with the function of the room, but maybe the room's architecture, for that day, was shaped by the quality of your thinking. First, I breathed the steps to my house, and then I descended them."[62] What does it mean to "[breathe] the steps to [one's] house"? I picture a character who takes a breath before going down a flight of stairs. But the phrasing hints at something else, something more: the character seems to breathe the steps into existence before descending them. In the previous sentence, the phrase "an essay you wrote as you breathed" may indicate that breathing and writing are concurrent or that breathing extends into writing. Earlier in the same sentence, "each room" is said to hold writing and breathing, and later, "the room's architecture, for that day, [is] shaped by the quality of your thinking"; causes and effects are interchangeable. Breathing steps, breathing an essay: those are figurative uses of respiration. The figure of speech before us isn't so much a metaphor as a hyperbole. Gladman merely exaggerates something rather mundane: the way breath propels activities, like construction and writing, whose outcomes we are likelier to consider tangible and social. In the introduction to the 1976 edition of *The Left Hand of Darkness*, Ursula K. Le Guin likens science fiction to a thought experiment that describes "reality, the current world," and records peculiarities already visible "at certain odd times of day in certain weathers."[63] Gladman's architecture, wherein "light shined in at odd angles," produces a similar effect. Seen through the respiratory processes upon which their existence is contingent, the structures that organize the way we live become uncannily fluid.

An attention to breathing enables Gladman to inhabit the cusp of actuality and virtuality. In *Architecture from the Outside: Essays on Virtual and Real Space* (2001), which Gladman has cited as an inspiration, Elizabeth Grosz describes the city "as a (collective) body-prosthesis or boundary that enframes, protects, and houses while at the same time taking its own forms and functions from the (imaginary) bodies it constitutes."[64] To actualize the virtual is to activate dormant corporeal "novelties": "Thus the virtual *requires* the actual to diverge, to differentiate itself, to proceed by way of division and disruption, forging modes of actualization that will transform this virtual into others unforeseen by or uncontained within it."[65] Grosz's city isn't built around "a single goal or ideal"; it instead responds to "the multiplicity of bodies and their varying political interests and ideals" or "a multiplicity of idealized solutions to living arrangements, arrangements about collective coexistence."[66] To breathe is to be in relation; any rendering of the city as epiphenomenal to respiratory flows disrupts its self-identicality and makes available dormant modes of organization. Gladman's city is a product of speculation, where *speculation* entails not the predictive analytics of the smart city but a commitment to asking questions about communal living amid crisis without expecting to learn what is already known.

This speculative practice is best encapsulated by the term *respiracy*, a portmanteau for respiratory piracy.[67] Buuck elaborates the concept of respiracy in *Site Cite City* (2015), a compendium of the performance protocols, scores, and transcripts of his Bay Area Research Group in Enviro-aesthetics (BARGE). Respiracy, Buuck muses, is "a term that will have had to have been concocted to somehow capture the vernacular practice of 'respiratory piracy,' by which air quality and environmental inequality are confronted head-on by those affected populations and their partisans."[68] Buuck's use of the passive voice and future perfect is noteworthy. Buuck overlays his proposed terminology with the claim that a term "will have had to have been concocted." By whom? And if not now, when? The definition's anachronism reflects the book's: in *Site Cite City*, the San Francisco Bay Area's gentrified, segregated, and polluted present is haunted by its past and its future. Many of the performances outlined have taken place, or may in some near or distant future take place, on Treasure Island, an artificial island that was home to the Golden Gate International Exposition of 1939 and, from the 1940s to the 1990s, to a military base. The poet describes Treasure Island as "a man-made land-mass designed to house a past's version of the future."[69] As a weapons storage and test site, Treasure Island has been a "rehearsal site for its own destruction, whether by quake or rising sea levels, fire or ecological disasters."[70] The respiration in *respiracy* figures and materializes an exposure to environments and an encounter with history that do not isolate resource from threat. The treasure and fever that in Robert Louis Stevenson's *Treasure Island* coexist—"I don't know about treasure . . . but I'll stake my wig there's fever here"—become irremediably entangled in *Site Cite City*: "If we are to take in the treasures, we must likewise taste of the fever."[71] The following section asks how respiratory variations and interruptions, those symptoms of the Ravickian fever, come to register as treasures or as ethical and political resources.

Symptomatic Breathing

Characters immersed in the Ravickian smog focus on their breathing to estimate their relative position. As they do so, they turn their respiration into the kind of proprioceptive device I discussed in chapter 1. Monitoring the air that moves in and out of their bodies prompts the characters to reencounter themselves beyond or beside themselves. In *The Ravickians*, Luswage Amini details the phenomenology of public speaking as a respiratory sequence:

It is dramatic and wonderful and isolating to present your work before an audience. You have got to hide your sweat and pretend your back fat does not bother you. Whatever shirt you are wearing, it must fit comfortably over your breasts yet let a little cleavage show. Dramatic, because you must connect with the piece you are reading, even if at present you do not. Wonderful, because you remember to breathe in from your navel region, but isolating when you forget to blow out, when you are breathing twice as hard as you would were you using normal breaths. Dramatic, remembering your nose and breasts.[72]

Amini describes the work of communicating, and connecting with, a text of her own as "dramatic and wonderful and isolating." As she reads to her audience, Amini gathers proprioceptive data from surrounding smells and the feeling of fabric on her skin. When she inhales deeply from her navel region, Amini is in sync with herself. But when she fails to follow up with an adequate exhale, she is suddenly at odds with her audience. In *Morelia*, the narrator's quest for information about her body and its location is similarly predicated on an attention to respiration. "I can't see myself sleeping but I feel my breathing," the narrator says; "I identify a certain sensation as my mouth. It's opening and asking where I am."[73] Conscious respiration might enable us to locate or center ourselves, but the realization that we are contingent beings exposed to a world of difference also estranges us from ourselves and others. Breathing does not so much provide answers as it yields new questions.

How does respiration—an imperfect proprioceptive device, an interrogative practice, a process of (self-)estrangement—shape encounters and relations in the smog-filled city? An episode featuring Ulchi, an interlocutor of *Event Factory*'s narrator, provides a way through this question. "One's senses eventually grow accustomed to the environment in which one is living," the narrator remarks; "So when I woke and quickly identified the green of dawn, I simultaneously smelled what appeared to be sulfur."[74] Increasingly frequent and intense, Ulchi's coughing shocks the narrator into noticing something beyond the sulfurous smog. Ulchi identifies his cough as a symptom of Ravicka's crisis: "'Something is not right in Ravicka,'" he says in a voice barely audible.[75] "Something had not been right there for a long time now," the narrator amends, "so the situation must be escalating. But why was it affecting him physically?" To ponder this question, she first proceeds comparatively, trying to "register [her] own health." But this focus conduces to sensory depletion: "The signals from my body were scattered and despondent. I decided to ignore this information entirely." The narrator thus turns to Ulchi, who, she says, "had just one symptom: he could not breathe."[76] She notices that his breathing has reached a critical point:

> Ulchi's brown had turned a deepening purple and his body appeared gripped against an oncoming seizure; he reached for me. He wanted something. One hand was opening and closing repeatedly. I managed to make out the word "*tirím*," which in Ravic means pen. It was the pen in my hand he wanted. I gave it to him. He used it to make a mark on his stomach that resembled an "o." He said, "*Ha meyeni.*" Push me. I did. I pushed fastly. With all my weight, I settled on that point, pressed as if a door might open. He let out a belch and beautiful yellow began to flow into his lungs; I could almost smell it.
> "What happened," I asked once he had recovered.
> "I don't know, but this wasn't the first time."
> "You've lost your breath before?"
> "Earlier."
> "When?"
> "Not long ago, but . . ." And in high Ravickian form he began to gesticulate dramatically, to "hide the story in the dance," as they say there. I did not take his subversion personally. This was Ravicka. Though, whatever had stopped his breathing then re-started it was symptomatic of the bigger problem with this city. "Ulchi, where do people go here to find the truth?" I got the question out, but figured it would be difficult for him to answer. Ravickians prefer not to share this kind of information: it belongs to the community. If you do not know it, this is because you are not supposed to.[77]

The phrasing "Ulchi's brown" could refer to the color of his skin. But instead of giving us information about Ulchi, this descriptor induces a crisis in meaning. We don't know if Ulchi's skin acquires a purple tint, or if it outright goes from brown to purple. Also unclear is whether the narrator perforates Ulchi's body to let air in or puts pressure on the "o" as a means to facilitate air flow through the respiratory tract. Nonetheless, the narrator assesses that "whatever had stopped [Ulchi's] breathing and then re-started it was symptomatic of the bigger problem with this city." She infers that the cause of Ulchi's symptom is the crisis playing out in Ravicka, but she lacks a language for articulating what experience, exactly, the crisis causes and the symptom expresses.

Something of Ulchi's experience gets lost in translation. Respiration and communication appear closely related throughout the Ravicka novels; the disruption of one doubles as a disruption of the other. In her impossible quest to uncover the true nature of the Ravickian crisis, the narrator of *Event Factory* meets the Esaleyons. Following a rebellion, the once-Ravickian Esaleyons became a faction with a language of their own, Esaléye. The narrator is fluent in Ravic but unfamiliar with Esaléye. She understands the Esaleyons to "speak in gaps and air"—or, as Gladman puts it in correspondence, in "gasps of the intelligible, a kind of embodied absence or unknown, a way of giving the unknown a shape."[78] The inversion of "gaps" and "gasps" is noteworthy: Gladman and her narrator associate gaps with air and gasps with unintelligibility, when the opposite—gasps of air, gaps in meaning—would be more intuitive. From the perspective of *Event Factory*'s narrator, the breathing of the Esaleyons is lost in translation, and their language lost in breathing. Were she to account for their communication, she would need a symbol "to represent air."[79]

Translation, with Gladman, thematizes the mediated nature of embodiment and experience. Early in *The Ravickians*, Amini introduces what we're reading in English as though it had originally been written in Ravic. The expression of a Ravickian's experience in a language other than Ravic, she says, is an expression of lack, of need: "To say you have been born in Ravicka in any other language than Ravic is to say you have been hungry."[80] Fractional translation also typifies geoscography, which, as previously indicated, names the study and measure of the migration of buildings. Ravicka's houses breathe, but their fluidity and motion aren't detectable by all characters. In the first section of *Houses of Ravicka*, Jakobi says of one house, "Not only did it fail to present a door, there also appeared to be no windows. It was one solid, unbroken, cascade of wall."[81] "The material," Jakobi adds, "was stone or stucco, I couldn't tell."[82] Descriptions of interiors defy physics; descriptions of façades are eerily matter-of-fact. Gladman's architecture breathes but is not transparent. Its paranormal intricacies don't translate. Although we may be tempted to conclude from these examples that experience, in Ravicka, is insider knowledge—that characters' experiences are transparent only to those who belong to the same group and speak the same language—many Ravickian-to-Ravickian interactions suggest otherwise. All encounters are translational, and a certain degree of familiarity isn't enough to overcome the variability of experience.

Ulchi's lost breath in *Event Factory* suggests that he is experiencing Ravicka's socioecological crisis in an acute way, but it doesn't grant the narrator access to the quality of this experience. Somewhat like Jacques Lacan's symptom or *sinthome*, Ulchi's labored and erratic breathing marks a node in the exchange of signifiers where meaning undoes itself.[83] Edelman explains that "though it functions as the necessary condition of the subject's engagement of Symbolic reality, the sinthome refuses the Symbolic logic that determines the exchange of signifiers; it admits no translation of its singularity and therefore carries nothing of meaning."[84] Ulchi's respiratory symptom may not carry "nothing of meaning," but it invites its interpreter to loosen her attachment to meaning. Through Ulchi's symptom the narrator comes to terms with the fact that the crisis isn't affecting her the same way it is him, and that it couldn't mean to her what it does to him: "The crisis ravaging Ravicka's population still had not become *my* crisis; the Ravickians would not allow it. The architecture said no."[85] By protecting the opacity of experience, Gladman does not intend to isolate or alienate her characters and readers. "In fact," she says in an interview, "I want the reader to get as close as possible to the conditions I experience while writing whatever is being read at that time. The reason that there is all this foreign-ness and untranslatability and shifts in knowing and seeing is because these are the qualities of experience that make me most aware of being a person in a very large world."[86] For Gladman's characters, recognizing the limits of what is graspable about experience is a necessity for, rather than an obstacle to, being in relation. As John Vincler notes, "In Gladman's work, especially in the Ravickian novels, when language fails to be comprehensible (the language spoken in Ravicka is an invented one), the movements of bodies become a means for maintaining communication or *some approximation of understanding*."[87] The narrator of *Event Factory* cannot access Ulchi's thoughts or feelings through his breathing, but the two can cultivate proximity by considering breath a shared alterity. They are, as Stefanie Heine might put it, "*breathing together-apart*."[88]

The interaction between the narrator of *Event Factory* and Ulchi is organized by symptomatic breathing, an interpretive attitude that recognizes as partial and, perhaps, inexact any information about the experience of crisis derived from respiratory symptoms. The term *symptomatic breathing*, of course, riffs on symptomatic reading. My aim is not to launch a substantive intervention into the debates on symptomatic versus nonsymptomatic reading or, in broader terms, critique versus postcritique.[89] I should nonetheless note that breathing calls for a concept of symptomaticity that dedramatizes symptomatic interpretation as it has recently been described—for instance, by Sharon Marcus and Stephen Best, as "a 'way' of interpreting" that takes "meaning to be hidden, repressed, deep, and in need of detection and disclosure by an interpreter."[90] Gladman's characters—ethnographers, linguists, novelists, comptrollers—are expert or amateur interpreters of the respiratory symptom. They ask what it means, what caused it. Yet they would struggle to sustain an attachment to ideals of total "detection and disclosure." There is a universe of atmospheric mediation between a respiratory symptom and its referent. To practice symptomatic breathing is to learn and relearn the impossibility of what we could call, after Fredric Jameson and Jonathan Flatley, a total psychosomatic mapping of crises.[91]

And really, there's no reason to tie symptomaticity to totalization. Julie Orlemanski explains that the ancient Greek term for symptom originally designated a mischance; only late in the development of Greek medical writing did *sumptōmata* come to refer to the bodily phenomena from which disease is inferred.[92] Both accident and sign, the symptom disturbs "somatic operation," "[troubling] the body's easy absorption into the self and [insisting] that we feel its burden."[93] Brooke Holmes similarly observes that the "fuzzy . . . line between the symptom and the feeling of a self" confronts us with "an inhuman otherness within the self" or the fact that we always, and at times despite ourselves, "[incorporate] much of [an] unseen world."[94] Respiratory symptoms linked to internal and external causes raise a vital contradiction: all living organisms are both themselves and not-themselves. They are what they breathe. Or breathing keeps them from being entirely themselves.

The symptom qua "somatic disturbance," notes Orlemanski, "provokes interpretation" and activates an "etiological imagination": "Hermeneutic instructions are not *in* symptoms . . . but rather in the discursive environment where the body is embedded and becomes legible."[95] The Ravicka novels make such legibility an ever-receding horizon, or more accurately a horizon clouded by smog. The symptom stimulates interpretation while deflating the certainty that the activity will yield satisfying conclusions. To regard breathing as a symptom is to give alterity minimal shape. It is to treat respiration as an object of knowledge without settling on its content. The respiratory symptom doesn't reveal much, but it's something to work with and around, together.

The Ethics and Politics of Opacity

Although it narrates and performs interpretive glitches, the Ravicka cycle does not endorse willful ignorance in the face of socioecological crisis, and neither do I. Such a program, or such absence of a program, would invalidate any struggle for justice. As Dorceta E. Taylor and Traci Brynne Voyles have shown, it's in part by legally and rhetorically detaching consequences (various conditions and illnesses) from their causes (acute toxicity) that corporations and governments continue to perpetrate environmental harm.[96] Abundant evidence of environmental harm doesn't automatically lead to accountability and redress, but compiling and circulating evidence remain the most reliable ways to demand a political response. The crisis plaguing Ravicka isn't equally enigmatic to everyone. And neither Gladman's characters nor her readers are dissuaded from seeking information about it. My point isn't that Ravicka's smog should not dissipate but that the fact of its presence triggers relational adjustments that in turn provide a template for building coalitions amid uneven geographies of asphyxiation. The monumental and ubiquitous smog pressures characters to improvise crisis sociality as again and again they lose the fantasy that knowing experience, their own and others', is what makes assembly both possible and desirable.

To ponder modes of relation that defetishize transparency, I turn to theories of racial and sexual opacity, thereby revisiting my earlier claim that the Ravicka books are novels of queerness and Blackness. Extending the synesthesia of Parikka's account of smog as breathable screen, I describe a visual phenomenon, opacity, in respiratory terms. Amid Ravicka's thick, yellowish smoke, a smoke that saturates the negative space between bodies and moves in and out of them, we may reimagine opacity as visual as well as atmospheric (tactile, gustatory, olfactory). Opacity, for Zach Blas, Christina A. León, Shaka McGlotten, and Thea Quiray Tagle, names a tactic of resistance within racist and homophobic regimes of surveillance.[97] León explains, for instance, that opacity resists a patriarchal and colonial gaze that seeks mastery.[98] Blas further argues that opacity, "an alterity that is unquantifiable, a diversity that exceeds categories of identifiable difference," "must be defended in order for any radically democratic project to succeed."[99] These critics attend to intentional performances of opacity—performances that are staged by individual subjects but hint at a collective response to surveillance. Much of the scholarship on opacity within the fields devoted to the study of minoritized subjectivities is propelled by the writings of the Martinican poet and philosopher Édouard Glissant. Glissant's philosophy focuses less on how to will opacity into existence than on the dynamics of recognizing or disavowing this existential, though historically and environmentally situated, condition. For Glissant—as for Gladman, I would venture—opacity is a given; the ethics and, on a larger scale, politics of opacity are activated when it is accepted as a condition of being in relation. Glissant:

> "Being is relation": but Relation is safe from the idea of Being.
> The idea of relation does not limit Relation, nor does it fit outside of it.
> The idea of relation does not preexist (Relation).
> Someone who thinks Relation thinks by means of it, just as does someone who thinks he [sic] is safe from it.
> Relation contaminates, sweetens, as a principle, or as flower dust.
> Relation enferals, lying in wait for equivalence.
> That which would preexist (Relation) is vacuity of Being-as-Being.

Being-as-Being is not opaque but self-important [*suffisant*].
Relation struggles and states itself in opacity. It defers [*diffère*] self-
importance.[100]

Against a self-sufficient and self-identical concept of Being-as-Being, Glissant posits relation as that which "enferals," or that which defers or induces difference in—the French *diffère* suggests both—Being-as-Being. Glissant insists that no one is unsusceptible to opacity and relation, and that those who think they can abstract themselves from such conditions think by way of them in the first place.

Zakiyyah Iman Jackson specifies that opacity does not deny interiority but protects against the grasping or seizing of interiority.[101] Glissant indeed writes that "to feel in solidarity with [the Other] or build with him [*sic*] or to like what he [*sic*] does, it is not necessary for me to grasp him [*sic*]."[102] Betsy Wing's translation of the French *comprendre* as "grasp," rather than "understand," emphasizes the act of *prendre* (to take, to steal, to make one's own) embedded in *comprendre*.[103] In an essay on her writing process, Gladman refutes the notion that the novel ought to make subjectivity graspable: "I think particularly of the English sentence, which forces one to begin with a subject, a kind of encapsulated self or other that speaks, sees, knows, or, in the case of objects, *a subjectivity that presumes grasp-ability*."[104] Kevin Everod Quashie's *The Sovereignty of Quiet: Beyond Resistance in Black Culture* (2012) offers one framework for thinking subjectivity beyond graspability. Quashie denounces the tendency of some antiracist discourses to validate Blackness only when it is expressive and dramatic, or when it performs something legible as resistance. Quashie makes room for a Black experience whose value is not contingent on its transparency.[105] Transposed into Quashie's idiom, Gladman's choice not to fix her characters' racial identity—and in some cases their gender identity—protects them against instrumentalization. We, as readers, must unlearn the idea that characters are worthy of our attention only insofar as their interiority is expressed. Where Quashie departs from both Glissant and Gladman is in his delineation of Black inner life as a locus of sovereignty.[106] Whereas for Quashie the quiet designates a register wherein Black individuals can be present to themselves, for Glissant and Gladman the relational nature of being is such that one is necessarily opaque to oneself, and hence not self-identical. One cannot possess alterity in oneself any more than in others.

The ethics and politics of what Tagle calls "being abstract together" prove pertinent beyond Ravicka's confines.[107] One logic that infiltrated popular US discourse in 2020 maintained that the COVID-19 pandemic had turned "I can't breathe" into a collective emission indicative of a generalized condition. Choy recalls, "A transpersonal gestural enactment of momentarily shared pandemic respiratory thickening paired incommensurably yet viscerally with linguistic and textual repetitions of racialized respiratory violence."[108] That incommensurability was often disregarded or minimized, such that anti-Black asphyxiation was recognized only insofar as anti-Blackness itself was denied. Pushing the denial of structural and environmental racism to its extreme, some "anti-maskers" appropriated the "I can't breathe" motto to denounce a method for limiting viral transmission that in their view encroached on their individual freedom. In refusing to abide by health and safety protocols, antimaskers put the lives of populations with limited or no access to medical care at greater risk. In this context, an interpretive practice calibrated to opacity insists on the non-transferability of experience. While it doesn't on its own rectify structural and environmental inequalities, this practice establishes parameters for coalitional action, including the principle that being breathless together does not make us breathless in the same way.[109]

One site where such coalitional action is sparked is the protest. In the wake of the 2014 police murder of Eric Garner, I partook in protests led by Black Lives Matter and Chicago-based organizations. When the crowd chanted, "I can't breathe" and "we can't breathe," I noticed that something was happening on a collective scale. Numerous protesters seemed to run out of breath as they chanted louder and louder. I didn't chant. I don't know whether or not this was the right thing to do; I simply felt, as a white individual, that asphyxia was not my experience to formulate in the first person, singular or plural. Still, when breathing is named, it draws attention to itself. As the chanting went on, I noticed that I was breathless—a product of exhaustion, rage, and hope. To some extent, the protesters who had assembled shared breathlessness. But my breathlessness couldn't be equated with the breathlessness of protesters asphyxiated by environmental racism, police violence, or microaggressions. My breathlessness tells me very little about someone else's. The ethics and politics of opacity make themselves available to us when, confronted with the impossibility of grasping the experiences of others, we continue to show up for them.

Respiratory Politics (a Précis)

Over the course of chapters 3 and 4, I have drawn the contours of a minoritarian aesthetics wherein responses to the environmental, social, and political crises of the late twentieth and early twenty-first centuries are guided by the principle that we are all breathers, but none of the same kind. To consider the widespread effects of climate crisis in tension with the acute vulnerability of members of marginalized populations, I have mapped out two ecologies of the particular: the breathing rituals of Black and Indigenous feminisms and an aesthetics of smog sensing that situates queerness and Blackness in an atmospherics. In chapter 3, I argued that ceremonial poetry and the novel of healing ritualize breathing to manage vulnerabilities and articulate collective survival while destabilizing the wholeness or wellness thereby afforded. In the present chapter, I have described breathing as a locus where the opacity of embodiment and experience reveals itself as a resource for ethics and politics.

It seems apt, at the close of a pair of essays on respiratory politics, to return to the question of the breathing *we* I first brought up in the introduction to *Breathing Aesthetics*. Earlier, I wrote that my use of the first-person plural was catachrestic—that it heralded its own impossibility. In *Unthinking Mastery: Dehumanism and Decolonial Entanglements* (2017), Julietta Singh writes that the pronoun *we* is inescapable in critical theoretical projects committed to social justice: "I am not uncritical of my recurring use the term 'we' across these pages, but it is one I cannot do without."[110] Inspired by Jeanne Vaccaro, Singh offers that *we* "is a question as much as it is a hopeful summons to the (always imagined) future readers of this text who might be or might become invested in collective reorientations in the world."[111] The *we* of *Breathing Aesthetics* is similarly aspirational. When I use *we*, it is not because I believe that breathers share some universal attributes despite the uneven distribution of risk. Much like Singh's, my use of *we* emerges in the midst of "collective reorientations." It is through the recognition that breathing at once deindividualizes and deuniversalizes embodiment and experience that it becomes possible to speak of a breathing *we*.

Death in the Form of Life

This final chapter zooms in on, appropriately, the last breath, the experience of which cannot be communicated. To relay how the last breath feels, the dying individual would have to keep breathing. Yet witnesses regularly comment on the experience, interpreting the nonviolent last breath, specifically, as evidence of the dying's presence of mind, control over their conditions, and readiness to die. A paradox animates such interpretation. A so-called good death, under a Western medical regime characterized by life support technologies and palliative care services, designates a situation where the dying is not entirely conscious or responsive, often due to analgesic drugs. At the same time, the frequent declaration by the living that in the last breath the dead "left peacefully" retroactively conjures a subject of consciousness and intention from the slow drift of terminality. This is a subject who returns to depart, one who is, for an instant, present enough to choose absence.

Chapter 4 advocated an estrangement from the assumption that breathing makes experience transparent and graspable. Here I append an asterisk to my reasoning. The fantasy that the nonviolent last breath, in particular, dispenses evidence that the dying has encountered mortality on their own terms enables witnesses to manage grief and loss. I've insisted throughout *Breathing Aesthetics* that we never breathe strictly on our own terms, and this chapter does not reverse course at the eleventh hour. The emphasis in the above statement should be on *fantasy*: the last breath accommodates one—that the dying individual is, if fleetingly, capable of deliberation and control—and its circulation serves a need. The last breath makes itself available to the living as a heuristic device for speculating an exception to contingency from contingency itself. Momentarily exempting the dying from contingency is but a way for those who survive them to bear their own. This management is discursive, which is to say social, but it does not cohere into an explicit ethics or politics of mourning—hence this chapter's protruding from the diptych on the respiratory commons formed by chapters 3 and 4. It makes narrative sense for the last chapter to address the last breath. It makes even more sense, given my sustained attention to the respiratory enmeshment of vitality and morbidity, for this chapter to deflate the last breath's fatality and finality, and to examine how it is received by the people who must keep breathing in its wake.

What constitutes a good death is historically and culturally variable. In the nineteenth century, the tubercular's death, ameliorated by opium, generally took place in the home. Let us picture this scene, narrated by John Anthony Tercier: "the family gathered around the bedside, a few murmured farewells, and then an exit 'gentle into that good night.'"[1] Although the good death might still happen in the home if individualized care can be afforded, it most often happens in a hospital or hospice room, which Bruce Buchan, Margaret Gibson, and David Ellison describe as "a borrowed space of transition rather than belonging."[2] Until the early twentieth century, hospitals provided care mostly to travelers, the destitute, the orphaned, and the poor.[3] The First and Second World Wars made the hospital the locus of caregiving. Palliative care practices transformed the hospital once more, this time into the place where we go to die.[4] In the era of palliative care, medicine, no longer just curative, produces the good death.[5] Medical professionals are tasked with managing the suffering of patients while helping them and their kin to accept the inevitability of death.[6]

The term *good death* indexes the dying's wealth; it is often preceded by the attribute *bourgeois* or, in Simone de Beauvoir's famous account of her mother's passing, "upper-class" ("*une mort de prévilégiée*").[7] It also signals luck, accidents not being, by definition, fully preventable. The term reveals little, however, about the dying's experience. Its oxymoronic quality—can a death really be good?—is exacerbated when we consider its application in cases where the dying display signs of discomfort such as strained or interrupted respiration.[8] Deaths qualify as good not necessarily because the dying don't suffer (a fact impossible to ascertain if, for example, the dying cannot, under the influence of analgesic drugs, self-report pain) but because they have been granted some relief: the gift of a partial or total absence from the site of their own suffering.

The good death supplies the conditions for the nonviolent last breath to be monitored, and for this monitoring to be welcome—although, as we shall see, the one last breath is more elusive than the discourse it inspires might suggest.[9] Access to the nonviolent last breath has been proven a matter of racial privilege for the dying and their witnesses alike by the necropolitics of anti-Black asphyxiation articulated in prior chapters. Nonviolent last breaths are not forcibly induced. And when they are recorded, their circulation neither casualizes anti-Black violence nor reproduces the trauma of being its target.

Throughout this chapter, I accompany the individuals who show up to the scene of the nonviolent last breath. By *scene*, I mean, in a loosely psychoanalytic sense, a relational configuration in which participants fulfill rough roles or functions (parent-child, doctor-patient) and manage the fantasies that bind them to various objects, including each other.[10] I use the term to refer as well to a film scene, or the action taking place in a single location (a matter of mise-en-scène) in continuous time (a matter of storytelling). The two senses of *scene* are inseparable in a pair of specimens of cinema vérité I examine in this chapter, namely, Frederick Wiseman's *Near Death* (1989) and Allan King's *Dying at Grace* (2003).[11] Shot in black and white, Wiseman's six-hour marathon follows doctors, nurses, and their terminally ill patients in Boston's Beth Israel Hospital. King's comparatively brisk, two-and-a-half-hour "actuality drama" profiles five patients, all elderly, from their admission into Toronto's Grace Health Centre until their demise.[12] Without voice-over narration or confessional interviews to fill in the gaps, we know as much about the subjects' biography as they disclose in the flow of conversation. In *Dying at Grace*, it is a great deal, and in *Near Death*, it is very little; even names are hard to catch in Wiseman's film. As they partake in the highly organized hospital setting's highly ritualized interactions, on-screen subjects, however complex their portrayal may be, take on the archetypal roles of the death scene: the dying, the dying's relative, the medical worker, and the occasional religious representative.

These interactions create a context for the dying's last breath to be watched and interpreted. Inspired by Ludwig Wittgenstein, Veena Das and Stanley Cavell name such a context a "form of life." "A form of life," Das and Clara Han explain, "rests on nothing more than that we agree, or find ourselves agreeing, on the way that we size things up, or respond to what we encounter."[13] To define the perimeter of this form of life, I propose, improbably, a comedic interlude. Nowhere are the stakes of being included in or excluded from this or any form of life starker than in the realm of humor. Characters in comedies often bring the norms governing social situations into sharp relief by transgressing them, intentionally or not, and consciously or not. Recent television comedies elicit physical and emotional reactions by testing, stretching, and crossing the limits of the form of life organizing the witnessing of the last breath. Three TV episodes—from *One Mississippi* (2015–17), the US remake of *Getting On* (2013–15), and *Veep* (2012–19)—share a premise: a woman asks or is asked to witness her mother's last breath, emitted either too early or too late. Witnessing the last breath, as these comedies reveal, is a problem of timing: to be on time would be to receive the dying's last breath as a farewell rather than just the cessation of biological functions. In these mother-daughter scenes, the last breath mirrors the first breath. The first breath heralds one's entry into the world, and the last breath one's exit. Both are narrated not by the subjects who breathe them but by witnesses.

In the pilot episode of Tig Notaro and Diablo Cody's tragicomedy *One Mississippi*, Tig (Notaro) stands at her mother Caroline's bedside.[14] Tig remarks that her mother, unresponsive and on life support, isn't fully herself—an observation that Tig's stepfather Bill (John Rothman), in one of the series's less convincing experiments with the setup-punchline form, takes literally. This chapter attends to the discourses that suffuse the death scene, so here and elsewhere I quote the dialogue at length.

TIG: It's just not her.

BILL: It most certainly is her, Tig. Look at the ID on the bed.

TIG: I know it's her. It's just ... Never mind.

DOCTOR: So, the nurse is going to go ahead and disconnect the respirator. Any questions?

TIG: About death?

DOCTOR: About the process.

REMY: Is she going to die right away?

DOCTOR: Possibly. But it could take hours, even days. Are we ready?

TIG: Yeah, she wouldn't want to be like this.

The respirator is unplugged, and Caroline inhales laboriously, then coughs. In between jump cuts indicating the passage of time, Tig requests assistance, suspecting that her mother is about to die or perhaps has already died. Tig once asks Nurse Mellie (Lorrie Chilcoat), "My mother stops breathing for ten seconds, and I keep thinking it's going to be her last breath. Is that going to happen ... soon?" Later, she requests, "Could you do that thing again where you clear out her throat or her lungs or something? She can't breathe." Pragmatically, tenderly, the nurse replies, "That's kind of the point, hon." Caroline's breaths get further and further apart, and uninterrupted silence eventually takes Tig out of her reverie. The last breath doesn't rise to the status of event; Tig knows it happened only after the fact, once no other breaths are detectable. She presses the call button one last time. In her next interaction with Nurse Mellie, the mood shifts rapidly from anxious to hysterical:

TIG: I think, I think my mother . . .

NURSE MELLIE: Yes, I'm sorry, she's gone.

TIG: What happens now? Do I just leave?

NURSE MELLIE: (bursting out laughing) Do you just leave!? No! You can't just leave your mother! Oh my gosh, that would be straight-up nuts!

TIG: (also laughing) I'm realizing that now!

Laughter, says Norbert Elias, breaks the rhythm of breathing with "rhythmical jerks and jolts[:] we expel more air than we inhale until, in the end of the hearty laugh, we are out of breath."[15] Tig and Nurse Mellie's breathless laughter resounds as a nonfatal counterpoint to Caroline's understated last breath. The awkwardness of not knowing how to react, paired with the relief that nothing worse can happen (Caroline is dead), causes the tension accumulated in the anticipation of the last breath to spill over into laughter. Comedy doesn't strictly dispel anxiety, and here laughter also visceralizes the news of Caroline's demise.[16]

Characters in the political satire *Veep* and the workplace sitcom *Getting On* either fail to meet the last breath with decorum or try to ceremonialize it tardily. In an episode of *Veep* titled "Mother," US president Selina Meyer (Julia Louis-Dreyfus) is encouraged by a forecasted spike of her favorability rating to expedite her mother's death.[17] When Selina unplugs the artificial respirator, a corrosive version of *One Mississippi*'s "Is she going to die right away?" exchange occurs between Selina and Dr. Mirpuri (Sarayu Blue):

SELINA: So in your experience, how long does that sort of thing . . . ?

DR. MIRPURI: Usually minutes. I've seen hours. Days are very rare.

SELINA: (cringing) Well, that's not going to work because . . . for me . . . with my . . . schedule—life.

Selina's mother dies within a few seconds—so quickly that the president asks to "have a moment." This instant of reverence is cut short by an aide who tells

Selina about the success of a political maneuver. "Oh! My prayer worked!" Selina shouts. Her daughter Catherine (Sarah Sutherland), who wished to be present for her grandmother's last breath, arrives too late and is puzzled by the festivities.

"The Concert," an episode of *Getting On*, also plays the denial of access to the dying's last breath for laughs.[18] The episode's opening act is a vaudeville. Due to Dr. Jenna James's (Laurie Metcalf) volatile medical advice, Phyllis Marmatan (Molly Shannon) repeatedly enters and exits the palliative care unit where her mother is staying. Phyllis misses her mother's last breath due to a hallway argument about this senseless back and forth. Back in the hospital room, Dr. James states the obvious before partially taking it back, realizing that her mercuriality caused a scene of intimacy to implode:

DR. JAMES: She's gone. . . . She's *barely* gone. Sit. She's *almost here.*

PHYLLIS: Can she still hear me?

DR. JAMES: (*squinting*) Ummmm . . . ?

Dr. James approximates a nod before leaving the room, withdrawing from a conversation that, because of her mixed signals, is about to take a paranormal turn.

The characters who populate these television series inhabit a shared form of life: they know to shape a nonevent or anticlimax (breathing's gradual extinction) into an event or climax (one last breath). But they do it all wrong. Tig too hastily declares every breath the last one. Distracted and flippant, Selina fails to perform emotions deemed appropriate within the death scene. And Phyllis, coaxed by Dr. James's vague statements, hopes to ritualize the witnessing of what is no longer witnessable. Comedy, as we know well, is a matter of timing. In *One Mississippi*, *Veep*, and *Getting On*, characters appraise the last breath either too early or too late. Comic value derives from the fact that characters show up to fill the temporal gap between the act of witnessing and the witnessable last breath with their respective rigidities: Tig's maladroitness, Selina's impatience, Dr. James's tendency to deflect blame.

The comedies examined here raise some questions, catalyzed by the medicalization of dying, regarding what constitutes life, death, and the capacity to determine our fate. Kristin Savell makes the claim that artificial ventilation and other life-sustaining technologies have inaugurated an entirely new type of decision: the decision not to endure treatment, to be made by a competent patient or, alternatively, a guardian or relative.[19] A series of "fictions" simplify the death scene's complex reality: one, "a competent patient can refuse medical treatment for any or no reason even if it means they will die"; two, "the doctor's removal of life-supporting technology does not entail responsibility for the resulting death"; and three, "such deaths are natural deaths."[20] To respond to the shifting landscape of dying, Robert Kastenbaum developed a new taxonomy of deaths in the 1960s. Phenomenological death occurs when "so-called heroic measures" maintain feeble signs of life even as "the person inside the body"—let us note the Cartesian split—"gives absolutely no indication of his [*sic*] continued existence."[21] Social death occurs when the living behave toward the dying as they would toward a dead person.[22] Modern medicine has pluralized the temporality of death. A patient can be phenomenologically dead or brain dead or clinically dead minutes, hours, or days before being legally pronounced dead.

The promise of the last breath, even when noticed too early or too late, is to organize those noncoinciding temporalities. This promise is so enticing that, according to the neurosurgeon Thomas B. Freeman, the last breath is worth faking.[23] Freeman's nephew suffered a closed head injury and, following an unsuccessful surgery, was declared brain dead. To be donated, functional organs must be harvested at this stage, inasmuch as the relatives of an organ donor rarely witness the last breath or heartbeat. Freeman recounts that his niece couldn't process that her brother was practically dead: "she felt that he was somehow still alive, since he was breathing on a ventilator and his heart was beating."[24] So, Freeman made a suggestion:

> I asked her if she would want to be with her brother when the ventilator was temporarily disconnected. My niece understood that in this way she could be present for her brother's final breath, and participate in his death by being at his side when he stopped breathing. I let her know that the alarms would be turned off, there would be a quiet and reverent atmosphere in the room, and the family would be with her for support as well as to say good-bye. In other words, I offered her the opportunity to be present at her brother's death, focusing on his breathing.[25]

The family greenlit Freeman's plan: the neurosurgeon's niece witnessed her brother's "final breath" and left the room before the latter's oxygen saturations began to fall and the ventilators had to be reconnected. The last breath, as Freeman stages it, operates as a gimmick. In Sianne Ngai's account, the gimmick appears both prematurely and belatedly, and works at once too hard and not hard enough.[26] The simulated last breath, a trick for providing closure, betrays its inner workings: this simple ruse in fact necessitates careful planning and costly medical technology. To Freeman and his niece, the last breath temporarily reconfigures the respiratory enmeshment of vitality and morbidity. A narrative threshold imposes itself. All that precedes it is reduced to life, all that follows it to death.

Buchan, Gibson, and Ellison contend that "the death scene is inherently dramatic."[27] I would counter that we process the death scenes of literary and screen cultures as dramatic, comedic, or both based on how they play with time, specifically untimeliness, to withhold or precipitate an emotional release. *Dying at Grace* couldn't be further, tone-wise, from the comedies I have probed. As the documentary's title suggests, Grace, the hospital, is where grace, the virtue, can be contemplated. By contrast, and perhaps surprisingly, *Near Death* and those television shows are not so tonally discordant. *Near Death* accrues all the aggression of a workplace comedy while allowing none of the release. All cringing, no laughing. We're given few if any outlets, in the form of a narrative climax or a tender moment, to let go of the tension. The experience is bewilderingly noncathartic—for nearly six hours. I turn to *Near Death* next.

Managing Respiration: Frederick Wiseman's *Near Death*

Wiseman's camera in *Near Death* may be invasive, but most of the patients and medical workers remain unnamed until the closing credits. As is customary with the filmmaker, portraits of individuals are secondary to a study of the institution in which they participate. We join conversations in medias res and exit them abruptly. Murmurs and mumbles are not closed-captioned. Through Wiseman's lens, the function of an institution like Boston's Beth Israel Hospital is to manage breath and its surrounding discourses. Early on, *Near Death* problematizes the witnessing of someone else's breathing. A mere three minutes into the documentary, a young medical worker suggests that a patient's respiratory settings be changed "in such a way that it doesn't look like he's breathing so hard." He goes on, "I think it's a bit disconcerting for the family to come in here and see him struggling like that. It's just an idea, just a passing idea." If the medical worker proposes to modulate respiration, it's not so much to guarantee the patient's comfort as to produce an image of comfort that could, in turn, reduce the family's own discomfort. Breathing, as chapter 1 and its theory of spectatorship established, is contagious.[28] Watching someone unable to take a full breath may be agonizing. It may cause witnesses to experience respiratory discomfort themselves. The dying rarely breathe alone. Witnesses, who aren't entirely resistant to the erratic rhythms they closely monitor, breathe along. When Wiseman's subjects talk about a patient's breathing, in particular a patient's experience of difficult breathing, they are often talking about their own, as well.

Conversations about breathing abound in *Near Death,* and they are jarring. As they try to get patients to adopt or reject treatment options, medical workers are emphatic, at times even aggressive. For their part, patients, many of whom are intubated, on painkillers, and visibly overwhelmed by the stakes of the decisions they're asked to make, tend to remain quiet. In an early scene, a female medical worker loudly tells a male patient, "On a scale of one to ten—of your lungs—ten being good and one being bad, you're a one. You have really poor, poor breathing." The aim of this performance assessment is for the patient to decide whether he wants to be intubated again if his state deteriorates. "Do you understand what intubation means?" the worker asks (figure 5.1). The patient nods. He ventures, "Freeze you off." His words are barely audible, and his lips are concealed. He is shot in profile, with a breathing mask covering his face's lower half. She corrects him:

> No, that's not what it means. Intubation means—it's an act of putting a tube in your mouth and into your lungs, and we attach it to a machine through tubes, and we help you breathe. Okay? And we wait for your lungs to get better, and then we take you off the machine. As you get better, you're allowed, you're able to breathe better on your own, and the machine does less and less work. Unfortunately, your lungs aren't going to get better. So the act of putting you on the machine is almost a futile effort. The machine is there to help you, and then when you get better, we can take the machine away gradually. What's going to happen if we put you on the machine is, is that you're not going to get better. This is you. It's sad, and it's frustrating, and it's anger provoking. But your lungs are about as bad as they can get, you know. Your breathing test tells us. You know, the breathing test? Not the little aerosol thing but the breathing test on the big machine. That tells us what you're like. And your body is telling us is that your lungs don't have much left.

Repetitions and amendments delineate a zone where the patient, the state of his lungs, and the quality of his breathing are one and the same: the breathing test "tells us what you're like"; "you're a one"; "this is you." The medical worker tries to guide the patient toward the realization that intubation isn't worth pursuing in case of relapse because he, his lungs, and his breathing are all near death. She asks him to confirm what his body, through something like "organ speech," is already saying: that when the prospects of recovery are naught, it is best to let go.[29] Breathing cannot be rebooted infinitely.

Throughout *Near Death,* medical workers ask patients whose health is on the decline to decide on treatments to be administered immediately or in case of

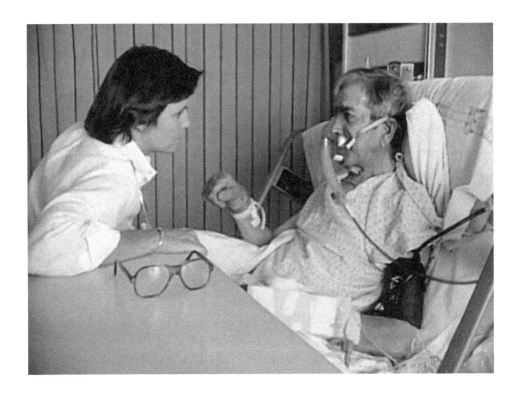

Figure 5.1. Still from *Near Death* (1989), directed by Frederick Wiseman. Zipporah Films.

emergency. The subtext of most conversations is that the decision isn't really one because death is on its way. An exchange between a male doctor and a female patient revolves around the tracheostomy, a surgical procedure wherein an incision in the windpipe relieves an obstruction to breathing. Although it temporarily facilitates respiration, the procedure damages the airways. The doctor breaks down the situation for his patient: "If you want to go on, if you want to live, then tracheostomy is your option." He asks her whether she's afraid to die. She isn't. He asks instead if she's afraid that her husband will react negatively to her turning down the surgery. She is. The doctor brusquely tells his patient that her husband might very well have a heart attack if she forewent the surgery and took the risk of dying sooner, though more comfortably. She raises her hand ever so slightly, in a horizontal position, as if to silence him. The doctor returns later in the film for another perplexing intervention. Arched over a bed on which an unidentifiable patient is lying, the doctor exclaims, "Today is the day! We're going to get that tube out today! Big day today!" The patient's stasis clashes with the doctor's manic enthusiasm. In *Near Death*, patients often fail to provide the soundbite requested by medical workers. Breathing activates a discursive machine that runs in overdrive. The patients whose breathing fuels this discourse contribute to it less and less as their state worsens.

In between doctor-patient or nurse-patient conversations about treatment options, medical workers debate among themselves the stakes of the actions, such as stopping life support, that they must ultimately perform. These are routine tasks, and yet the workers describe them as uncanny. One worker says of a patient, "So if he stops breathing, we just let him stop breathing?" The colleague nods: "Uh huh." "That's *so* weird," the former replies. Medical workers ponder whether life support is "a political question or an ethical one" and whether artificial respiration counts as "life" or as "purgatory." They lament that there exists no "blood test for terminality" or "litmus test for competence." And when relatives or guardians must make decisions for patients, "emotions get in the way." One especially exasperated worker deplores that life support produces an illusion of aliveness: "When we say, 'brain dead,' what we should say is, 'Your family member has passed away, and the only reason you see a heartbeat is because we're artificially keeping the body, essentially, alive—or going, keeping the heart rate going because of the oxygen.' Because the longer we procrastinate, in that particular instance, the longer we keep the heart going, the more confused the family is going to become." What the worker calls an "illusion of aliveness" may be parsed out as life without evidence of the feeling of being alive.

Phenomenologists have sought to determine how the feeling of being alive arises. Thomas Fuchs insists that "the body is not simply the accidental carrier of the brain as an information-processing machine that produces consciousness out of itself."[30] Mind and body, Fuchs explains, are involved in the dynamics that produce "the conscious manifestations of life itself."[31] Evan Thompson's "enactive approach" similarly stipulates that "the human mind emerges from self-organizing processes that tightly interconnect the brain, body, and environment at multiple levels."[32] The feeling of being alive, Fuchs posits, develops at "the turning point between the *vital processes* of an organism's self-preservation in its continuous exchange with the environment and the *psychic processes* of sentience and agency based on the organism's sensorimotor interaction with its surroundings"—which is to say in the interstice between life and experience.[33] The illusory aliveness mentioned by some medical workers in *Near Death* refers to a situation in which dying people display no signs of autoaffection, or no signs that they are aware of their existence as individuals somewhat distinct from their milieus. In this context, body and mind no longer seem co-constitutive—hence the Cartesian split in Kastenbaum's claim that phenomenological death has occurred when "the person inside the body" shows no more signs of life.[34] Patients "[watch] life erode," as Janet Maslin puts it in a 1989 review of *Near Death*, until they no longer can and medical workers, relatives, and the film's spectators must take over.[35]

What remains unsaid in Wiseman's documentary is that staying alive, even maintaining an illusion of aliveness, is expensive. *Near Death* is a depiction of for-profit health care, declining social services, and surging insurance premiums in the United States of the late 1980s. Maintaining the fiction of the natural death requires muting economic considerations. Once its ties to managerial and actuarial calculations are revealed, the act of stopping life support appears denatured. It's partly in order for the decisions and actions of relatives and medical workers not to register as actual decisions and actions that the dying individual is, in the last breath, made into a subject of consciousness and intention. *Dying at Grace* documents this process.

Leaving Peacefully: Allan King's *Dying at Grace*

Near Death stays near death: not too close, at the safe distance of a medium shot. In Wiseman's sterile documentary, corpses are sealed off in body bags. By contrast, *Dying at Grace* prompts spectators to confront dying, its images and its sounds. King zooms in on faces: on wrinkles, thin white hair, worried gazes, and open mouths. His attention to the last breath and the passage from life to death it narrates poses a problem for cinema, a medium that from its inception, Louis-Georges Schwartz recounts, has carried a promise of immortalization.[36] Schwartz belongs to a critical tradition that describes cinema as a ghost story of sorts. André Bazin, a key figure in this tradition, argues that the screen, contra the photographic frame, functions as a mask: characters survive even as they walk out of the camera's field of vision.[37] For Gilberto Perez, cinema personifies a possible absence, and its image is a "true hallucination" or "material ghost."[38] The last breath magnified and amplified by *Dying at Grace* implies a tension between two configurations of life and death: a sequential one (first life, then death) and a concurrent one (life and death, presence and absence).

Capturing the last breath poses not just a philosophical problem but a technical one. Jennifer Malkowski notes that recording the last breath requires audiovisual equipment that can fit in compact hospital rooms and run for hours at a manageable cost.[39] Although we may choose when to unplug an artificial respirator, the dying's last breath, as we have seen, cannot be timed with exactitude. Moreover, the last breath can be named as such only retroactively: when no other breaths follow and the dying, now dead, is silent and immobile.[40] *Near Death* is the rare deathbed documentary shot on celluloid—a fact that, for Malkowski, speaks to Wiseman's pedigree as an established filmmaker.[41] King, also a celebrated filmmaker, shot *Dying at Grace* with handheld video cameras, likely because they guaranteed more flexibility. King enjoyed longer shooting days, and he could plan one at short notice if the health of one of his subjects deteriorated. That *Near Death*, unlike *Dying at Grace*, doesn't actually show anyone's last breath possibly points to a directorial decision. At the same time, it exposes the limitations of celluloid, a material perhaps too onerous to capture something as fleeting as the last breath.[42]

King's film is more graphic than Wiseman's, but also quieter and more meditative. The opening titles read, "This film is about the experience of dying"; "Five patients in a palliative care ward for the terminally ill agreed to share their experience in the hope that it will be useful for the living." Few of the documentary's subjects—Carmela Nardone, Joyce Bone, Richard Pollard, Lloyd Greenway, and Eda Simac—got to know each other during the shoot, and for a while King considered turning *Dying at Grace* into five short films.[43] The feature film that King ultimately released is remarkably cohesive; it's in fact almost repetitive. We watch one subject die, then another, and so on. Each subject's last breath, whether depicted or just discussed, marks the limit of the biographical— the point beyond which life must be formulated in the past tense.

The first patient we meet, Carmela, is diabetic. In one scene, the resident chaplain, Phyllis, addresses palliative care with Carmela's daughter:

PHYLLIS: How are you doing?

DAUGHTER: *(pauses and sighs)* Trying to cope. You know, sad.

PHYLLIS: It's not very easy.

DAUGHTER: No, it isn't easy. You know, just waiting for the inevitable to come. I would rather it be a surprise, you know what I'm saying?

PHYLLIS: Yes, we don't have a choice.

DAUGHTER: There's no choice. As long as she's not in pain. . . .

PHYLLIS: And when she does leave us, she will leave in peace.

DAUGHTER: She will leave in peace because, you know,
she's a good woman.

As the two women talk, Carmela's eyes are wide open. She doesn't appear to be looking at anything in particular. An oxygen tube connects her nostrils to a ventilator. Later in the film—though we don't know how many hours, days, or weeks later in Carmela's life—her congestion worsens. She widens her mouth to take in some air. Her breaths become louder and less frequent. When two nurses enter the room, Carmela has already died. One of them pulls out a stethoscope and waits for a heartbeat that never makes itself heard. They work quietly, nodding and whispering only when needed. Theirs is the breathing now audible. After they exit the room, one of them makes a phone call: "Carmela passed away within the past twenty minutes—very peacefully, quietly, just the way you had left her."

King's second subject, Joyce, believes that she's "not handling [her cancer diagnosis] very well." She's "letting it get to" her. If she had her way, she asserts, she would move into a corner, cross her legs, and wait until she died. "Is that because you feel weak?" Phyllis offers. "No," says Joyce, whose two sons were killed and whose husband committed suicide, "I just feel—finished." In another scene, a nurse comes in to measure the interval between each breath. King cuts to a winter sunrise, trading the confined space for sublime imagery. A nurse dictates her report: "6:04, bed two, Joyce Bone. When we first came on she had indicated that she wanted something for pain and shortness of breath. She was able to verbalize that. Her congestion and respiratory difficulty were obvious at that point. And Joyce's respiration ceased at 9:35. In the end it was a rapid decline with respiratory distress, and then a peaceful last breath." Halfway through the report, we return to the hospital room. The scene before us—Joyce, dead, with her eyes and mouth wide open—darkens the sunrise's symbolism. Bearing traces of discomfort and restlessness, Joyce's inert body refutes the nurse's report, in particular the claim that the patient's last breath was peaceful.

A nurse makes a similar postmortem declaration about Richard, who at the time he's introduced suffers from lung cancer and hepatitis C related to smoking and heavy drug use. As the film progresses, Richard shows more symptoms of dementia, even threatening the medical staff. As he breathes, an evidently painful process, he alternates between laughing and crying. After he dies, someone notes, off-frame, "He looks like a Renaissance painting . . . the agony of Rick." And yet, a medical worker states, "He did struggle, but in the end he went peacefully."

Two last breaths are shown explicitly in *Dying at Grace*. The first is Lloyd's. By the time he joins the cast, Lloyd communicates in a manner only his brother Norm can grasp. The two are tight-knit. As Lloyd gets sicker, his breaths turn to grunts. He has difficulty inhaling and swallowing, inasmuch as two nurses must work collaboratively to close his mouth once they have sprayed medication into it. Hugging and kissing him, his relatives encourage him to "let go" (figure 5.2). After he has a spasm, speculation ensues. Will another breath follow, or will this have been Lloyd's last? After a while, a relative risks, "He went so peacefully." "He did, he did," everyone agrees.

King's fifth and last subject, Eda, experiences a less linear decline. Introduced early in the film, she moves out of the Grace Health Centre when her cancer symptoms wane. Her stay out of the palliative care unit is brief, however, and she returns visibly enfeebled. As Phyllis prays for her, Eda breathes loudly. She has a series of short spasms, followed by a more dramatic one. Then, stillness. The film ends with a close-up of Eda's face. Having died seconds before, she appears to be gazing at the camera, urging us to intone the refrain: *she left peacefully*.

The events leading up to the last three deaths are interwoven. Twenty or so minutes before the end credits roll, King, who otherwise favors lengthy scenes, cuts rapidly between Richard, Lloyd, and Eda. Continuity is ensured by the movement, rhythm, and noise of the patients' breathing. It becomes unclear whose breathing we're hearing; any given transition could be a match cut (two shots share a composition), an L cut (the audio from the preceding scene overlaps the picture from the following scene), or a J cut (the audio from the following scene overlaps the picture from the preceding scene). The deaths appear concurrent, but they likely were not. Known to take liberties at the editing stage, King probably aligned Richard's, Lloyd's, and Eda's arcs to build toward a climax. And it works: the filmmaker conditions his spectators to expect the last breath. In an early viewing of *Dying at Grace*, I tried to capture the last breath.

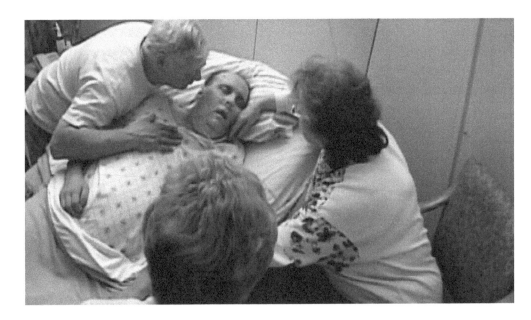

Using my computer's screenshot function, I generated stills of Lloyd's and Eda's last moments. I included those shots in a previous iteration of this chapter, before concluding that my stills were mere approximations of, and thus mere attempts to stabilize, an elusive process. Evidence of a nonviolent last breath, it now seems to me, isn't primarily visual (or even audiovisual) but discursive. The last breath occurs if the living generate a discursive context in which it can signify.

Breathing after Death

Malkowski writes that "Eda's loss of self is a consequence of modern dying and . . . especially of hospice and palliative care, whose mission to provide comfort and suppress pain requires medications that inhibit alertness and eventually consciousness."[44] The loss of self observed by Malkowski, paired with the refrain of the peaceful departure, returns us to the paradox that opened this chapter. To leave peacefully, the dying must no longer be present to their own suffering, but to leave, they must not yet be absent. Marshaling what Mel Y. Chen describes as the "alchemical magic of language," the discourse of the last breath projects onto a body that cannot remain animate on its own a subject able to opt out of life.[45]

In "Sociality and Sexuality," Leo Bersani sets out to imagine an origin myth for sociality. He explains, "I am of course not referring to a historically locatable moment, one at which each human subject—and not only human subjects— might have the option of *not* moving, of *not* connecting. Such beginnings are both inexistent—there was never any moment when we were not already in relation—and structurally necessary: it is perhaps only by positing them that we can make existent relations intelligible."[46] The scene of the nonviolent last breath tells something of a concluding myth for sociality. Whereas sociality's origin story, for Bersani, has to do with the subject's narcissistic extension into the world, through which their ego boundary shatters and they find themself in relation, the discourse of the last breath manifests a unitary, ego-bound subject capable of escaping the scene of breathing, which is to say the scene of relation, of their own volition. Bersani sees in his origin myth "a heuristic device designed to help us see the invisible rhythms of appearance and disappearance in all being."[47] The discourse of the last breath operates as a similar heuristic device, this one programmed to help the living to envision an exception to contingency from its very throes.[48]

Within the form of life that is the scene of the last breath, the peaceful departure registers as nonsuicidal. Debates on suicide have long revolved around the action's rationality or irrationality. From philosopher David Hume's standpoint, suicide is justified if one judges one's life to conflict with public interest.[49] Human life, for Hume, is not fundamentally worthier of preservation than the life of any other organism. From another philosophical standpoint, Immanuel Kant's, to kill oneself is to treat oneself as a means to an end rather than an end in itself.[50] Suicide for Kant is irrational, for it is specifically the duty of self-preservation that makes human beings rational agents.[51] Veering away from both Hume and Kant, Christopher Cowley argues that suicide is neither rational nor irrational, for these discrete rubrics do not account for the complicated feelings—the unease, perhaps the acrid relief—that suicide engenders.[52] The discourses of the last breath sustain an attachment to the idea of dying on one's own terms while streamlining the complicated feelings that accompany anything recognizable as a suicide.[53] In the last breath, intentional death appears not as the consequence of an exceptional gesture but as something close to universal.

The trope of the peaceful departure also speaks to a desire on the part of the living to deal with the unresponsiveness of the dying or the dead. Barely or not alert, the dying personify Catherine Malabou's "destructive plasticity": a shattered identity that has no biographical precedent, an identity that doesn't recognize itself and is unrecognizable to others.[54] Within the physician Georges Canguilhem's framework, what Malabou calls destructive plasticity would correspond to a pathology that has strayed so far from an anomaly that it calls into question the dynamic polarity of life.[55] Destructive plasticity constitutes an accident that yields existential improvisation.[56] Malabou, as I mentioned in chapter 3, contends that even destructive plasticity is productive, insofar as it makes room for a new identity. But debilitated and sedated patients in deathbed documentaries eventually fail to express anything recognizable as an identity, old or new. In the interval of the last breath, its emptiness, its infinity, relatives and medical professionals conjure a familiar self. The momentary endowment of the dying with the capacity to make a decision, even the decision to exit life, makes them relatable again. Discourses of the last breath, as Anne-Lise François might say, "make an open secret of fulfilled experience."[57] They make an open secret of the idea that fantasies of consciousness and intention are meant to appease the living. When witnesses in King's documentary claim that through the last breath the dead departed peacefully, they are also commenting on the quality of their own breathing, now more peaceful. There is relief in no longer watching and being disorganized by someone else's labored respiration. But along with peace comes pain. If we're still breathing, we're still living, with loss.

Tercier decries the impulse to tie up death, grief, and mourning around the moment of the last breath as "a denial of loss": "The eternity of extinction for the victim and loss for the survivor becomes marked by an attempt to remove death from time, to make it an instantaneous event."[58] He goes on, "The paradigms of the death-with-dignity and the hi-tech death are, in the end, idealized fantasies. They are tropes, the former nostalgic and the latter heroic, used by those unexposed to the realities of the deathbed."[59] Tercier presumes that witnesses of the last breath attach to the fantasy of a peaceful departure because they don't know any better. Witnesses, he believes, should instead face "the realities of the deathbed." Tercier's is a cynical and moralistic account of fantasy, one that disregards its function in organizing all attachments. The language of the peaceful departure isn't wrong; it is euphemistic. To breathe is, as this book has shown, to be near death. Discourses of the last breath do not deny this reality so much as they frame it within a form of life. Those are the stories we tell ourselves in order to keep breathing.

Coda. A Queer Theory of Benign Respiratory Variations

Our lives must go on in the wake of other people's last breaths, and so must this book.

Breathing Aesthetics has flowed from a pair of claims: that an aesthetics of respiration spanning literary, screen, and performance cultures indexes the intensified contamination, weaponization, and monetization of the air since the 1970s; and that the minoritarian manifestations of this aesthetics devise individual and collective practices of survival amid crisis. In expounding the latter claim, I have sought to underscore the contributions of aesthetic experimentation to (anti)disciplinary frameworks, such as environmental, disability, and sexuality studies, that locate embodiment and experience within ecologies of interconnection and interdependence. The aesthetics of breathing provides more than just a record of, say, the experience of urban smog or the phenomenology of allergy. While breathing isn't itself a resource for living under precarity, aesthetic mediation turns it into one.

When I say that the aesthetics of breathing is a resource, I don't mean, as should now be clear, that it neutralizes or eliminates breathlessness. It bears repeating that breathlessness is one mode of breathing, not its antithesis. In the preceding chapters, I laid out tactics and strategies for managing breathlessness. Discussed in the opening chapter, the elemental media of Ana Mendieta and Amy Greenfield cultivate, along with uneasy breathing, a critical spectatorial disposition toward the pastoral's anachronistic ideals of natural purity and vitality as well as the imperial and colonial project they mask. Chapter 2 attended to Dodie Bellamy's, CAConrad's, and Bob Flanagan and Sheree Rose's queer life writing and performance, wherein the notation of labored breathing minimally organizes desire amid crises ranging from the personal to the planetary. In the third and fourth chapters, I shifted gears, and scales, by sketching minoritarian models of collective life inspired by respiration. Toni Cade Bambara's and Linda Hogan's Black and Indigenous feminist respiratory rituals destabilize the provisional wellness and wholeness they afford. Renee Gladman's aesthetics of smog sensing, specifically its treatment of respiratory interruptions as symptoms of crisis, suggests an ethics and politics of opacity. In chapter 5, I amplified the discourses around the nonviolent last breath in Frederick Wiseman's and Allan King's cinema vérité. These discourses' circulation signals a desire on the part of the living to manage their own respiratory confrontations with finitude.

Toward the end of the introduction to *Breathing Aesthetics*, I came closest to making a prescriptive claim by calling for an imaginary that accommodates the fullness of breathing, including a range of benign respiratory variations. I now return to this concept. I adapt the phrase *benign respiratory variations* from Gayle Rubin's concept of "benign sexual variation," developed in "Thinking Sex: Notes for a Radical Theory of the Politics of Sexuality."[1] First presented in 1982 and published in 1984, this essay, key to the emergence of queer studies, regards sex law as an instrument of erotic persecution. The state, Rubin explains, intervenes in the realm of sexuality to an extent that wouldn't be tolerated in other areas of social life. Systems of sexual judgment attempt to determine on which side of "the line" a particular act, practice, or identity falls, and "only sex acts on the good side of the line are accorded moral complexity."[2] The sexual stratification induced by moral panics quickly calcifies as social stratification, for stigma renders sexual dissidents morally defenseless. To contest the "fallacy of misplaced scale," or the burdening of sexual acts "with an excess of significance," Rubin calls for a pluralistic sexual ethics rooted in a concept of benign sexual variation.[3] Rubin clarifies, "Variation is a fundamental property of all life, from the simplest biological organisms to the most complex human social formations. Yet sexuality is supposed to conform to a single standard."[4] Rubin's hope is that a notion of benign sexual variation would protect consensual acts that are neither harmful nor hostile from stigmatization and legislative overreach.

I use the phrase *benign respiratory variations* cautiously, without implying a one-to-one analogy between sex and breath. In 2020, the shakiness of this analogy was made glaring by the proliferation on social media of comparisons between the HIV/AIDS epidemic and the coronavirus pandemic. What exactly was being compared? Epidemiologists and medical humanities scholars have been right to note that, in response to both epidemics, the US government imposed xenophobic restrictions on travel and immigration, disguising a public health threat as a threat to national security.[5] But other efforts to posit a more direct comparison—the likening of masks to condoms, for instance—have been tenuous.[6] Rather than enforcing a strict analogy, I venture that there exist some parallels between the hypervisibility and violent repression of sex that Rubin witnessed in the early 1980s (and we still witness today, under minimally altered configurations) and the hypervisibility and violent repression of breath of the early 2020s. Within the crisis in breathing, the state claims a monopoly over the interruption of respiration via police violence, environmental threats, and unaffordable health care. To generate accessible and accountable breathing publics, we must accommodate and valorize benign respiratory variations and interruptions. Those include the Blackpentecostal practices of shouting, tarrying, whooping, and speaking in tongues inventoried by Ashon Crawley as well as Conrad's breathtaking confrontations with planetary crisis, Flanagan and Rose's breathless performances at the junction of sadomasochism and cystic fibrosis, and the ecstatic experience of the public reading in Gladman's fiction.

The imperfect analogy between sex and breath is such that what counts as a benign sexual variation does not necessarily count as a benign respiratory variation, and vice versa. The friction between the two concepts is manifest in Trisha Low's description of a sadomasochistic (SM) waterboarding workshop, which appears halfway through the book-length essay *Socialist Realism* (2019). Low has been associated with the legacies of conceptualism and New Narrative.[7] As I noted in chapter 2, respiration is one of the objects that New Narrative has taken up as it has extended its sex writing practice to different scenes of relation, openness, and vulnerability. Waterboarding is a form of torture in which water is poured over a cloth covering the face and breathing passages of an immobilized person who, as a result, experiences drowning. By giving an account of waterboarding's uses and misuses in the context of SM, Low points to the fragile conditions in which it is possible to enjoy a willful interruption of respiration. Low begins,

> We sit in rows and watch as a woman chokes and retches under the soaked cotton of a drenched T-shirt, as she has fizzy Mountain Dew dripped slowly into her nostrils so the airways can never clear from the sugar. The workshop covers all the essentials: the history of waterboarding in a specifically S-M context, what to tell your TSA officer if your carry-on luggage is full of waterboarding equipment, the physiology of

oxygen deprivation, how to emergency-respond if something goes wrong. The man doing the demonstration is obviously hard through his tight black jeans; he's stroking his cock with a zipper half open while he tells us this information. Occasionally he giggles, nervous and high pitched. His wife burbles under the cloth and jerks feebly before he removes it and spits in her face. I recognize the dazed look in her eyes, and it might not seem like it, but I know she feels delirious and relieved, the world turning green and torn apart as though it were dispensable, as though it were no longer hers. Her knees jerk up. I see the cotton worm its way into her mouth and pucker.[8]

Following a digression, Low resumes the account:

It's hour two and there's equipment set out so we can experiment on our own. The workshop leaders watch. It's my turn. I'm no stranger to asphyxiation, and the cool drip of water is starting to make the intensity in my chest burn from the lack of oxygen even as it calms me, but suddenly, the towel is ripped away from my face, an unwelcome gasp of air screeching through my lungs. And amidst my gasping, the woman who's helping me shrieks, "Oh god, stop, you're a breath holder!" as though it is some terrible accusation. I'm confused. As it turns out, what makes for successful waterboarding is our body's instinctive urge to inhale when denied oxygen. What makes it so painful is the convulsive gasping that comes from trying to suck in life-affirming air but finding in its place only damp, suffocating moisture.

Waterboarding is no match for me. Years of training as a synchronized swimmer have dulled my urge to inhale when deprived of oxygen. Instead, I hold my breath stubbornly until I can't help but pass out. I don't suffer as dramatically, but it also means that my body doesn't express any symptoms before I move swiftly on my way to permanent brain damage. "Most people kick or struggle when they're waterboarded, you know, from the panic, which is part of the enjoyment," the woman explains. "But if you're holding your breath, you'll just be as still as a rock, and how would we know—how could your partner know then—if you're," she pauses, looking confused. "Well, if you're already dead."[9]

Low describes a breathing public as well as a sexual public. In the SM workshop, pleasurable respiratory interruptions become a matter of collective responsibility and accountability. We may be tempted to perceive waterboarding, as it is practiced in this space, as a benign sexual variation and a benign respiratory variation. But in Low's account, "the woman" acts as though she were operating with a concept of benign respiratory variation that did not exactly map onto a concept of benign sexual variation. We know that the author consents to being waterboarded, and consent is, to Rubin, an essential criterion for the "benign sexual variation" designation. We also know that the author finds the experience pleasurable and soothing: "the cool drip of water," she writes, "is starting to make the intensity in my chest burn from the lack of oxygen even as it calms me." Yet the burning and calming asphyxia is interrupted by "an unwelcome gasp of air screeching through [the] lungs." "The woman" communicates two reasons for cutting the experiment short: first, that Low, however much she may have enjoyed herself, didn't display the panicked enjoyment expected of people who practice waterboarding; and second, that by holding her breath, Low didn't supply cues that would indicate mortal danger. Noticing that Low's breath holding, an endurance skill she developed as an athlete, deviates from waterboarding's breathlessness script, the instructor prevents a respiratory interruption from causing serious injury, or becoming malign. Variations in the intensity of breathing say something that consent does not. Whereas the criterion of consent implies individual personhood and presence to oneself, a system of responsibility and accountability calibrated to respiratory variations is premised on the fact of being in relation, or the fact that our ability to withstand breathlessness is contingent on the ways other people interact with, and respond to, the instincts and reflexes we do or do not display.

The principle that animates such a system is compatible with those of the sexual cultures of people with disabilities. As Tobin Siebers writes, "Being able-bodied assumes the capacity to partition off sexuality as if it were a sector of private life."[10] Deriving parameters for collective life from the negotiation of respiratory variations and interruptions unmoors embodiment and experience from an ideology of "private ownership."[11] The system I advocate also matches Stacy Alaimo's and Nicole Seymour's calls for a queer ecological framework that values the pleasures and surprises in ethical modes of inhabiting compromised ecosystems.[12] Abundant neologisms have been coined to describe the experience of the present crisis, from "ecological grief" to "solastalgia" to "pretraumatic stress syndrome."[13] Within environments so hostile that existence itself is described in pathological terms, we must generate, through practices of mutual care, publics wherein breathlessness isn't fatal. Breathing is inevitably morbid, but I want it, I need it, to be life-giving and life-affirming as well.

Introduction

Excerpts from Orlando White's "NASCENT," from LETTERRS (2015), are reprinted by permission of Nightboat Books. Excerpts from *Scree: The Collected Earlier Poems, 1962–1991,* © 2015 Fred Wah, Talonbooks, Vancouver, BC, are reproduced by permission of the publisher.

1   *Toxin* refers to a poison produced within the living cells or organs of plants and animals, and *toxicant* to a synthetic, human-made chemical. Liboiron, *Pollution Is Colonialism*, 94.

2   Eigen, *Toxic Nourishment*, 3, 1, xiii.

3   Eigen, *Toxic Nourishment*, 3.

4   Eigen, *Damaged Bonds*, 32.

5   On the synergic operation of Michel Foucault's biopolitics and Achille Mbembe's necropolitics, see Puar, *Terrorist Assemblages*, 32–36.

6   Hsu, *The Smell of Risk*, 6. "These problems with olfactory epistemology and representation," Hsu goes on, "have contributed to the denigration of smell in Western aesthetics. At least since the Enlightenment, smell has been framed as too immersive, imprecise, subjective, interactive, involuntary, material, promiscuous, and ineffable to convey aesthetic experience" (6).

7   Zhang, "Notes on Atmosphere," 124. Further complicating atmospheric description and theorization is the fact that "sensing an atmosphere cannot be reduced to the perception of any discrete elements or limited to any one sensory mode. Instead, such perception responds to the relation between all the elements in a

setting as they interact with each other in the environment created by their co-presence." Zhang, *Strange Likeness*, 79.

8   Cha, *DICTEE*, 3.

9   Theresa Hak Kyung Cha, "Artist's Statement/Summary of Work," Cha Collection, Berkeley Art Museum and Pacific Film Archive, Berkeley, California, n.d., http://www.oac.cdlib.org/ark:/13030/tf4j49n6h6/?order=3&brand=oac4.

10 Cha, *DICTEE*, 3, 4.

11 Cha, *DICTEE*, 3.

12 Cha, *DICTEE*, 4.

13 Cha, *DICTEE*, 4.

14 Cha, *DICTEE*, 5.

15 Originally from Tółikan, Arizona, White is Diné of the Naaneesht'ézhi Tábaahí and born for the Naakai Diné'e.

16 White, *LETTERRS*, 13.

17 White, *LETTERRS*, 17.

18 White, *LETTERRS*, 23, 43, 59, 67, 68, 71, 72.

19 White, *LETTERRS*, 21.

20 Simmons, "Settler Atmospherics."

21 Simmons, "Settler Atmospherics."

22 Simmons, "Settler Atmospherics."

23 Braun, *Breathing Race into the Machine*, 13, 26. The history of aerial and respiratory colonialism also includes the circulation, until the late nineteenth century, of humoral and climate theories, with their anti-Black and anti-Indigenous concepts of racial difference and morphological change. See LaFleur, *The Natural History of Sexuality in Early America*, esp. 32–62.

24 Brugge and Goble, "A Documentary History of Uranium Mining and the Navajo People," 25–47.

25 Dillon and Sze, "Police Power and Particulate Matters," 13.

26 Sharpe, *In the Wake*, 109.

27 "Asthma and African Americans," Office of Minority Health of the U.S. Department of Health and Social Services, accessed February 11, 2021, http://minority health.hhs.gov/omh/browse.aspx?lvl=4&lvlid=15; "Inequitable Exposure to Air Pollution from Vehicles in California," Union of Concerned Scientists, January 28, 2019, https://www.ucsusa.org/clean-vehicles/electric-vehicles/CA-air-quality -equity#.XFxySIxKhyx.

28 Taibbi, *I Can't Breathe*, 74.

29 Laurel Wamsley, "Erica Garner, Who Became an Activist after Her Father's Death, Dies," NPR, December 30, 2017, https://www.npr.org/sections/thetwoway /2017/12/30/574514217/erica-garner-who-became-an-activist-after-her-fathers -death-dies.

30 Oliver Laughland, Jessica Glenza, Steven Trasher, and Paul Lewis, "'We Can't Breathe': Eric Garner's Last Words Become Protesters' Rallying Cry," *Guardian*, December 4, 2014, https://www.theguardian.com/us-news/2014/dec/04/we -cant-breathe-eric-garner-protesters-chant-last-words.

31   Lucy Tompkins, "Here's What You Need to Know about Elijah McClain's Death," *New York Times*, June 30, 2020, https://www.nytimes.com/article/who-was-elijah-mcclain.html. In photos taken at a memorial site for McClain, Aurora police officers are seen smiling, with one of them re-creating the carotid control hold that their colleagues put on McClain. Bill Chappell, "Three Police Officers Fired over Photos at Elijah McClain Memorial," NPR, June 30, 2020, https://www.npr.org/sections/live-updates-protests-for-racial-justice/2020/06/30/885178533/colorado-police-officers-under-investigation-for-photos-at-elijah-mcclain-memori.

32   Two autopsies have determined Floyd's death to be a homicide. Whereas the Hennepin County medical examiner concluded that Floyd had died by cardiac arrest while restrained by officers employing "neck compressions," an independent autopsy commissioned by Floyd's family found "evidence . . . of mechanical or traumatic asphyxia" as the cause of death. Frances Robles and Audre D S. Burch, "How Did George Floyd Die? Here's What We Know," *New York Times*, June 2, 2020, https://www.nytimes.com/article/george-floyd-autopsy-michael-baden.html. When the full Hennepin County report was released, the public learned that Floyd, who had lost his security job at a bar and restaurant forced to comply with pandemic closure rules, had tested positive for COVID-19 in early April. Scott Neuman, "Medical Examiner's Autopsy Reveals George Floyd Had Positive Test for Coronavirus," NPR, June 4, 2020, https://www.npr.org/sections/live-updates-protests-for-racial-justice/2020/06/04/869278494/medical-examiners-autopsy-reveals-george-floyd-had-positive-test-for-coronavirus.

33   Larry Buchanan, Quoctrung Bui, and Jugal K. Patel, "Black Lives Matter May Be the Largest Movement in US History," *New York Times*, July 3, 2020, https://www.nytimes.com/interactive/2020/07/03/us/george-floyd-protests-crowd-size.html.

34   Zoe Cormier, "How Covid-19 Can Damage the Brain," BBC FUTURE, June 22, 2020, https://www.bbc.com/future/article/20200622-the-long-term-effects-of-covid-19-infection; "Post-COVID Conditions," Centers for Disease Control and Prevention, accessed September 16, 2021, https://www.cdc.gov/coronavirus/2019-ncov/long-term-effects.html.

35   "Health Equity Considerations and Racial and Ethnic Minority Groups," Centers for Disease Control and Prevention, accessed April 19, 2021, https://www.cdc.gov/coronavirus/2019-ncov/community/health-equity/race-ethnicity.html; Chowkwanyun and Reed, "Racial Health Disparities and Covid-19." On the inadequacy of public health infrastructures and the displacement of risk onto private households in the context of the COVID-19 pandemic, see Mitropoulos, *Pandemonium*. In reaction to the June 2020 Black Lives Matter protests and under the guise of ensuring public safety, Los Angeles County, in California, temporarily closed nineteen of its thirty-six free COVID-19 testing sites, preventing members of disenfranchised populations from accessing the service. Sareen Habeshian, "Half of L.A. County's COVID-19 Testings Sites Remain Closed as Protests against

George Floyd's Killing Continue," KTLA, June 1, 2020, https://ktla.com/news
/local-news/half-of-l-a-countys-covid-19-testings-sites-remain-closed-as-protests
-against-george-floyds-killing-continue/.

36 Crawley, *Blackpentecostal Breath*, 1. See also Crawley, *The Lonely Letters*, 41.

37 Fanon, *Black Skin, White Masks*, 226.

38 See, e.g., Theodore Richards, "I Can't Breathe," *Re-imagining*, accessed September
3, 2021, https://reimaginingmagazine.com/project/i-cant-breathe/.

39 Fanon, *A Dying Colonialism*, 65. See also Perera and Pugliese, "Introduction," esp.
1–4; Rose, "Combat Breathing in Salman Rushdie's *The Moor's Last Sigh*," 118.

40 Crawley, *Blackpentecostal Breath*, 38, 63.

41 Tremblay, "How Sia Kept Breathing and Became a Formalist."

42 Tompkins, "Crude Matter, Queer Form," 267–68.

43 Engelmann, "Toward a Poetics of Air," 431.

44 Puar et al., "Precarity Talk," 166.

45 Puar et al., "Precarity Talk," 169.

46 Nayar, *Ecoprecarity*, 8–9.

47 Marder, "Being Dumped," 180.

48 Marder, "Being Dumped," 182.

49 Marder, "Being Dumped," 182.

50 Marder, "Being Dumped," 188–89.

51 Taylor, *Toxic Communities*, 1; Taylor, *The Environment and the People in American
Cities*. See also Zimring, *Clean and White*.

52 Hsu, *The Smell of Risk*, 12.

53 Sloterdijk, *Terror from the Air*, 14.

54 Michael Crowley, "Drawing the Line: Regulation of 'Wide Area' Riot Control
Agent Delivery Mechanisms under the Chemical Weapons Convention," Brad-
ford Non-lethal Weapons Project and Omega Research Foundation, April 2013,
https://omegaresearchfoundation.org/sites/default/files/uploads/Publications
/BNLWRP%20ORF%20RCA%20Munitions%20Report%20April%202013_0.pdf.
Despite a ban on use of chemical weapons across state lines, US border agents
gathered media attention when in 2018 they fired tear gas grenades into Mexico, making explicit the role of asphyxia in the preemptive control of migration.
"How Tear Gas Became a Favorite Weapon of U.S. Border Patrol, Despite Being
Banned in Warfare," Democracy Now!, November 28, 2018, https://www
.democracynow.org/2018/11/28/how_tear_gas_became_a_favorite.

55 Feigenbaum, *Tear Gas*, 70.

56 See Doyle, *Campus Sex, Campus Security*, 91–92.

57 Régine Debatty, "Using Respiration to Mine Crypto-Currencies," *We Make
Money Not Art*, December 5, 2017, http://we-make-money-not-art.com/using
-respiration-to-mine-crypto-currencies/.

58 Kelly Conaboy, "The Business of Breathing," *Damn Joan*, 2018, https://damnjoan
.com/business-breathing.

59 Conaboy, "The Business of Breathing."

60 Kressbach, "Breath Work," 185.

61 "About Us," Spire, accessed November 1, 2018, https://web.archive.org/web /20181128091724/https://spire.io/pages/about.

62 "About Our Products," Vitality Air, accessed September 3, 2021, https://vitalityair .ph/about-our-products/.

63 Katie Hunt, "Canadian Start-Up Sells Bottled Air to China, Says Sales Booming," CNN, December 16, 2015, http://www.cnn.com/2015/12/15/asia/china-canadian -company-selling-clean-air/.

64 Ahmann and Kenner, "Breathing Late Industrialism," 417.

65 Ahmann and Kenner, "Breathing Late Industrialism," 422. Ahmann and Kenner continue, "To study late industrialism is to reject the idea that we are living in the twilight of a once-ideal system, struggling to deal with unexpected glitches. Instead, we are living at a moment when industrialism's systemic harms have begun to spill out of our blind spots" (422).

66 Choy, *Ecologies of Comparison*, 157.

67 Kim, *Unbecoming Language*, 169.

68 McCormack, *Atmospheric Things*, 32.

69 Simondon, *L'individu et sa genèse physico-biologique*, 21–23. I translate the French *"couple individu-milieu"* as "individual-milieu couple," rather than "pair individual-environment," Gregory Flanders's translation as it appears in Simondon, "The Position of the Problem of Ontogenesis," 5.

70 Read, *The Politics of Transindividuality*, 5–6.

71 Alaimo, *Bodily Natures*, 2.

72 Siebers, "Disability and the Theory of Complex Embodiment," 284.

73 Kenner, *Breathtaking*, 5.

74 Toxicology reports pin this gender asymmetry on a host of biological and social factors, such as the constitution of women's immune system; their generally higher proportion of body fat, which tends to retain chemicals; their lower percentage of alcohol dehydrogenase, an enzyme that breaks down toxins; and their traditionally higher exposure to household chemicals. Alaimo, *Bodily Natures*, 117.

75 Bellamy, *When the Sick Rule the World*, 27.

76 Murphy, *Sick Building Syndrome and the Problem of Uncertainty*, 6.

77 Alaimo, *Bodily Natures*, 117; Seymour, *Strange Natures*, 75–76, 90. On environmental illness in racially differentiated atmospheres, see also Hsu, *The Smell of Risk*, 52–54.

78 Ray and Sibara, "Introduction," 1–5. The term "eco-crip theory" appears in the collection's subtitle. Versions of Ray and Sibara's research question are posed, elsewhere in the volume, in Johnson, "Bringing Together Feminist Disability Studies and Environmental Justice"; Kafer, "Bodies of Nature." See also Cella, "The Ecosomatic Paradigm in Literature."

79 Puar, *The Right to Maim*, xiii–xiv.

80 Puar, *The Right to Maim*, 135, 136.

81 Puar, *The Right to Maim*, 135.

82 Mitchell and Snyder, "Is the Study of Debility Akin to Disability Studies without Disability?," 665.

83 Mitchell and Snyder, "Is the Study of Debility Akin to Disability Studies without Disability?," 665, emphasis removed.

84 Connor, *The Matter of Air*, 9.

85 Menely, "Anthropocene Air," 100.

86 Bachelard, *L'air et les songes*, 269, 265.

87 Irigaray, *L'oubli de l'air chez Martin Heidegger*, 9.

88 On Irigaray's substitution of *interval* with *breath*, see Tremblay, "An Aesthetics and Ethics of Emergence," 290.

89 Irigaray, *To Be Two*, 11. I add "aerial" to "ethereal," Monique M. Rhodes and Marco F. Cocito-Monoc's translation of "*aérienne*," to reflect the literary and figurative sense of Irigaray's term of choice in *Être deux*, 26.

90 Irigaray, *To Be Two*, 2.

91 Lévinas, *Otherwise Than Being*, 181.

92 Marder, "Breathing 'to' the Other," 98; Cavarero, *For More Than One Voice*, 31; Feron, "Respiration et action chez Lévinas," 203.

93 Škof, *Breath of Proximity*, 143, 5.

94 Škof and Berndtson, *Atmospheres of Breathing*.

95 For instance, Margareta Ingrid Christian observes in Aby Warburg's dissertation on Sandro Botticelli that literal and figurative uses of the air pivot on the notion of inspiration, from the Latin *inspiratio* (to breathe in). Warburg believed that the reigning spirituality and mentality of Botticelli's surroundings, or what was figuratively in the air, inspired depictions of actual air in motion in his painting—for example, Venus's flowing hair in the *Nascita di Venere*. Christian, "*Aer, Aurae, Venti*," 405.

96 Ursell, "Inspiration," 709–10.

97 Mackey, "Breath and Precarity," 5.

98 Olson, "Projective Verse," 239.

99 Stefanie Heine identifies such a compositional principle in writing by Allen Ginsberg and Jack Kerouac (*Poetics of Breathing*, 49–116). Jason R. Rudy reads Olson's focus on energy as evidence of "the staying power of Victorian physiological poetics, as well as the continued imbrication of physiological poetics with the language of electric charge" (*Electric Meters*, 185). Physiological poetics encompasses "Alfred Tennyson's 'poetics of sensation,' the midcentury 'Spasmodic phenomenon, [and] the so-called fleshy school of the 1870s," all of which demand "to be read as physiologically inspired: rhythms that pulse in the body, a rhetoric of sensation that readers might feel compelled to experience" (2).

100 Mackey, "Breath and Precarity," 6.

101 Grobe, *The Art of Confession*, 45.

102 Mackey, "Breath and Precarity," 9.

103 With "Breath and Precarity," Mackey reframes as a respiratory matter the tension between Black Mountain poetry or projectivism and Black experimental aesthetics that lies at the heart of his 1993 monograph, *Discrepant Engagement*.

104 Moten, *The Little Edges*, 4.

105 Michel, *Le souffle coupé*, 27, 73. Eve Kosofsky Sedgwick would later make the more

sophisticated point that Proust's interest in the weather problematized the relation between open and closed systems (*The Weather in Proust*, 4).

106 Michel, *Le souffle coupé*, 181.

107 Rose, "Combat Breathing in Salman Rushdie's *The Moor's Last Sigh*," 113; Rose, "In the Wake of Asbestos," 140.

108 Diffrient, "Dead, but Still Breathing."

109 Williams, "Film Bodies," 3.

110 Williams, "Film Bodies," 4.

111 Williams, "Film Bodies," 4.

112 Quinlivan, *The Place of Breath in Cinema*, 10–11, 48, 168.

113 Jones, "Do(n't) Hold Your Breath."

114 Buell, *The Future of Environmental Criticism*, 117; Heise, *Sense of Place and Sense of Planet*, 39.

115 Zhang, "Notes on Atmosphere," 123–24.

116 The ecocritical equation between aesthetic experience and the acquisition of civic virtues informs a wave of self-branded empirical research that purports to measure the influence of climate fiction based on responses reported by readers. This research presents some shortcomings: one, it presumes that readers are always present to their experiences, leaving out the role of the unconscious in processes of socialization and politicization; two, it flattens aesthetic experience by rerouting all responses toward such familiar destinations as liberal and conservative attitudes; and three, it produces a contradiction between the content of much climate fiction (depictions of radical vulnerability or multispecies entanglement) and the assumed subject consuming it (an agentive, reasonable, and rational subject). See, e.g., Schneider-Mayerson, "The Influence of Climate Fiction"; Schneider-Mayerson, "'Just as in the Book'?"; Schneider-Mayerson et al., "Environmental Literature as Persuasion."

117 Wah, *Scree*, 439.

118 See, e.g., Povinelli, "Hippocrates' Breaths," esp. 32, 34–35; Povinelli, *Geontologies*, 42–43; Kean, *Caesar's Last Breath*.

119 Wah, *Scree*, 441.

120 Wah, *Scree*, 455.

121 Wah, *Scree*, 459.

122 On Wah's poetics of ethnicity as "betweenness," see Wah, "A Poetics of Ethnicity," 108; Wah, "Is a Door a Word?," 39; Saul, *Writing the Roaming Subject*, 105.

123 Wah, *Scree*, 439.

124 In their introduction to the issue, Oxley and Russell write, "Despite the merits of exploring breath as a phenomenon that is at once intrinsically shared but contextually distinct, the meanings and embodiment of breath [have] seldom been examined as a central research theme in the humanities and social sciences" ("Interdisciplinary Perspectives on Breath, Body and World," 4). Jane Macnaughton, a contributor, adds, "Nothing is so much taken for granted as breath, the literal source of our lifeblood. . . . So entangled is breath in everything bodies are, experience and do that it gets taken for granted, lost from view and is rarely a direct

focus of attention. Putting breath under the spotlight is, therefore, a daunting task" ("Making Breath Visible," 30–31).

125 Macnaughton, for instance, attempts "to bring breath into visibility" ("Making Breath Visible," 33).

126 Górska, *Breathing Matters*, 22, 284. Borrowing from the nomenclature of feminist science studies, specifically Karen Barad's agential realism, Górska describes breath as a political process of "corpo-affective, material-discursive and situatedly dispersed agential intra-active enactments, metabolizations, transformations and resistances of intersectional power relations, and an enactment of alternatives" (284).

127 Stewart, *Ordinary Affects*, 2; Berlant, *Cruel Optimism*, 262–63.

128 Heine, *Poetics of Breathing*, 3, 6, 31.

129 Berardi, *Breathing*, 17. I discuss the pamphlet and its case studies in my review (Tremblay, "*Breathing*").

130 Scappettonne, "Precarity Shared," 47.

131 Crawley, *Blackpentecostal Breath*, 23.

132 Hsu, *The Smell of Risk*. On smell and the negotiation of "privacy in public, a norm of personal territory that involved managing the boundaries of the body and its intrusion into circumambient space," in the context of eighteenth-century sociability, see Tullett, *Smell in Eighteenth-Century England*, 2. On the politics of smell in nineteenth-century cities facing sanitary challenges amid rapid urban and industrial growth, see Kiechle, *Smell Detectives*.

133 Lewis, *Air's Appearance*, 6.

134 Mbembe, "The Universal Right to Breathe," s61.

135 Mbembe, "The Universal Right to Breathe," s61.

1. Breathing against Nature

1 "Breathing," written and performed by Kate Bush and directed by Keith MacMillan (EMI Records, 1980).

2 Berlant, *The Queen of America Goes to Washington City*, 1. The nation in Berlant's study is the United States, but the figure of the fetus has dominated antiabortion rhetoric well beyond the United States.

3 On the "lead panic" sparked by potentially toxic toys associated with Chinese manufacturers, Chen observes, "There is in fact very little that is new about the 'lead panic' in 2007 in the United States. . . . In fact, anxieties about intoxications, mixings, and Chinese agents have steadily accompanied U.S. cultural productions and echo the Yellow Peril fears articulated earlier in the twentieth century. That lead was subject to an outbreak narrative works synergistically with these anxieties, and these narratives may indeed have been partially incited or facilitated by them" (*Animacies*, 169). Chen adds, "The recent lead panic echoes, yet is a variation of, the turn-of-the-century Orientalized threat to white domesticity" (170).

4 Sheldon, *The Child to Come*, vii, 2–3.

5   Alaimo, *Exposed*, 1.

6   Spahr, *This Connection of Everyone with Lungs*, 19, 23, 26, 28, 29, 34, 35, 38, 42, 58, 61, 63.

7   Spahr, *This Connection of Everyone with Lungs*, 10.

8   Masco, *Nuclear Borderlands*, 28.

9   The practices and artworks I categorize as elemental media highlight and make use of the elements' status as sites of mediation. John Durham Peters claims that the elements are "agencies of order," "vessels and environments, containers of possibility that anchor our existence and make what we are doing possible" (*The Marvelous Clouds*, 1, 2). He continues, "The old idea that media are environments can be flipped: environments are also media. Water, fire, sky, earth, and ether are elements—homey, sublime, dangerous, wonderful—that sustain existence and we still haven't figured out how to care for them; our efforts to do so constitute our technical history" (3). Although I regard air and breath as environments of mediation, I wouldn't go so far as to subsume them into specific media concepts that, as Melody Jue notes, are calibrated for "anthropogenic technologies of storage and transmission" (*Wild Blue Media*, 24). By classifying cinema dance and earth-body sculpture as elemental media, I also seek to respond to the call made by scholars of media ecologies to investigate connections between "media *about* the environment and media *in* the environment." Walker and Starosielski, "Introduction," 3; see also Parks and Starosielski, "Introduction"; Mukherjee, *Radiant Infrastructures*. These scholars have insisted that the representational practices of media cultures rely on infrastructures that are themselves situated in environments. Rather than tallying the environmental impact of large-scale technologies of diffusion, I focus on small-scale avant-garde interventions that problematize their environmental embeddedness and enable us to see environments as something more than media's unconscious or repositories of media's debris.

10   Osterweil, "Bodily Rites."

11   Viso, *Ana Mendieta*, 41–42.

12   Griefen, "Ana Mendieta at A.I.R. Gallery," 171.

13   Blocker, *Where Is Ana Mendieta?*, 1–4.

14   León, "Trace Alignment."

15   Osterweil, "Bodily Rites."

16   Haller, *Flesh into Light*, 99.

17   Tierney, *What Lies Between*, 13.

18   Haller, *Flesh into Light*, 18.

19   Haller, *Flesh into Light*, 49.

20   Mulvey, "Visual Pleasure and Narrative Cinema," 715.

21   Lacan, *Le séminaire de Jacques Lacan: Livre II*, 98.

22   McGowan, "Looking for the Gaze," 29. See also Carlsson, "The Gaze as Constituent and Annihilator," esp. 2.

23   Bush's stare operates somewhat like the absent World Trade Center in the introduction to Eve Kosofsky Sedgwick's "Shame, Theatricality, and Queer Performativity: Henry James's *The Art of the Novel*": "In the couple of weeks after the World

Trade Center was destroyed in September 2001, I had a daily repetition of an odd experience, one that was probably shared by many walkers in the same midsouthern latitudes of Manhattan. Turning from a street onto Fifth Avenue, even if I was heading North, I would feel compelled first to look south in the direction of the World Trade Center, now gone. The inexplicably furtive glance was associated with a conscious wish: that my southward vista would again be blocked by the familiar sight of the pre–September 11 twin towers, somehow come back to loom over us in all their complacent ugliness. But, of course, the towers were always still gone. Turning away, shame was what I would feel" (*Touching Feeling*, 35).

24 Many thanks to Steven Swarbrick, whose generous response to a draft of this chapter strengthened its conceptual architecture.

25 Gifford, "Gods of Mud." See also Gifford, "Judith Wright's Poetry and the Turn to the Post-pastoral."

26 Gifford, "Pastoral, Anti-pastoral, and Post-pastoral," 26.

27 Gifford, "Pastoral, Anti-pastoral, and Post-pastoral," 28.

28 Gifford, *Pastoral*, 1–2.

29 Robertson, *XEclogue*, n.p. The definition comes from a story that the poet is told by her ancestress while dreaming.

30 Buell, *The Environmental Imagination*; Emerson, *Nature*; Thoreau, *Walden*.

31 Carson, *Silent Spring*, 1; Buell, "Toxic Discourse," 648.

32 Carson, *Silent Spring*, 39; Schuster, *The Ecology of Modernism*, 132–35.

33 On the role of *Silent Spring* in the rise of the sustainability discourse in the 1960s and 1970s, see Du Pisani, "Sustainable Development," 89.

34 Cronon, "The Trouble with Wilderness," 10.

35 Kant, *Critique of the Power of Judgment*, 132.

36 Ngai, *Ugly Feelings*, 6.

37 Raquel Cecilia, the artist's niece and associate administrator for the Estate of Ana Mendieta Collection, explains, "Ana never really considered herself a feminist because she felt it was a movement that only related to white middle-class women. . . . While Ana was a member of A.I.R. Gallery, she curated an exhibition, *Dialectics of Isolation: An Exhibition of Third World Women Artists of the United States*, to bring an awareness to the *other* women who weren't included in the feminist discussions." Rosen, "Ana Mendieta Fought for Women's Rights."

38 Daly, *Pure Lust*, 3, 17.

39 Daly, *Pure Lust*, 17.

40 Daly, *Gyn/Ecology*, 9.

41 Irigaray, "The Age of Breath," 165, 166–67.

42 Irigaray, *Marine Lover of Friedrich Nietzsche*; Irigaray, *The Forgetting of Air in Martin Heidegger*. Rounding out the elemental cycle are Irigaray, *Sharing the Fire*; Irigaray, *Elemental Passions*; Irigaray and Marder, *Through Vegetal Being*.

43 See Daly, *Gyn/Ecology*, 70–71.

44 Godart, "Silence and Sexual Difference," 11; Poe, "Can Luce Irigaray's Notion of Sexual Difference Be Applied to Transsexual and Transgender Narratives?," 112. See also Gill-Peterson, "The Miseducation of a French Feminist."

45 Tremblay, "An Aesthetics and Ethics of Emergence," 286–87.

46 Grosz, *Time Travels*, 214.

47 Wilson, *Psychosomatic*, esp. 3; Wilson, *Gut Feminism*, esp. 1–17.

48 See Tremblay, "Breath," 95.

49 Schneider, *The Explicit Body in Performance*, 2.

50 Schneider, *The Explicit Body in Performance*, 2.

51 Simondon, *L'individu et sa genèse physico-biologique*, 21–23.

52 Simondon, *L'individu et sa genèse physico-biologique*, 106; Manning, *Always More Than One*.

53 Manning, *Relationscapes*, 70; Manning, *Always More Than One*, 76.

54 Connor, *The Matter of Air*, 194.

55 Fay, *Inhospitable World*, 4, 10.

56 Osterweil, "Bodily Rites."

57 Blocker, *Where Is Ana Mendieta?*, 74.

58 Christine Redfern imagines a dialogue between Mendieta and site-specific sculptors in the comic book *Who Is Ana Mendieta?*, 30.

59 Blocker, *Where Is Ana Mendieta?*, 74.

60 Merewether, "Ana Mendieta," 40.

61 Muñoz, "Vitalism's After-Burn," 193.

62 Muñoz, "Vitalism's After-Burn," 191.

63 Greenfield, "The Kinesthetics of Avant-Garde Dance," 21.

64 Gibson, "Breathing Looking Thinking Acting."

65 Artaud, *Le théâtre et son double*, 130, 139, 200. See also Derrida and Thévenin, *The Secret Art of Antonin Artaud*, esp. 61, 63–65, 85, 91, 103; Grammatikopoulou, "Theatre Minus Representation."

66 Peterson, "Barbara Hammer's *Jane Brakhage*," 73.

67 Peterson, "Barbara Hammer's *Jane Brakhage*," 73, 86.

68 Peterson, "Barbara Hammer's *Jane Brakhage*," 86.

69 Peterson, "Barbara Hammer's *Jane Brakhage*," 89.

70 Quinlivan, *The Place of Breath in Cinema*, 168.

71 Sobchack, *The Address of the Eye*, 3, 5.

72 On proprioceptive cinema, see Richmond, *Cinema's Bodily Illusions*, 6–7.

73 On panic's respiratory circuits of contagion, see Orr, *Panic Diaries*, 213.

74 Tompkins, "Crude Matter, Queer Form," 266.

75 Duncan, "The Dance of the Future," 262–63.

76 Peterson, "Barbara Hammer's *Jane Brakhage*," 88.

77 Haller, *Flesh into Light*, 49.

78 Marks, *The Skin of the Film*, 188.

79 Lefebvre, *The Social Production of Space*, 31.

80 Ghosh, "Petrofiction," 29.

81 Seymour, *Bad Environmentalism*, 26.

82 Haraway, *Staying with the Trouble*, 44.

83 Ben Guarino, Zara Stone, and Sawsan Morrar, "California's Deadliest Wildfire Is Also a Massive Air-Quality Problem," *Washington Post*, November 14, 2018,

https://www.washingtonpost.com/nation/2018/11/15/californias-deadliest-wildfire
-is-also-massive-air-quality-problem/.

84 Clark and Yusoff, "Queer Fire," 9.

85 On queer theory's pastoralism, see Swarbrick, "Nature's Queer Negativity."

86 A like-minded thinker would be Carolyn Merchant. When in 1990 Merchant announced the death of nature, she cautiously eulogized the organic paradigm that had kept it alive, so to speak. While the mechanistic worldview that replaced the organic paradigm sanctioned the exploitation of nature, it is also true that female figurations of nature (as a benevolent nurturer, as a force of chaos and destruction) had disenfranchised women. Merchant, *The Death of Nature*, 1–2.

87 Federici, *Caliban and the Witch*, 11–15, 140–41, 150.

88 Pinkerton et al., "Women and Lung Disease," 11–16.

89 Viso, *Ana Mendieta*, 60.

90 On the accusations of essentialism launched at Mendieta, see Heathfield, "Embers," 31; Pollock, *Generations and Geographies*.

91 Viso, *Ana Mendieta*, 46–47; Cruz, "Ana Mendieta's Art," 227.

92 Hyacinthe, *Radical Virtuosity*; Viso, *Ana Mendieta*, 63.

93 Alaimo, *Undomesticated Ground*, 9.

94 Heathfield, "Embers," 31.

95 Rosenthal, "Ana Mendieta," 6.

2. Aesthetic Self-Medication (Three Regimens)

Portions of chapter 2 are derived from Jean-Thomas Tremblay, "Aesthetic Self-Medication: Bob Flanagan and Sheree Rose's Structures of Breathing," *Women and Performance: a journal of feminist theory* 28, no. 3 (2018): 221–38, https://doi.org/10.1080/0740770X.2018.1524621.

Excerpts from *The TV Sutras*, © 2014 Dodie Bellamy, are reproduced with the permission of the author and Ugly Duckling Presse. Excerpts from CAConrad's "POETRY is DIRT as DEATH is DIRT," "QUALM CUTTING AND ASSEMBLAGE," and "(Soma)tic Poetry at St. Mark's Poetry Project, NYC," from *A Beautiful Marsupial Afternoon: New (Soma)tics* (2012), are reproduced with the permission of the author and Wave Books. Excerpts from Bob Flanagan's *The Pain Journal* (2000) are reproduced with the permission of Semiotext(e).

1 Derrida, *Of Grammatology*, 98; Leder, *The Absent Body*, 15.

2 Derrida, *On Touching*, 197–200; Malabou, "How Is Subjectivity Undergoing Deconstruction Today?," 113; Clough, *Autoaffection*, 17–18. In *Poetics of Breathing*, Stefanie Heine describes breaches in autoaffection in both sonic and respiratory terms: "The sound entering our ears insinuates that we never own the air we breathe; that we continually depend on a physiological mechanism we cannot control; that it is an alien, inanimate substance that keeps us alive by entering and leaving our body, something we take but cannot keep, in a process of perpetual loss" (xix).

3 Anzieu, *The Skin-Ego*, 59–72.

4 Balint, *The Basic Fault*, 136, 67. On breathing and air as exemplars in Balint's psychoanalysis, see Sedgwick, *The Weather in Proust*, 13.

5 Fradenburg, "Breathing with Lacan's Seminar X," 164.

6 Saoji, Raghavendra, and Manjunath, "Effects of Yogic Breath Regulation," 57.

7 Saoji, Raghavendra, and Manjunath, "Effects of Yogic Breath Regulation," 57. Increased awareness of the benefits of pranayama practices is one of many factors behind the expansion of the yoga industry. In 2020, the business consulting firm Allied Market Research projected that the global yoga market value would reach $66.2 billion by 2027, up from $37.5 billion in 2019. "Yoga Market Expected to Reach $66.2 Billion by 2027—Allied Market Research," AP News, September 21, 2020, https://apnews.com/press-release/wired-release/virus-outbreak-corporate-news-physical-fitness-diseases-and-conditions-products-and-services-a934442a159df4a9e87beb745b10bd42.

8 The dynamic between agency or control and openness or receptivity is a familiar refrain in critical theory. It shows up as the capacity to affect and be affected in affect theory, as the interplay between self-organizing systems and emergent processes in phenomenology, and as the double meaning of plasticity as giving and taking form in theoretical engagements with neurobiology. See Massumi, "Notes on the Translation and Acknowledgements," xvi; Thompson, *Mind in Life*, ix, 37, 44; Malabou, *The New Wounded*.

9 I discuss Bellamy's writing on multiple chemical sensitivity or idiopathic environmental intolerance as well as the ways environmental illness challenges the category of disability in the introduction to this volume.

10 Kafer, *Feminist, Queer, Crip*, 4.

11 Kuppers, *The Scar of Visibility*, 3.

12 Erevelles, *Disability and Difference in Global Contexts*, 8.

13 Russell and Malhotra, "Capitalism and Disability."

14 Bellamy, *The TV Sutras*, 13.

15 Conrad, *A Beautiful Marsupial Afternoon*, 1.

16 Most scholarship wrongly attributes Flanagan and Rose's collaborative work to Flanagan alone. Dominic Johnson's explanation for this omission is that Flanagan's "signature goofball style" drew more attention to itself than did "Rose's deadpan" (*The Art of Living*, 107). In the introduction to the collection *Rated RX*, Yetta Howard "considers what it means to decenter the male artist as the site of innovation and to reorient sexist approaches to curation and the politics of the archive through Rose's art practices" (3). Howard's corrective approach, which makes claims of authorship on the basis of Rose's status as "*the Dominant* in her relationship with Flanagan," oddly casts being a submissive (a sexual preference) and being an author (artistic labor) as irreconcilable (7). The introduction has the curious effect of minimizing Flanagan's artistic contributions: the erasure of one artist is rectified by the erasure of another. I take a different approach. Unless I refer to work authored by Flanagan on his own or produced by Rose after Flanagan's death, I insist on their status as collaborators.

17   Bob Flanagan, "Visiting Hours," n.d., box 22, Bob Flanagan Collection, Rare Books and Manuscripts Library, The Ohio State University, Columbus, Ohio.

18   Flanagan, *The Pain Journal*, 142.

19   Kafer, *Feminist, Queer, Crip*, 43.

20   In the Enlightenment tradition of autobiography, a sovereign subject having achieved reason takes a retrospective, chronological look at life events. Written in the midst of crisis, the works I compile in this chapter do not display the privileges of sovereignty and retrospection. These works best fit the capacious rubric of *life writing* as Sidonie Smith and Julia Watson define it: "writing that takes a life, one's own or another's, as its subject" (*Reading Autobiography*, 4).

21   Foucault, *Histoire de la sexualité 3*, 123.

22   Spatz, *What a Body Can Do*, 1. Performance, as defined by Richard Schechner, includes disparate aesthetic practices: in theater, dance, and music, in rites and ceremonies, and in everyday greetings, displays of emotion, and professional roles (*Performance Theory*, xvii). Although performance (the set of practices) and performance art (the art form) have long, variegated prehistories, Diana Taylor situates the coalescence of these rubrics in the 1960s and 1970s. Performance art, Taylor explains, aims to "challenge regimes of power and social norms" by "placing . . . FRONT AND CENTER" bodies that are "no longer the [objects] depicted in paintings, or sculpture, or film, or photography but the living flesh *and breath* of the act itself" (*Performance*, 1, 41, emphasis added). On the generation of knowledge about racialized, émigré, sexually nonnormative, or disabled subjectivities in minoritarian or transnational performance, see Sell, *Avant-Garde Performance and the Limits of Criticism*; Johnson, "Black Performance Studies," 446–47.

23   In a 1977 piece titled "Breathing In/Breathing Out (Death Itself)," Marina Abramović, the patron-saint-slash-bad-mother of performance art, and her then-partner Ulay connected their mouths and breathed in a "closed circuit"—though there is no absolutely closed circuit when it comes to breathing—for almost twenty minutes. A reflection on aggression in artistic collaboration, the piece shows the depletion of bodies forced to take in increasing amounts of carbon dioxide. Abramović and Ulay's sustained exchange of toxic air, which relies on a combination of control and abandonment, renders breathing not as something we all do but as a perfectible technique for pushing bodies to their limits—limits beyond which lies "death itself." "Marina Abramovic & Ulay," Pomeranz Collection, 2017, http://pomeranz-collection.com/?q=node/39.

24   The language of performance appears in the author's reflection on her own writing in Bellamy, *the buddhist*, 84, 89.

25   Doyle, "Dirt Off Her Shoulders," 423.

26   O'Brien, "Performing Chronic," 55.

27   O'Brien, "Performing Chronic," 55.

28   Brookes, *Catching My Breath*, 17.

29   Rothenberg, *Breathing for a Living*, 171–233.

30   Kalanithi, *When Breath Becomes Air*, 213, 214. I return to the scene of the last breath in chapter 5.

31 Bellamy, *The TV Sutras*, 105.

32 Bellamy, *The TV Sutras*, 13.

33 Dorothea Lasky denounces the classification of poems and corpuses as projects,
    a term inherited from business, science, and visual art. "I think that if you really
    are a poet, you don't think this is how poetry works," Lasky opines. She adds
    that poetry ought to be "intuited" instead of conceptually devised first and ex-
    ecuted second: "Naming your intentions is great for some things, but not for
    poetry." Lasky, "Poetry Is Not a Project." Even if we accept the tenets of Lasky's
    argument—Bellamy is certainly sympathetic to them, as she mentions in an in-
    terview by David Buuck published in *BOMB* magazine—*The TV Sutras*, in which
    Bellamy states her intentions and sets parameters for intuition, remains a proj-
    ect. Buuck, "Dodie Bellamy by David Buuck."

34 Bellamy, *The TV Sutras*, 13.

35 Bellamy, *The TV Sutras*, 13.

36 Bellamy, *The TV Sutras*, 13,

37 Bellamy, *The TV Sutras*, 14.

38 The 1960s witnessed the birth of New Age and contemporary Western Paganism.
    As Michael York explains, the former "[redesigned] the global polity to reflect a tran-
    scendental hegemony," while the latter "[restructured] the world in line with envi-
    ronmental and ecological holistics" (*Historical Dictionary of New Age Movements*, 4).
    Sixties psychedelic experiments precipitated the makeshift synthesis of mysticism,
    contemplation, and spirituality of New Age. Yet the roots of New Age extend fur-
    ther into the past. They lie in Western occult-metaphysical traditions, Eastern spir-
    ituality, and the rise of psychology. Specific influences include, in the nineteenth
    century, American spiritualism, New Thought, Theosophy, and transcendentalism;
    in the twentieth century, reflexology, Scientology, Gestalt therapy, transpersonal
    psychology, and Reichian therapy; and within a broader historical frame, Zen or Ti-
    betan Buddhism, Hinduism, and the holistic perspective. See Archibald, *The Evolu-
    tion of Self-Help*, 9; Drury, *The New Age*, 39, 76; Kyle, *The New Age Movement in American
    Culture*, 13; York, *Historical Dictionary of New Age Movements*, xix–xxvi, 17–18, 30, 38. Bel-
    lamy's New Age approach to the sutra brings up questions of cultural appropriation.
    On the politics of appropriation in New Narrative, Bellamy's primary affiliation, see
    Halpern, "'Where No Meaning Is'"; Tremblay, "Together, in the First Person."

39 Bellamy, *The TV Sutras*, 41.

40 Buuck, "Dodie Bellamy by David Buuck."

41 Bellamy, *The TV Sutras*, 190.

42 Bellamy, *the buddhist*, 75.

43 Harris, "New Narrative and the Making of Language Poetry," 808. See also
    Halpern and Tremblay-McGaw, "'A Generosity of Response,'" 7–11.

44 Kevin Killian offers, "'Sex writing' . . . differs from other forms of representa-
    tion in that it has some kind of chemical effect on the reader. I get hard, I can't
    contain myself. A fugue results, between the closed system of language and the
    complex system of molecules that holds my body together a real communication
    begins" ("Sex Writing and the New Narrative," 293).

45 Bellamy, *The TV Sutras*, 106.

46 Robert Glück nonetheless specifies that New Narrative was never an outright repudiation of the Language school. The Language poets, he recalls, reinvigorated a dormant San Francisco writing scene. They had the audacity to propose a poetics of their own and made it possible for authors to position themselves in relation to that proposition: "Suddenly people took sides, though at times these confrontations resembled a pastiche of the embattled positions of earlier avant-guards [*sic*]. Language Poetry seemed very 'straight male'—though what didn't?" (*Communal Nude*, 14). See also Chisholm, *Queer Constellations*, 55–56; Bellamy and Killian, "Introduction."

47 Harris, "Avant-Garde Interrupted," 654.

48 Bellamy's turn to New Age is in fact a return: she joined a religious cult in the early 1970s, before becoming a member of New Narrative. "With New Narrative," she tells Buuck in their *BOMB* interview, "I was getting out of one cult and leaping into another" (Buuck, "Dodie Bellamy by David Buuck").

49 Bellamy, *The TV Sutras*, 106. Unlike vomit for Jacques Derrida or the abject for Julia Kristeva, the vulgar in Bellamy's project shatters neither representation nor being. Derrida, "Economimesis," 90; Kristeva, *Powers of Horror*.

50 Bellamy, *The TV Sutras*, 190.

51 Jean-Christophe Bailly writes that breathing produces "living, . . . until the end, as a porosity" ("The Slightest Breath," 5).

52 Bellamy, *The TV Sutras*, 33.

53 Bellamy, *The TV Sutras*, 103.

54 Bellamy, *The TV Sutras*, 22.

55 Bellamy, *Academonia*, 15.

56 Buuck, "Dodie Bellamy by David Buuck."

57 Bellamy, *The TV Sutras*, 102.

58 Bellamy, *The TV Sutras*, 102.

59 Bellamy, *The TV Sutras*, 102.

60 See Bellamy, *The Letters of Mina Harker*; Bellamy, *When the Sick Rule the World*, 25–44, 185–243.

61 Buuck, "Dodie Bellamy by David Buuck." Shambhala is an international network of mindfulness meditation centers.

62 Buuck, "Dodie Bellamy by David Buuck"; Bellamy, *The TV Sutras*, 186.

63 Cameron, *Impersonality*, 86.

64 Cameron, *Impersonality*, viii–ix.

65 Emerson, *The Portable Emerson*, 212.

66 Eve Kosofsky Sedgwick notes New Age's proximity to corporate ideology: "The stigmatizing rubrics of 'self-help,' 'New Age,' and 'therapy-like' have suggested a [less than] respectable market-niche specification for [non-Western] teachings aimed at non-Asian consumers" (*Touching Feeling*, 155–56).

67 Conrad, *A Beautiful Marsupial Afternoon*, 2.

68 Conrad, *Ecodeviance*, xi.

69 In an email dated February 24, 2016, Conrad told me an anecdote about their in-

terest in Olson's poetics: "When I was working with Jonathan Williams on *The Book of Frank* I would bug him with questions about Olson. He finally was caught in a mood where he didn't mind the question after decades of people hammering him (hammering is another kind of sequential breath) about Olson. He told me that one day after Olson played (I can't remember the composer) music as loud as he could on the record player, Olson told everyone to LEAVE the building at once, to RUN across the field of flowers and to write on the other side of the field AND AS THEY WERE LEAVING THE BUILDING HE SAID that the sunlight and flowers would be there in the poems AND I KNEW THE MOMENT I HEARD THIS that Olson meant the essence. Not documentary poetics. The experiential poetics instead."

70 Conrad, *A Beautiful Marsupial Afternoon*, 36.
71 Conrad, *Ecodeviance*, xi.
72 Conrad, *Ecodeviance*, xi.
73 Conrad, *Ecodeviance*, xi; Conrad, *A Beautiful Marsupial Afternoon*, 1
74 Buuck, "Dodie Bellamy by David Buuck."
75 Conrad, *A Beautiful Marsupial Afternoon*, 1.
76 Conrad, *A Beautiful Marsupial Afternoon*, 1.
77 Conrad, *A Beautiful Marsupial Afternoon*, 56; Conrad, *Ecodeviance*, 109.
78 Soto, "CA Conrad."
79 *The Book of Conrad*, dir. Belinda Schmid and David Cranstoun Welch (2015).
80 Conrad, *While Standing in Line for Death*, 1.
81 Conrad, *While Standing in Line for Death*, 8.
82 Conrad, *While Standing in Line for Death*, 12.
83 Conrad, *A Beautiful Marsupial Afternoon*, 149, emphasis added.
84 Conrad, *A Beautiful Marsupial Afternoon*, 147–48.
85 Berlant, "The Commons," 405; Spahr, *This Connection of Everyone with Lungs*.
86 Winnicott, *Reading Winnicott*, 160, 41–43.
87 Conrad, *A Beautiful Marsupial Afternoon*, 12.
88 Freudenthal, *Aristotle's Theory of Material Substance*, 106–7; Reich, *Selected Writings*, 164, 241. The psychoanalyst Jean-Louis Tristani draws on Reich to hypothesize an "érogénéité respiratoire" (respiratory erogeneity) (*Le state du respir*, 7). Revisiting Freud's writings on Dora's hysteric coughing, Tristani claims that breathing is one of the ego's drives, along with nutrition. Inhalation is analogous to oral ingestion; and exhalation, though also oral, is analogous to anal expulsion. Hysteria interferes with free respiration, thereby expanding to the entire body an erogenous zone typically limited to nasal and buccal intake and outtake (56, 134–35, 159).
89 Willis, *The Essential Ellen Willis*, 105, 186–87, 500, 504. Willis's feminist recuperation of Reich clashes with the feminist critique of Reich, which posits, by and large, that Reich's model hinges on biological determinism and figures emotional release in terms that are both phallocentric and specific to male ejaculation.
90 For examples of Conrad's nonbinary poetics, see Conrad, WRITING IN ALL CAPS IS THE BREATH MINT OF THE SOUL, esp. 18; Conrad, *The Book of Frank*, esp. 11. For an analysis of this poetics, see Tremblay, "Poetics of Gender Self-Determination."

91 Conrad, *A Beautiful Marsupial Afternoon*, 183.

92 Sandilands, "Melancholy Natures, Queer Ecologies," 342. For a critique of queer theory's melancholic relation to nature, see Tremblay and Swarbrick, "Destructive Environmentalism."

93 Muñoz, *Cruising Utopia*, 1; Halberstam, "Go Gaga," 126.

94 Halberstam, "Go Gaga," 127.

95 Conrad, *A Beautiful Marsupial Afternoon*, 2.

96 The trouble with wildness as an ideal is twofold. First, it locates a fantasy of the untamable within a past that never actually happened. Second, it downplays the role of colonialism and imperialism in shaping this fantasy. Writing about wilderness, the spatialization of wildness, William Cronon argues that "we mistake ourselves when we suppose that wilderness can be the solution to our culture's problematic relationships with the nonhuman world" ("The Trouble with Wilderness," 7–8). The figuration of wilderness areas as uninhabited land is premised on the erasure of Indigenous life. Peter Coviello makes a complementary point by arguing that Henry David Thoreau's treatment of the wild in *Walden*—a "carnal delightedness . . . not separable from sex . . . but neither . . . reducible to it"— foreshadows sexuality's entry into a regime of biopower ("The Wild Not Less Than the Good," 510).

97 CAConrad, "(Soma)tic Poetry," workshop at the University of Chicago, January 25, 2017.

98 Garland-Thomson, "Seeing the Disabled," 358.

99 Jennifer Doyle, "Sheree Rose: A Legend of Los Angeles Performance Art," KCET, June 20, 2013, https://www.kcet.org/shows/artbound/sheree-rose-a-legend-of-los-angeles-performance-art.

100 *Sick: The Life and Death of Bob Flanagan, Supermasochist*, dir. Kirby Dick (1997).

101 Juno and Vale, *Bob Flanagan*, 27.

102 Flanagan, Rose, and Rugoff, "Visiting Hours," 65.

103 Quoted in Jones, *Body Art/Performing the Subject*, 233.

104 Garland-Thomson, "Staring Back," 334, 335, 338n4.

105 Lorenz, *Queer Art*, 78–79; Kuppers, *The Scar of Visibility*, 78–80, 94.

106 McRuer, *Crip Theory*, 193.

107 Kauffman, *Bad Girls and Sick Boys*, 21.

108 McRuer, *Crip Theory*, 183.

109 Flanagan and Rose's papers and other artifacts are held by the Ohio State University and the ONE National Gay and Lesbian Archives, housed by the University of Southern California. Flanagan's solo bibliography also includes three collections of poems: *The Kid Is the Man*, *The Wedding of Everything*, and *Slave Sonnets*.

110 Bob Flanagan, journal, 1979, Bob Flanagan and Sheree Rose Collection, ONE Gay and Lesbian Archives, University of Southern California Library, Los Angeles, California. In his incomplete manuscript of the "Book of Medicines," Flanagan mentions a journal he wrote, at least in part, in 1979 (439). I believe it is the late -1970s journal I consulted in the archive.

111 Bob Flanagan, journal, 1985, Bob Flanagan and Sheree Rose Collection.

112 Flanagan, *Fuck Journal*, 56.

113 Bob Flanagan, journal, 1986, Bob Flanagan and Sheree Rose Collection.

114 Flanagan, "S," 24–30.

115 Bob Flanagan, "Underdog," 1995, box 16, Bob Flanagan Collection.

116 Michel, *Le souffle coupé*, 196.

117 Michel, *Le souffle coupé*, 16.

118 Michel, *Le souffle coupé*, 7.

119 Flanagan, *The Pain Journal*, 24. I have kept all excerpts from *The Pain Journal* intact, without correcting syntactical, grammatical, or typographical errors.

120 Doyle, *Hold It against Me*, 20.

121 Flanagan, *The Pain Journal*, 34.

122 Flanagan, *The Pain Journal*, 156–57.

123 "Understanding Changes in Life Expectancy," Cystic Fibrosis Foundation, accessed September 3, 2021, https://www.cff.org/Research/Researcher-Resources/Patient-Registry/Understanding-Changes-in-Life-Expectancy/.

124 Flanagan, *The Pain Journal*, 125.

125 Bob Flanagan, "Dead Air," undated, box 18, Bob Flanagan Collection.

126 Sheree Rose, journal, 1977, box 3, Bob Flanagan and Sheree Rose Collection.

127 Sheree Rose, interview by author, May 3, 2016.

128 Flanagan, *The Pain Journal*, 152.

129 Flanagan, *The Pain Journal*, 55, 67, 140–41.

130 Flanagan, *The Pain Journal*, 141–42.

131 Flanagan, *The Pain Journal*, 12, 120.

132 Flanagan, *The Pain Journal*, 58.

133 Flanagan, *The Pain Journal*, 58.

134 Flanagan, *The Pain Journal*, 89.

135 Flanagan, *The Pain Journal*, 85.

136 Flanagan, *The Pain Journal*, 52.

137 Phillips, *On Kissing, Tickling, and Being Bored*, 68. Elizabeth S. Goodstein calls Phillips's essay "an intriguing reading of boredom from an object relations perspective" (*Experience without Qualities*, 2n2). Goodstein's definition of boredom as an "experience without qualities" is not so different from Phillips's model, insofar as both authors gesture toward a dissatisfying lack. Lars Svendsen similarly describes boredom as "a lack of personal meaning" amid "objects and actions [that] come to us fully coded" (*A Philosophy of Boredom*, 31).

138 Phillips, *On Kissing, Tickling, and Being Bored*, 77.

139 Phillips, *On Kissing, Tickling, and Being Bored*, 78, 70.

140 Quoted in Phillips, *On Kissing, Tickling, and Being Bored*, 74.

141 A particular structure of desire, not age, defines the subject of Phillips's essay on boredom, the child. Flanagan's boredom picks up where his masochism left off, which is to say in the realm of infantile desire. Flanagan was candid about the impact of the care and attention he received as a sick child on his development as a masochist. In an undated performance of the "Death Monologue," Flanagan revisits the origin tale: "I have to go to the CF clinic, which is still in a pediatri-

cian's office. I sit in these little chairs, and stuff. That's where I get a lot of new inspiration for my work." Bob Flanagan, "Death Monologue," box 7, Bob Flanagan Collection. In the May 1, 1995, entry of *The Pain Journal*, Flanagan attributes a brief resurgence of his "SM frame of mind" to Sheree's travels: "I think it's like being a kid again, with the parents out" (47).

142 Doyle, *Sex Objects*, xxviii.

143 Doyle, *Sex Objects*, xxix.

144 Flanagan, "Book of Medicines," 439.

145 Kafer, *Feminist, Queer, Crip*, 25.

146 For an adroit psychoanalytic reading of the erotics of care in Rose's solo and collaborative performances, see Musser, "Sheree Rose, the Maternal, and the Erotics of Care."

147 Ngai, *Ugly Feelings*, 284. The shocking quality of Flanagan's symptomatologies conjures, if involuntarily, the mid-nineteenth-century "Spasmodic school," as Sydney Dobell's and Alexander Smith's detractors called it. Rudy, *Electric Meters*, 14. Jason A. Rudy writes that rhythm, for Dobell in particular, "expresses metonymically the physiological conditions of the human body—its pulses either harmonize with or strain against the throbbing of our physical being" (14). Dobell's poetry is thus "meant to be felt like a literal, bodily shock" (14).

148 Ngai, *Ugly Feelings*, 255.

149 Tim Goodman, "Milton Berle 1908–2002," *SFGate*, March 28, 2002, http://www .sfgate.com/news/article/MILTON-BERLE-1908-2002-Mr-Television-dies-at -2861231.php.

150 Flanagan, *The Pain Journal*, 62.

151 Laird, "Musical Styles and Song Conventions," 34.

152 Bersani, *Is the Rectum a Grave?*, 64. See also Bersani and Phillips, *Intimacies*, 85. By proposing that the therapeutic valence of masochism is transduced as aesthetic form in *The Pain Journal*, and that the formalism of sexuality hinges on the interpretation of pain as something potentially pleasurable, I combine aspects of Bersani's two formal theories of sexuality. The first, found in *The Freudian Body*, posits that the psychoanalytic validity of Freud's theory of sexuality hinges on the collapse of representational discourse. Any theory of sexuality, by seeking to contain or repress the destabilizing force of the sexual, constitutes a normalizing enterprise (15). A theory of sexuality can be accurate only in an aesthetic sense: if, as a function of its development, it gives in to the perturbations of the sexual. In his work from the 1990s and 2000s, Bersani overhauls this model. Rather than viewing the sexual as a disturbance of structure, he tracks the structuring of the sexual. Proposing what would later be known as the antisocial thesis in queer theory, Bersani claims in *Homos* that "homoness," or the desire for sameness, propels sex (7). The narcissism of homoness can produce a hyperbolizing image of the self, but also initiate the subject into seductive self-dissolution, shattering, or "nonsuicidal disappearance," thereby causing this subject to extend into and reappear in the external world (99, emphasis removed). In Bersani's first model, the formalization of the sexual becomes legible through the erosion of mechanisms

of expository writing. In his second model, the formalism of sexuality orchestrates the masochistic management and interpretation of libidinal investments.

153 Flanagan, *The Pain Journal*, 110, 111.

154 Sheree Rose, interview with unknown interviewer, 1998, Bob Flanagan and Sheree Rose Collection.

155 Sheree Rose, interview with unknown interviewer, 1998, Bob Flanagan and Sheree Rose Collection.

156 Rose, "Life Is Still Possible in This Junky World," 108.

157 Sheree Rose, draft of an interview by Tina Takemoto, undated, box 3, Bob Flanagan and Sheree Rose Collection.

158 Sheree Rose, interview by author, May 3, 2016.

3. Feminist Breathing

An early version of this chapter appeared as Jean-Thomas Tremblay, "Feminist Breathing," *differences: A Journal of Feminist Cultural Studies* 30, no. 3 (2019): 92–117.

Excerpts from Linda Hogan's "Old Ocean, She," "Morning's Dance," and "The Other Side," from *Dark. Sweet. New and Selected Poems* (2012), are reproduced with the permission of Coffee House Books.

1 Sarachild, "Consciousness-Raising," 147. Anita Shreve reminds us that CR and the women's movement ought not to be conflated: "Although most members of the Women's Movement did at one time or another try CR (and although many CR groups were composed of committed feminists), some women who joined CR groups never considered themselves part of the Women's Movement at all" (*Women Alone*, 5–6).

2 Cornell, "Las Greñudas," 1033.

3 See Hanisch, "The Personal Is Political," 204–5; hooks, *Feminism Is for Everybody*.

4 Sarachild, "Consciousness-Raising," 144, emphasis removed.

5 "Guide to Consciousness-Raising," 118.

6 Allen, *Free Space*, 17–18.

7 Stimpson, Shulman, and Millett, *"Sexual Politics,"* 32, 33.

8 Ephron, *"Crazy Salad,"* 93.

9 Freedman, *Feminism, Sexuality, and Politics*, 82. Janet L. Freedman explains that the women's studies class, in its goals and methods, descends from the CR meeting (*Reclaiming the Feminist Vision*, 104, 109).

10 Wittig and Zeig, *Brouillon pour un dictionnaire des amantes*, 43; Irigaray, *To Be Two*, 2.

11 Alluding to the internal disputes and general political losses of 1975, including a leadership crisis within the National Organization for Women and a failed attempt to get the progressive states of New York and New Jersey to ratify the Equal Rights Amendment, Betty Friedan argues in her "Open Letter to the Women's Movement" that the "diversion into in-fighting and dead ends has been a by-product of the opposition economic equality . . . [faced] from big business, church and state" (*It Changed My Life*, 372).

12 Firestone, *Airless Spaces*; Firestone, *The Dialectic of Sex*.

13 Ngai, "Shulamith Firestone's *Airless Spaces*."

14 Weeks, "The Vanishing *Dialectic*," 745.

15 Weeks, "The Vanishing *Dialectic*," 746.

16 Firestone, *Airless Spaces*, 132; Solanas, SCUM *Manifesto*.

17 Elliott, "The Currency of Feminist Theory," 1697.

18 Moraga, "Preface," xv.

19 Reagon, "Coalition Politics," 359.

20 Reagon, "Coalition Politics," 356.

21 Alaimo, "Trans-corporeal Feminisms and the Ethical Space of Nature," 261.

22 Hogan, *Dark. Sweet*, 55.

23 See Cook, "From the Center of Tradition," 11.

24 Mishuana R. Goeman (Tonawanda Band of Seneca) and Jennifer Nez Denetdale (Diné) hint at Native feminism's spatial imaginary when they claim, not arbitrarily, "We desire to *open up spaces* where generations of colonialism have silenced Native peoples about the status of their women and about the intersections of power and domination that have also shaped Native nations and gender relations" ("Native Feminisms," 10, emphasis added).

25 Hogan, *Dwellings*, 37.

26 Hogan, *Dwellings*, 37.

27 Allen, *The Sacred Hoop*, 62. See also Chandler, "Terrestrial Spirituality," 24.

28 Simpson, "Land as Pedagogy," 11.

29 Hogan, *Dark. Sweet*, 196, 197.

30 Hogan, *Dark. Sweet*, 385.

31 Hogan, *Dark. Sweet*, 385.

32 Hogan, *Dark. Sweet*, 385.

33 Hogan, *Dark. Sweet*, 386.

34 Philip, "The Ga(s)p," 31. Although I would favor the term *parent* over *mother*, I have decided against tweaking Philip's phrasing. As I discuss in chapter 1, the very idea of a female breath situates femaleness in exchanges and transactions that exceed any one individual, thus contesting its own essentialism.

35 Philip, "The Ga(s)p," 31.

36 Philip, "The Ga(s)p," 32.

37 Philip, "The Ga(s)p," 34. While Philip's and Hogan's poetics of maternal breathing resonate with one another, to conflate them would erase some of the specific ways Black women's bodies have been seized and controlled in US history. From the late eighteenth century through the end of the Civil War, some Chickasaw individuals held people of African descent in slavery. As Barbara Krauthamer argues, slavery in the antebellum Chickasaw Nation rested on racial and gender ideologies that justified the enslavement of Black women and men's bodies, labor, and reproduction (*Black Slaves, Indian Masters*, 4). Chickasaw matrilineality concurred with a distinct application of the concept, one that reproduced the exploitation of Black people by decreeing that children of Black slave women would follow their mothers into slavery. Krauthamer, *Black Slaves, Indian Masters*,

5; St. Jean, *Remaining Chickasaw in Indian Territory*, 46. The history of chattel slavery in the Chickasaw Nation sheds light on Black women's alienation from their life-giving and life-sustaining force. Read alongside this history, Hogan's female figuration of the breath of creation gives us the opportunity to consider the racial inequalities that enclose radical hospitality.

38 See St. Jean, *Remaining Chickasaw in Indian Territory*, 19.

39 Allen, *The Sacred Hoop*, 209.

40 Allen, *The Sacred Hoop*, 2, 30.

41 Hogan, *Dark. Sweet*, 59.

42 Hogan, *Dark. Sweet*, 59.

43 Hogan, *Dark. Sweet*, 79.

44 Bell, "Introduction," 3.

45 Shotwell, *Against Purity*, 9.

46 Shotwell, *Against Purity*, 15.

47 Hogan, *Dark. Sweet*, 362.

48 Hogan, *The Woman Who Watches Over the World*, 16.

49 Hogan, *The Woman Who Watches Over the World*, 16.

50 Hogan, *The Woman Who Watches Over the World*, 18.

51 Hogan, *The Woman Who Watches Over the World*, 18.

52 Malabou, *The New Wounded*, 17.

53 Malabou, *The New Wounded*, 58, emphasis added.

54 Malabou, *The New Wounded*, 166.

55 Jackson, *Becoming Human*, 72–73.

56 Jackson, *Becoming Human*, 73. On the biopolitics of plasticity, or the cultivation of "the capacity to be formed by outside pressure, yet to maintain internal coherence all the while," see Schuller and Gill-Peterson, "Introduction," 4.

57 Bambara, *The Salt Eaters*, 56.

58 Bambara, *Gorilla, My Love*; Bambara, *The Sea Birds Are Still Alive*.

59 Willis, *Specifying*, 129.

60 Hull, "What It Is I Think She's Doing Anyhow," 124.

61 Bambara, "Preface," 7.

62 Bambara, interview with Claudia Tate, 13.

63 Bambara, interview with Claudia Tate, 13.

64 Bambara, *The Salt Eaters*, 258.

65 Bambara, *The Salt Eaters*, 258.

66 Willis, *Specifying*, 130.

67 Bambara, *The Salt Eaters*, 5.

68 Boyd, "'She Was Just Outrageously Brilliant,'" 90.

69 Bambara, interview with Claudia Tate, 16.

70 See Kelley, "'Damballah Is the First Law of Thermodynamics,'" 485; Wilentz, *Healing Narratives*, 55.

71 Toni Cade Bambara, "What It Is I Think I'm Doing Anyway," essay draft, 1979, box 7, Toni Cade Bambara Collection, Part I, Spelman College Archives, Atlanta, Georgia.

72 Bambara, "What It Is I Think I'm Doing Anyway."

73 Bambara's Black feminism is intersectional and coalitional. It stands in solidarity with other struggles for gender and racial equality. Bambara refutes the idea that being "both a feminist and a warrior of the race struggle" might constitute a contradiction: "I'm not aware of what the problem is for people who consider it a dilemma. I don't know what they're thinking because it's not as if you're a black *or* a woman. I don't find any basic contradiction or any tension between being a feminist, being a pan-Africanist, being a black nationalist, being an internationalist, being a socialist, and being a woman in North America." Quoted in Guy-Sheftall, "Toni Cade Bambara, Black Feminist Foremother," 125. Carter A. Mathes sums up: "Bambara's writing suggests conceptions of late-twentieth-century racial subjectivity that embrace the seeming chaos of multiplicity and interconnection, not as an erosion of particular identities and locations, but rather as crucial starting points for the realization of the political complexity within them" ("Scratching the Threshold," 370). Elliott Butler-Evans argues that scholarship on *The Salt Eaters* has prioritized the novel's cultural and historical relevance to African American culture over its feminist content (*Race, Gender, and Desire*, 171). I agree. This said, pertinent feminist readings of *The Salt Eaters* include Griffin, "Toni Cade Bambara"; Marshall, *Black Professional Women in Recent American Fiction*, 107; and Patton, *The Grasp That Reaches beyond the Grave*, 31–50.

74 Alwes, "The Burden of Liberty," 354–55.

75 Bambara, *The Salt Eaters*, 19.

76 Alwes, "The Burden of Liberty," 354.

77 Bambara, *The Salt Eaters*, 111.

78 Bambara, *The Salt Eaters*, 111, 112.

79 Bambara, *The Salt Eaters*, 6.

80 Bambara, *The Salt Eaters*, 7.

81 Bambara, *The Salt Eaters*, 7–8.

82 See Csikszentmihalyi, *Flow*; Stenner, "Being in the Zone and Vital Subjectivity."

83 Bambara, "What It Is I Think I'm Doing Anyway."

84 Bambara, *The Salt Eaters*, 263–64.

85 Stanford, "Mechanisms of Disease," 33.

86 Diouf and Nwankwo, *Rhythms of the Afro-Atlantic World*, 81.

87 Crawley, *Blackpentecostal Breath*, 202.

88 Daly, *Pure Lust*, 136.

89 Harries, *Forgetting Lot's Wife*, 15–16.

90 Bambara, "What It Is I Think I'm Doing Anyway."

91 Bambara, *The Salt Eaters*, 147.

92 Gordon, "Something More Powerful Than Skepticism," 187.

93 Bambara, *The Salt Eaters*, 258.

94 Stanford, "Mechanisms of Disease," 32. See also Thistlethwaite, "God and Her Survival in a Nuclear Age," 87.

95 Collins, "Generating Power," 37.

96 Bambara, *The Salt Eaters*, 243.

97 Bambara, *The Salt Eaters*, 212.

98 Hurley, *Infrastructures of Apocalypse*, 28.

99 Bambara, *The Salt Eaters*, 3.

100 Bambara, *The Salt Eaters*, 106.

101 Bambara, *The Salt Eaters*, 9.

102 Bambara, *The Salt Eaters*, 10.

103 Bambara, *The Salt Eaters*, 220.

104 Clare, *Brilliant Imperfection*, xvi.

105 Willis, *Specifying*, 129.

106 Stanford, "Mechanisms of Disease," 35.

107 *This Bridge Called My Back*, performed by Madelyne Beckles, Art Gallery of Ontario, Toronto, May 4, 2017.

108 "Don't Make Me Over," performed by Dionne Warwick, *Presenting Dionne Warwick*, 1963.

109 O'Brien, "Performing Chronic," 55.

110 My use of *durable breath* refers to Smelcer and Birchfield, *Durable Breath*.

111 Million, "Felt Theory," 54–55.

112 Simmons, "Settler Atmospherics"; Dillon and Sze, "Police Power and Particulate Matters."

113 Alexis Pauline Gumbs, "About," *Black Feminist Breathing Chorus*, accessed April 30, 2019, https://web.archive.org/web/20190417113309/http://blackfeministbreathing.tumblr.com/.

114 Alexis Pauline Gumbs, "Meditation #16: The Most Effective Way to Do It Is to Do It," audio file, accessed April 30, 2019, https://web.archive.org/web/20190321193132/http://blackfeministbreathing.tumblr.com/post/172251240385/blackfeministbreathing-iexhale-collage-by.

115 Gumbs, *Spill*, esp. 7, 13, 34, 84; Gumbs, *M Archive*, esp. xi, 6–7, 63, 79; Gumbs, *Dub*, esp. 13, 41; Gumbs, Martens, and Williams, *Revolutionary Mothering*. Gumbs's books of theoretical poetics are inspired primarily by the writings of Hortense Spillers, M. Jacqui Alexander, and Sylvia Wynter.

116 Sedgwick, *Touching Feeling*, 128.

117 Sedgwick, *Touching Feeling*, 150–51.

4. Smog Sensing

Excerpts from Renee Gladman's *Event Factory* (2010) are reproduced with the permission of Dorothy, a publishing project.

1 *Oxford English Dictionary Online* (2021), s.v. "smog," https://www.oed.com/view/Entry/182692?.

2 Brimblecombe, "Early Episodes," 11–15.

3 Hinrichs and Kleinbach, *Energy*, 250; *Encyclopedia Britannica*, s.v. "smog," accessed March 19, 2019, https://www.britannica.com/science/smog.

4 Parikka, "The Sensed Smog," 9, 4.

5 Parikka, "The Sensed Smog," 9.

6 Parikka, "The Sensed Smog," 1. Parikka here draws on Halpern, *Beautiful Data*, 27. On the datafication of the atmosphere, see Moro, "Grid Techniques for a Planet in Crisis." For a critique of the smart city, see Mattern, "A City Is Not a Computer."

7 Parikka, "The Sensed Smog," 9.

8 Zeiba, "City Writer"; "Renee Gladman," Foundation for Contemporary Arts, 2016, https://www.foundationforcontemporaryarts.org/recipients/renee -gladman.

9 See Clemmons, "Where Is Our Black Avant-Garde?"

10 See McNamara, "It Just Made Perfect Sense"; Rudick, "Press Pass."

11 Gladman, *Event Factory*, 11.

12 Gladman, *Event Factory*, 69–70.

13 Gladman, *The Ravickians*, 156.

14 Gladman, interview with the editors of *HAUS RED*, 14.

15 Hsu, *The Smell of Risk*, 12.

16 Rahm, "Meteorological Architecture"; Stavridou, "Breathing Architecture"; "Biomimicry 101," Biomimicry Institute, accessed September 3, 2021, https:// biomimicry.org/what-is-biomimicry/.

17 TPC Staff, "Doris Sung Creates Living Architecture."

18 Doroteo, "Let Your Building 'Breathe.'"

19 Campbell-Dollaghan, "5 Smart Building Skins That Breathe."

20 Campbell-Dollaghan, "5 Smart Building Skins That Breathe."

21 See Corton, *London Fog*, 93, 22–23, 148. For a comprehensive study of novelistic engagements with the London fog qua "artificial climate," see Jesse Oak Taylor, *The Sky of Our Manufacture*.

22 See the chapter "James's Air" in Zhang, *Strange Likeness*, 61–86, for a discussion of James's "ethereal preoccupations" (63) and of atmosphere as "a preeminent site of disclosure" (68) for the writer.

23 DeLillo, *White Noise*, 117.

24 Samuel R. Delany, journal 45, October 1972–May 1973, box 15, Samuel R. Delany Collection, Howard Goetlib Archival Center, Boston University, Boston.

25 Delany, *Dhalgren*, 72.

26 Delany, *Dhalgren*, 45.

27 Delany, *Dhalgren*, 75.

28 Delany, *Dhalgren*, 15.

29 Gladman, interview by the editors of *HAUS RED*, 10–11.

30 *Encyclopedia Britannica*, s.v. "smog."

31 Choy, *Ecologies of Comparison*, 157.

32 Zhang, "Notes on Atmosphere," 130.

33 Stewart, "Atmospheric Attunements," 445–46.

34 Stewart, "Atmospheric Attunements," 452.

35 Sedgwick, *Tendencies*, 9, xii.

36 Edelman, *No Future*, 5.

37 On the politics of queer kinship (normative, antinormative, and some combina-

tion thereof), see Amin, *Disturbing Attachments*; Bradway, "Slow Burn"; Delany, *Times Square Red, Times Square Blue*; Eng, *The Feeling of Kinship*; Freeman, *Time Binds*; Rodríguez, *Sexual Futures, Queer Gestures*.

38 Berlant and Edelman, *Sex, or the Unbearable*, viii. "Sex is exemplary in the way it powerfully induces such encounters," Berlant and Edelman clarify, "but such encounters exceed those experiences we recognize as sex" (viii).

39 Cohen, "Punks, Bulldaggers, and Welfare Queens," 438; Ferguson, *Aberrations in Black*, 3; Johnson, "'Quare' Studies," 3.

40 Buuck, "A Walking Measure," 145.

41 Buuck, "A Walking Measure," 145.

42 Wilkinson, "An Interview with Renee Gladman."

43 Gladman, *Morelia*, 30, 12, 20.

44 Gladman, *Morelia*, 10.

45 Braun, *Breathing Race into the Machine*; Mitman, *Breathing Space*, 65, 145.

46 On *Dhalgren* and the Watts Rebellion, see Tucker, *A Sense of Wonder*, 79; Jerng, "A World of Difference," 259; Comer, "Playing at Birth," 173. On environmental racism and segregation, see Taylor, *The Environment and the People in American Cities*.

47 Dillon and Sze, "Police Power and Particulate Matters," 13.

48 Dillon and Sze, "Police Power and Particulate Matters," 19.

49 Carter and Cervenak, "Black Ether," 205.

50 Cervenak, "'Black Night Is Falling,'" 167. Cervenak draws on Fred Moten's claim that Blackness "has been associated with a certain sense of decay, even when that decay is invoked in the name of a certain (fetishization of) vitality" (Moten, "The Case of Blackness," 177).

51 Gladman, *Calamities*, 19.

52 See Anderson and Jones, "Introduction," vii–viii; Dery, "Black to the Future," 189–90; Nelson, "Introduction," 1–15; Womack, *Afrofuturism*, 126.

53 Wilkinson, "An Interview with Renee Gladman," emphasis added.

54 Cain and Gladman, "Amina Cain and Renee Gladman." See also DiFrancesco, "The Shifting Literary and Ecological Landscapes of Renee Gladman's *Calamities*."

55 Gladman, *Ana Patova Crosses a Bridge*, 14.

56 Gladman, *Ana Patova Crosses a Bridge*, 80.

57 Gladman, *Houses of Ravicka*, 125.

58 Gladman, *Ana Patova Crosses a Bridge*, 92–93.

59 Gladman, *Prose Architectures*, viii.

60 Gladman, *Prose Architectures*, xi.

61 Gladman, *Houses of Ravicka*, 144.

62 Gladman, *Houses of Ravicka*, 139–40.

63 Le Guin, *The Left Hand of Darkness*, xiv, xviii. Le Guin's musings pertain to the gender identity of the characters in *The Left Hand of Darkness*: "Yes, indeed the people in it are androgynous, but that doesn't mean that I'm predicting that in a millennium or so we will all be androgynous, or announcing that I think we damned well ought to be androgynous. I'm merely observing, in the pecu-

liar, devious, and thought-experimental manner proper to science fiction, that if you look at us at certain odd times of day in certain weathers, we already are" (xvii–xviii). Le Guin's stance on gender nonconformity resonates with that of the Ravicka series. Although I wouldn't call Jakobi androgynous—androgyny being more stable an identity than whatever we may intuit from *Houses of Ravicka*—the character's gender presentation does waver.

64 Gladman, "The Person in the World," 46–49; Grosz, *Architecture from the Outside*, 48.

65 Grosz, *Architecture from the Outside*, 129.

66 Grosz, *Architecture from the Outside*, 149.

67 Buuck, *Site Cite City*, 55.

68 Buuck, *Site Cite City*, 55.

69 Buuck, *Site Cite City*, 34.

70 Buuck, *Site Cite City*, 51.

71 Quoted in Buuck, *Site Cite City*, 33; Buuck, *Site Cite City*, 35.

72 Gladman, *The Ravickians*, 35.

73 Gladman, *Morelia*, 6.

74 Gladman, *Event Factory*, 74.

75 Gladman, *Event Factory*, 75.

76 Gladman, *Event Factory*, 75.

77 Gladman, *Event Factory*, 76–77.

78 Gladman, *Event Factory*, 61; Renee Gladman, interview by author, May 30, 2016.

79 Gladman, *Event Factory*, 61.

80 Gladman, *The Ravickians*, 7.

81 Gladman, *Houses of Ravicka*, 60.

82 Gladman, *Houses of Ravicka*, 62.

83 Lacan, *Le séminaire de Jacques Lacan: Livre 23*.

84 Edelman, *No Future*, 35. The sinthome structures *jouissance*, a painful excess or waste that transcends a pleasure principle communicable through language, or containable by the Symbolic.

85 Gladman, *Event Factory*, 109.

86 Gladman, interview by the editors of *HAUS RED*, 17.

87 Vincler, "Dwelling Places," emphasis added.

88 Heine, *Poetics of Breathing*, 34.

89 For a cluster of reflections on critique and postcritique as well as the assumptions regarding collectivity, method, and temporality that inform polemics on "the way we read now," see Chew and Orlemanski, "We, Reading, Now."

90 Best and Marcus, "Surface Reading," 1.

91 Jameson, *Postmodernism*, 44; Flatley, *Affective Mapping*.

92 Orlemanski, *Symptomatic Subjects*, 17. While *Symptomatic Subjects* draws from a late medieval archive, Orlemanski insists that today, still, "medicine is one idiom among others for speaking about embodiment. . . . [The] project . . . of conceiving our lives in the full rush of the world's causes, where we suffer, seek care, and tell our stories[,] . . . continues into the present" (280).

93 Orlemanski, *Symptomatic Subjects*, 17, 19.

94 Holmes, *The Symptom and the Subject*, 275.

95 Orlemanski, *Symptomatic Subjects*, 16.

96 See Taylor, *Toxic Communities*, 1–3; Voyles, *Wastelanding*, 117–50.

97 Blas, "Opacities"; León, "Forms of Opacity"; Tagle, "Becoming Abstract Together"; McGlotten, "Black Data."

98 León, "Forms of Opacity," 378.

99 Blas, "Opacities," 149.

100 Glissant, *Poétique de la relation*, 199–200; Glissant, *Poetics of Relation*, 185–86. The French word for being, *être*, is most often uncapitalized in the original. I read Glissant's postulates as ontological and ontic, which is to say as addressing both Being itself and the experience of being a subject in the world. Thanks to Jordan Stein for guiding me toward this clarification.

101 Jackson, *Becoming Human*, 100.

102 Glissant, *Poetics of Relation*, 193.

103 Glissant, *Poetics of Relation*, 26; Glissant, *Poétique de la relation*, 39.

104 Gladman, "The Sentence as a Space for Living," 98, emphasis added.

105 Quashie, *The Sovereignty of Quiet*, 3–4.

106 Quashie, *The Sovereignty of Quiet*, 6, 115.

107 Tagle, "Becoming Abstract Together," 996, emphasis removed. Tagle uses this phrase to describe Takahiro Yamamoto's performance *Property of Opaqueness* and Asian American sociality more broadly. My description of symptomatic interpretation in the present chapter aligns with Tagle's account of the experience and reception of performances of opacity: "*Property of Opaqueness* seduces audiences into interpretation, in order to frustrate their desire to fix meaning to the dancers' bodies, gestures, and movements, or the performance as a whole" (996).

108 Choy, "A Commentary," 586.

109 It is possible to envision the just distribution of environmental risks and benefits without appealing to the criterion of recognition that much of the environmental justice movement considers synonymous with respect and dignity. The principle of opacity reminds us that recognition often is misrecognition by another name; the discomfort provoked by this fact is where the work of ethics and politics begins. See Schlosberg, "Reconceiving Environmental Justice," esp. 519–21.

110 Singh, *Unthinking Mastery*, 172.

111 Singh's statement reads, in full, "My own 'we' across *Unthinking Mastery* is a question as much as it is a hopeful summons to the (always imagined) future readers of this. It is also fundamentally a dehumanist 'we,' one that arises not on the grounds of Western scientific discourse and humanist politics but from the promises of those subjugated and emergent worldviews that recognize life, feel energy, and hear rhythms where now there appear to be none" (*Unthinking Mastery*, 173).

5. Death in the Form of Life

1 Tercier, *The Contemporary Deathbed Documentary*, 2.

2 Buchan, Gibson, and Ellison, "Reflections on the Death Scene," 5. In what has amounted to a massive shift in the organization of the medical and insurance industries and the management of life and death, dying has, over the past two centuries, left the everyday and the domestic to become a bureaucratic matter: actuarial, rationalized, depersonalized, and handled by experts. Moller, *Confronting Death*, 24.

3 Howarth, *Death and Dying*, 116.

4 Castra, *Bien mourir*, 3, 5.

5 Castra, *Bien mourir*, 5, 57.

6 Castra, *Bien mourir*, 210; Hockey, *Experiences of Death*, 57; Rosen, *Families Facing Death*.

7 De Beauvoir, *A Very Easy Death*, 95; de Beauvoir, *Une mort très douce*, 147.

8 For instance, in Simone de Beauvoir's account of her mother's death, a nurse sums up as "a very easy death" (*"une mort très douce"*) an episode of agony: "Maman had almost lost consciousness. Suddenly she cried, 'I can't breathe!' Her mouth opened, her eyes stared wide, huge in that wasted, ravaged face: with a spasm she entered into a coma" (*A Very Easy Death*, 88; *Une mort très douce*, 137). On de Beauvoir and the good death, see also Miller, *Bequest and Betrayal*, 53.

9 This elusive quality is the focus of conceptual artist Sophie Calle's *Pas pu saisir la mort* (2007), translatable as *couldn't grasp* or *catch death*, where *grasp* and *catch* mean both *capture* and *understand*. What would become an installation at the Italian Pavilion of the 2007 Venice Biennale began as a project to record the last three months of life of Calle's mother, Monique Sindler. Calle installed a camera at Sindler's bedside. "I wanted to make sure to be there," the artist recounts, "to hear her last words, to see her last smile, her last moment." Filming her mother's dying process allowed Calle to displace her anxiety. Rather than worrying about the days, hours, or minutes Sindler had left to live, Calle concerned herself with having to replace or rewind the tape. Calle was by her mother's side when the latter died. And yet, "Something strange happened, which was that I couldn't figure out when the last breath had taken place. I knew the last book she had read. I knew the last words she had said. I knew the last person she had met. But this . . . she had asked me that when she was about to die I put on a piece by Mozart, but I didn't know when to press *play*. There were tiny breaths and then, for eleven minutes, there was this moment between life and death when I didn't know if she was alive or dead. I couldn't put my finger on the last breath and on death itself. There was this no man's land between life and death where I couldn't catch death." Calle, "Lecture by Sophie Calle."

10 See Laplanche and Pontalis, "Fantasy and the Origins of Sexuality"; Berlant, *Desire/Love*, 74.

11 *Near Death* and *Dying at Grace* display the characteristics of cinema vérité listed by William Rothman, namely, the absence of screenplays and the filmmakers'

withdrawal from the worlds they portray (*The "I" of the Camera*, 282, 289–90). On Wiseman's style, see Nichols, "Fred Wiseman's Documentaries," 16–17.

12 King referred to his own films as "actuality dramas." See Dennis Lim, "A Second Look: Allan King's 'Actuality Dramas' Get a New Audience," *Los Angeles Times*, September 9, 2010, https://www.latimes.com/archives/la-xpm-2010-sep-19-la-ca -second-look-20100919-story.html.

13 Han and Das, "Introduction," 23. See also Han, "On Feelings and Finiteness in Everyday Life," 193; Cavell, *The Claim of Reason*, 308.

14 "Pilot," dir. Nicole Holofcener, *One Mississippi* (Amazon Prime Video, 2015).

15 Elias, "Essay on Laughter," 283.

16 The introduction to Lauren Berlant and Sianne Ngai's special issue of *Critical Inquiry* on comedy begins, "Comedy's pleasure comes in part from its ability to dispel anxiety, as so many of its theoreticians have noted, *but it doesn't simply do that*. As both an aesthetic mode and a form of life, its action just as likely produces anxiety: risking transgression, flirting with displeasure, or just confusing things in a way that both intensifies and impedes the pleasure. Comedy has issues" ("Comedy Has Issues," 233, emphasis added).

17 "Mother," dir. Dale Stern, *Veep* (HBO, 2016).

18 "The Concert," dir. Howard Deutch, *Getting On* (HBO, 2013).

19 Savell, "A Jurisprudence of Ambivalence," 53.

20 Savell, "A Jurisprudence of Ambivalence," 53. See also Seymour, "Revisiting Medicalisation and 'Natural' Death," 693.

21 Kastenbaum, "Psychological Death," 9, emphasis removed.

22 Kastenbaum, "Psychological Death," 15, emphasis removed. See also Kastenbaum, *The Psychology of Death*; Kastenbaum, *On Our Way*.

23 Freeman, "Death Perception," 9–12.

24 Freeman, "Death Perception," 9.

25 Freeman, "Death Perception," 10–11.

26 Ngai, *Theory of the Gimmick*, 1–3, 52–63.

27 Buchan, Gibson, and Ellison, "Reflections on the Death Scene," 4.

28 On breathing in cinema, specifically the relation between actor and spectator and the role of editors, directors of photography, and sound designers in shaping that relation, see Ferguson, "Painting in the Dark," 33; Greene, "The Labour of Breath," 112–13; Quinlivan, *The Place of Breath in Cinema*.

29 Drawing on Karl Abraham and Sigmund Freud, Elizabeth Wilson defines organ speech as a "biological performative" that, similarly to J. L. Austin's concept of performative utterance, "enacts the events it appears only to be symbolizing" (*Gut Feminism*, 76).

30 Fuchs, "The Feeling of Being Alive," 163.

31 Fuchs, "The Feeling of Being Alive," 163.

32 Thompson, *Mind in Life*, 37.

33 Fuchs, "The Feeling of Being Alive," 149.

34 Kastenbaum, "Psychological Death," 9, emphasis removed.

35 Janet Maslin, "Fredrick Wiseman's *Near Death*," *New York Times*, October 7, 1989,

http://www.nytimes.com/1989/10/07/movies/frederick-wiseman-s-near-death.html.

36 Schwartz, "Cinema and the Meaning of 'Life,'" 27.

37 Bazin, *What Is Cinema?*, 193.

38 Perez, *The Material Ghost*, 28.

39 Malkowski, *Dying in Full Detail*, esp. 3–8, 23–65.

40 Jaworski, "The Breath of Life and Death," 83.

41 Malkowski, *Dying in Full Detail*, 88. See also Aaron, *Death and the Moving Image*, 157–77.

42 Looking back on the making of *Dying at Grace*, King reported, "It was very difficult to find a place to film. Everybody wanted to watch over us to make sure we didn't injure somebody. The level of paranoia, the fear of filmmakers that has developed since I began is huge and almost crippling." King resorts to a disability analogy to describe his limited agency in a context where one workplace (the hospital) accommodates another (the film set), and one professional contingent (medical workers) is inconvenienced by the presence of another (crew members). So attached to the fiction that he is a victim of paranoia, King ignores that being invited to and remaining still within the deathbed scene depend largely on his social and economic status. In both *Dying at Grace* and *Near Death*, much of the work of adjusting respirators, measuring and reporting vital signs, reassuring patients, and accompanying relatives through the grieving process is performed by female-presenting nurses. In general, women of color are disproportionally expected to perform care work. The ability to capture the last breath in a medical setting isn't only a technical problem; it is also a labor question. Who, within the hospital room, is allowed to remain behind the camera without being asked to provide care? Glassman, "The POV Interview."

43 Glassman, "The POV Interview."

44 Malkowski, *Dying in Full Detail*, 105.

45 Chen, *Animacies*, 23.

46 Bersani, *Is the Rectum a Grave?*, 103.

47 Bersani, *Is the Rectum a Grave?*, 104.

48 Discourses that interpret the last breath as the swan song of a subject of consciousness mirror early modern poetry's fusion of the birth of consciousness and birth itself (the first breath). On the unlikely alignment of consciousness and natality in this poetry and in the Western philosophical tradition, see Harrison, *Coming To*, esp. 4–11, 235–43. In hinting at a speech act—"I leave peacefully"—in the absence of a speaking subject, the last breath concretizes the "impersonal enunciation" that, Christian Metz argues, all cinema allegorizes (*Impersonal Enunciation*, esp. 15–16).

49 Hume, "Of Suicide."

50 Kant, *Groundwork for the Metaphysics of Morals*, 47.

51 Kant, *Groundwork for the Metaphysics of Morals*, 47; Cholbi, "Kant and the Irrationality of Suicide," 159–60, 169; Clarke, "Autonomy, Rationality and the Wish to Die," 457–62.

52 Cowley, "Suicide Is Neither Rational nor Irrational."

53 Suicidality cannot be so easily brushed off in Peter Richardson's *How to Die in Oregon* (2011), a documentary about medical help in dying that follows individuals who face chronic pain or incurable diseases and choose to die, generally at home, through a lethal overdose of a prescribed substance. What difference exists between ingesting a lethal substance and being administered analgesic drugs to which one has consented? For one, lethal substances enable the dying to control their time of death with greater precision. What is more, even though, in both the medically assisted death and the nonviolent last breath, the ability to set the terms of one's passing are at stake, in the latter case it is the living who must ultimately endow the dying, now dead, with such an ability.

54 Malabou, *The New Wounded*, esp. 166–69.

55 Canguilhem, *The Normal and the Pathological*, 125–49.

56 Malabou, *Ontology of the Accident*.

57 François, *Open Secrets*, xvi.

58 Tercier, *The Contemporary Deathbed Documentary*, 20.

59 Tercier, *The Contemporary Deathbed Documentary*, 241.

Coda

Excerpts from Trisha Low's *Socialist Realism* (2019) are reproduced with the permission of Coffee House Books.

1 Rubin, *Deviations*, 154.

2 Rubin, *Deviations*, 151.

3 Rubin, *Deviations*, 149.

4 Rubin, *Deviations*, 154.

5 See Walters, "What the HIV/AIDS Pandemic Can Teach Us." On anti-Asian racism in the context of the coronavirus pandemic, see Lau, "On Virality, Corona or Otherwise." We may grasp xenophobic responses to the COVID-19 pandemic as the latest manifestation of what Hsuan L. Hsu terms "atmo-orientalism": "a discourse that frames Asiatic subjects (and particularly the Chinese) in terms of noxious atmospheres" (*The Smell of Risk*, 115). For a long history of pandemic discourses' marginalization of Asians and Asian Americans, see Kong, "Pandemic as Method."

6 See James Gorman, "Are Face Masks the New Condoms?," *New York Times*, April 18, 2020, https://www.nytimes.com/2020/04/18/health/coronavirus-mask-condom.html.

7 I address Low's ambivalent relation to New Narrative in Tremblay "Together, in the First Person." On Low's oscillation between conceptualism and confessionalism, see Siltanen, "Conceptual Confession."

8 Low, *Socialist Realism*, 112.

9 Low, *Socialist Realism*, 113–14.

10 Siebers, "A Sexual Culture for Disabled People," 39.

11 Siebers, "A Sexual Culture for Disabled People," 39. On disability justice's networks of care, see Piepzna-Samarasinha, *Care Work*, esp. 22, 33.

12 Alaimo, *Exposed*, esp. 17–40; Seymour, *Bad Environmentalism*, 23–24.

13 Cunsolo and Ellis, "Ecological Grief"; Albrecht, *Earth Emotions*, 27–62; Kaplan, *Climate Trauma*, 1, 40.

Aaron, Michele. *Death and the Moving Image: Ideology, Iconography and I.* Edinburgh: Edinburgh University Press, 2014.

Ahmann, Chloe, and Alison Kenner. "Breathing Late Industrialism." *Engaging Science, Technology, and Society* 6 (2020): 416–38.

Alaimo, Stacy. *Bodily Natures: Science, Environment, and the Material Self.* Bloomington: Indiana University Press, 2010.

Alaimo, Stacy. *Exposed: Environmental Politics and Pleasures in Posthuman Times.* Minneapolis: University of Minnesota Press, 2016.

Alaimo, Stacy. "Trans-corporeal Feminisms and the Ethical Space of Nature." In *Material Feminisms*, edited by Stacy Alaimo and Susan Heckman, 237–64. Bloomington: Indiana University Press, 2008.

Alaimo, Stacy. *Undomesticated Ground: Recasting Nature as Feminist Space.* Ithaca, NY: Cornell University Press, 2000.

Albrecht, Glenn. *Earth Emotions: New Words for a New World.* Ithaca, NY: Cornell University Press, 2019.

Allen, Pamela. *Free Space: A Perspective on the Small Group in Women's Liberation.* New York: Times Change, 1970.

Allen, Paula Gunn. *The Sacred Hoop: Recovering the Feminine in American Indian Traditions.* Boston: Beacon, 1986.

Alwes, Derek. "The Burden of Liberty: Choice in Toni Morrison's *Jazz* and Toni Cade Bambara's *The Salt Eaters.*" *African American Review* 30, no. 3 (1996): 353–65.

Amin, Kadji. *Disturbing Attachments: Genet, Modern Pederasty, and Queer History*. Durham, NC: Duke University Press, 2017.

Anderson, Reynaldo, and Charles E. Jones. "Introduction." In *Astro-Blackness*, edited by Reynaldo Anderson and Charles E. Jones, vii–xviii. Lanham, MD: Lexington, 2016.

Anzieu, Didier. *The Skin-Ego*. Translated by Naomi Segal. New York: Routledge, 2018.

Archibald, Matthew E. *The Evolution of Self-Help*. New York: Palgrave Macmillan, 2007.

Artaud, Antonin. *Le théâtre et son double, suivi de Le théâtre de Séraphin*. Paris: NRF Gallimard, 1964.

Bachelard, Gaston. *L'air et les songes: Essai sur l'imagination du mouvement*. Paris: Librairie José Corti, 1943.

Bailly, Jean-Christophe. "The Slightest Breath (On Living)." Translated by Matthew H. Anderson. *CR: The New Centennial Review* 10, no. 3 (2011): 1–11.

Balint, Michael. *The Basic Fault: Therapeutic Aspects of Regression*. London: Tavistock, 1968.

Bambara, Toni Cade. *Gorilla, My Love*. New York: Vintage, 1972.

Bambara, Toni Cade. Interview with Claudia Tate. In *Black Women Writers at Work*, edited by Claudia Tate, 12–37. London: Continuum, 1983.

Bambara, Toni Cade. "Preface." In *The Black Woman: An Anthology*, edited by Toni Cade Bambara, 7–12. Middlesex: Mentor, 1970.

Bambara, Toni Cade. *The Salt Eaters*. New York: Random House, 1980.

Bambara, Toni Cade. *The Sea Birds Are Still Alive: Collected Stories*. New York: Random House, 1977.

Bazin, André. *What Is Cinema?* Translated by Timothy Barnard. Montreal: Caboose, 2009.

Bell, Betty Louise. "Introduction: Linda Hogan's Lessons in Making Do." *Studies in American Indian Literatures* 6, no. 3 (1994): 3–5.

Bellamy, Dodie. *Academonia*. San Francisco: Krupskaya, 2006.

Bellamy, Dodie. *the buddhist*. San Francisco: Allone, 2012.

Bellamy, Dodie. *The Letters of Mina Harker*. Madison: University of Wisconsin Press, 2004.

Bellamy, Dodie. *The TV Sutras*. Brooklyn: Ugly Duckling Presse, 2014.

Bellamy, Dodie. *When the Sick Rule the World*. Los Angeles: Semiotext(e), 2015.

Bellamy, Dodie, and Kevin Killian. "Introduction." In Bellamy and Killian, *Writers Who Love Too Much*, i–xx.

Bellamy, Dodie, and Kevin Killian, eds. *Writers Who Love Too Much: New Narrative Writing 1977–1997*. New York: Nightboat, 2017.

Berardi, Franco "Bifo." *Breathing: Chaos and Poetry*. South Pasadena, CA: Semiotext(e), 2019.

Berlant, Lauren. "The Commons: Infrastructures for Troubling Times." *Environment and Planning D: Society and Space* 34, no. 3 (2016): 393–419.

Berlant, Lauren. *Cruel Optimism*. Durham, NC: Duke University Press, 2011.

Berlant, Lauren. *Desire/Love*. Brooklyn: Punctum, 2012.

Berlant, Lauren. *The Queen of America Goes to Washington City: Essays on Sex and Citizenship*. Durham, NC: Duke University Press, 1997.

Berlant, Lauren, and Lee Edelman. *Sex, or the Unbearable*. Durham, NC: Duke University Press, 2013.

Berlant, Lauren, and Sianne Ngai. "Comedy Has Issues." *Critical Inquiry* 43, no. 2 (2017): 233–49.

Bersani, Leo. *The Freudian Body: Psychoanalysis and Art*. New York: Columbia University Press, 1986.

Bersani, Leo. *Homos*. Cambridge, MA: Harvard University Press, 1995.

Bersani, Leo. *Is the Rectum a Grave? And Other Essays*. Chicago: University of Chicago Press, 2010.

Bersani, Leo, and Adam Phillips. *Intimacies*. Chicago: University of Chicago Press, 2008.

Best, Stephen, and Sharon Marcus. "Surface Reading: An Introduction." *Representations* 108, no. 1 (2009): 1–21.

Blas, Zach. "Opacities: An Introduction." *Camera Obscura* 31, no. 2 (2016): 149–53.

Blocker, Jane. *Where Is Ana Mendieta? Identity, Performativity, and Exile*. Durham, NC: Duke University Press, 1999.

Boyd, Valerie. "'She Was Just Outrageously Brilliant': Toni Morrison Remembers Toni Cade Bambara." In Holmes and Wall, *Savoring the Salt*, 88–99.

Bradway, Tyler. "Slow Burn: Dreadful Kinship and the Weirdness of Heterosexuality in *It Follows*." *Studies in the Fantastic*, no. 9 (2020): 122–44.

Braun, Lundy. *Breathing Race into the Machine: The Surprising Career of the Spirometer from Plantation to Genetics*. Minneapolis: University of Minnesota Press, 2014.

Brimblecombe, Peter. "Early Episodes." In *Air Pollution Episodes*, edited by Peter Brimblecombe, 11–26. Singapore: World Scientific, 2017.

Brookes, Tim. *Catching My Breath: An Asthmatic Explores His Illness*. New York: Random House, 1994.

Brugge, Doug, and Rob Goble. "A Documentary History of Uranium Mining and the Navajo People." In *The Navajo People and Uranium Mining*, edited by Doug Brugge, Esther Yazzie-Lewis, and Timothy H. Benally Sr., 25–47. Albuquerque: University of New Mexico Press, 2006.

Buchan, Bruce, Margaret Gibson, and David Ellison. "Reflections on the Death Scene." *Cultural Studies Review* 17, no. 1 (2010): 3–15.

Buell, Lawrence. *The Environmental Imagination: Thoreau, Nature Writing, and the Formation of American Culture*. Cambridge, MA: Belknap, 1995.

Buell, Lawrence. *The Future of Environmental Criticism: Environmental Crisis and Literary Imagination*. Malden, MA: Blackwell, 2005.

Buell, Lawrence. "Toxic Discourse." *Critical Inquiry* 21, no. 3 (1998): 639–65.

Butler-Evans, Elliott. *Race, Gender, and Desire: Narrative Strategies in the Fiction of Toni Cade Bambara, Toni Morrison, and Alice Walker*. Philadelphia: Temple University Press, 1989.

Buuck, David. "Dodie Bellamy by David Buuck." *BOMB*, January 1, 2014. https://bombmagazine.org/articles/dodie-bellamy/.

Buuck, David. *Site Cite City*. New York: Futurepoem, 2015.

Buuck, David. "A Walking Measure: Renee Gladman and City Writing." In Halpern and Tremblay-McGaw, *From Our Hearts to Yours*, 137–52.

Cain, Amina, and Renee Gladman. "Amina Cain and Renee Gladman" (interview). *BOMB*, November 21, 2013. https://bombmagazine.org/articles/amina-cain-renee-gladman/.

Calle, Sophie. "Lecture by Sophie Calle." Photography Lecture Series, California College of the Arts, San Francisco, March 30, 2011. https://www.youtube.com/watch?v=IMraLWWMvNw.

Cameron, Sharon. *Impersonality: Seven Essays*. Chicago: University of Chicago Press, 2007.

Campbell-Dollaghan, Kelsey. "5 Smart Building Skins That Breathe, Farm Energy, and Gobble Up Toxins." Gizmodo, September 5, 2013. http://gizmodo.com/5-smart-building-skins-that-breathe-farm-energy-and-g-1254091559.

Canguilhem, Georges. *The Normal and the Pathological*. Translated by Carolyn R. Fawcett and Robert S. Cohen. Brooklyn: Zone, 2007.

Carlsson, Mats. "The Gaze as Constituent and Annihilator." *Journal of Aesthetics and Culture* 4, no. 1 (2012): 1–7.

Carson, Rachel. *Silent Spring*. Boston: Houghton Mifflin, 2002.

Carter, J. Kameron, and Sarah Jane Cervenak. "Black Ether." *CR: The Centennial Review* 16, no. 2 (2016): 203–24.

Castra, Michel. *Bien mourir: Sociologie des soins palliatifs*. Paris: Presses Universitaires de France, 2003.

Cavarero, Adriana. *For More Than One Voice: Toward a Philosophy of Vocal Expression*. Translated by Paul A. Kottman. Stanford, CA: Stanford University Press, 2005.

Cavell, Stanley. *The Claim of Reason: Wittgenstein, Skepticism, Morality, and Tragedy*. New York: Oxford University Press, 2009.

Cella, Matthew J. C. "The Ecosomatic Paradigm in Literature: Merging Disability Studies and Ecocriticism." *ISLE: Interdisciplinary Studies in Literature and Environment* 20, no. 3 (2013): 574–96.

Cervenak, Sarah Jane. "'Black Night Is Falling': The Airy Poetics of Some Performance." *TDR: The Drama Review* 62, no. 1 (2018): 166–69.

Cha, Theresa Hak Kyung. *DICTEE*. 1982. Berkeley: University of California Press, 2001.

Chandler, Katherine R. "Terrestrial Spirituality." In Cook, *From the Center of Tradition*, 17–33.

Chen, Mel Y. *Animacies: Biopolitics, Racial Mattering, and Queer Affect*. Durham, NC: Duke University Press, 2012.

Chew, Dalglish, and Julie Orlemanski, eds. "We, Reading, Now" (colloquy). *Arcade*, 2015–16. http://arcade.stanford.edu/colloquies/we-reading-now.

Chisholm, Dianne. *Queer Constellations: Subcultural Spaces in the Wake of the City*. Minneapolis: University of Minnesota Press, 2005.

Cholbi, Michael J. "Kant and the Irrationality of Suicide." *History of Philosophy Quarterly* 17, no. 2 (2000): 159–67.

Chowkwanyun, Merlin, and Adolph L. Reed Jr. "Racial Health Disparities and Covid-19—Caution and Context." *New England Journal of Medicine* 383, no. 3 (2020): 201–3. https://www.nejm.org/doi/full/10.1056/NEJMp2012910.

Choy, Tim. "A Commentary: Breathing Together Now." *Engaging Science, Technology, and Society* 6 (2020): 586–90.

Choy, Tim. *Ecologies of Comparison: An Ethnography of Endangerment in Hong Kong.* Durham, NC: Duke University Press, 2011.

Christian, Margareta Ingrid. *"Aer, Aurae, Venti*: Philology and Physiology in Aby Warburg's Dissertation on Botticelli." *PMLA* 129, no. 3 (2014): 399–416.

Clare, Eli. *Brilliant Imperfection: Grappling with Cure.* Durham, NC: Duke University Press, 2017.

Clark, Nigel, and Kathryn Yusoff. "Queer Fire: Ecology, Combustion and Pyrosexual Desire." *Feminist Review* 118, no. 1 (2018): 7–24.

Clarke, David M. "Autonomy, Rationality and the Wish to Die." *Journal of Medical Ethics* 25, no. 6 (1999). 457–62.

Clemmons, Zinzi. "Where Is Our Black Avant-Garde?" *Literary Hub*, January 29, 2016. https://lithub.com/where-is-our-black-avant-garde/.

Clough, Patricia Ticineto. *Autoaffection: Unconscious Thought in the Age of Teletechnology.* Minneapolis: University of Minnesota Press, 2000.

Cohen, Cathy. "Punks, Bulldaggers, and Welfare Queens: The Radical Potential of Queer Politics?" *GLQ* 3, no. 4 (1997): 437–65.

Collins, Janelle. "Generating Power: Fission, Fusion, and Postmodern Politics in Bambara's *The Salt Eaters*." *MELUS* 21, no. 2 (1996): 35–47.

Comer, Todd A. "Playing at Birth: Samuel R. Delany's *Dhalgren*." *JNT: Journal of Narrative Theory* 25, no. 2 (2005): 172–95.

Connor, Steven. *The Matter of Air: Science and the Art of the Ethereal.* London: Reaktion, 2010.

Conrad, CA. *A Beautiful Marsupial Afternoon: New (Soma)tics.* Seattle: Wave, 2012.

Conrad, CA. *The Book of Frank.* Tucson, AZ: Chax, 2009.

Conrad, CA. *Ecodeviance: (Soma)tics for the Future Wilderness.* Seattle: Wave, 2014.

Conrad, CA. *While Standing in Line for Death.* Seattle: Wave, 2017.

Conrad, CA. *WRITING IN ALL CAPS IS THE BREATH MINT OF THE SOUL: PROSE POEMS OR SOMETHING.* Portland, OR: Bone Tax, 2014.

Cook, Barbara J. "From the Center of Tradition: An Interview with Linda Hogan." In Cook, *From the Center of Tradition*, 11–16.

Cook, Barbara J., ed. *From the Center of Tradition: Critical Perspectives on Linda Hogan.* Boulder: University of Colorado Press, 2003.

Cornell, Drucilla. "Las Greñudas: Recollections on Consciousness-Raising." *Signs* 25, no. 4 (2000): 1033–39.

Corton, Christine L. *London Fog: The Biography.* Cambridge, MA: Belknap, 2015.

Coviello, Peter. "The Wild Not Less Than the Good: Thoreau, Sex, Biopower." *GLQ* 23, no. 4 (2017): 509–32.

Cowley, Christopher. "Suicide Is Neither Rational nor Irrational." *Ethical Theory and Moral Practice* 9, no. 5 (2006): 495–504.

Crawley, Ashon. *Blackpentecostal Breath: The Aesthetics of Possibility.* New York: Fordham University Press, 2016.

Crawley, Ashon. *The Lonely Letters.* Durham, NC: Duke University Press, 2020.

Cronon, William. "The Trouble with Wilderness: Or, Getting Back to the Wrong Nature." *Environmental History* 1, no. 1 (1996): 7–28.

Cruz, Carlos A. "Ana Mendieta's Art: A Journey through Her Life." In *Latina Legacies: Identity, Biography, and Community*, edited by Vicki L. Ruiz and Virginia Sanchez Korrol, 225–39. Oxford: Oxford University Press, 2005.

Csikszentmihalyi, Mihaly. *Flow: The Psychology of Optimal Experience.* New York: Harper and Row, 2008.

Cunsolo, Ashlee, and Neville Ellis. "Ecological Grief as Mental-Health Response to Climate Change–Related Loss." *Nature Climate Change* 8, no. 4 (2018): 275–81.

Daly, Mary. *Gyn/Ecology: The Metaethics of Radical Feminism.* Boston: Beacon, 1990.

Daly, Mary. *Pure Lust: Elemental Feminist Philosophy.* Boston: Beacon, 1984.

de Beauvoir, Simone. *Une mort très douce.* Paris: Gallimard, 1964.

de Beauvoir, Simone. *A Very Easy Death.* Translated by Patrick O'Brian. New York: Pantheon, 1985.

Delany, Samuel R. *Dhalgren.* New York: Vintage, 2001.

Delany, Samuel R. *Times Square Red, Times Square Blue.* New York: New York University Press, 1999.

DeLillo, Don. *White Noise.* New York: Penguin, 1999.

Derrida, Jacques. "Economimesis." In *Mimesis des articulations*, edited by Sylviane Agacinski, 57–93. Paris: Aubier-Flammarion, 1975.

Derrida, Jacques. *Of Grammatology.* Translated by Gayatri Chakravorty Spivak. Baltimore: Johns Hopkins University Press, 1976.

Derrida, Jacques. *On Touching—Jean-Luc Nancy.* Translated by Christine Irizarry. Stanford, CA: Stanford University Press, 2005.

Derrida, Jacques, and Paule Thévenin. *The Secret Art of Antonin Artaud.* Translated by Mary Ann Caws. Cambridge, MA: MIT Press, 1998.

Dery, Mark. "Black to the Future: Interviews with Samuel R. Delany, Greg Tate, and Tricia Rose." In *Flame Wars: The Discourse of Cyberculture*, edited by Mark Dery, 179–222. Durham, NC: Duke University Press, 1994.

Diffrient, David Scott. "Dead, but Still Breathing: The Problem of Postmortem Movement in Horror Films." *New Review of Film and Television Studies* 16, no. 2 (2018): 98–122.

DiFrancesco, Alex. "The Shifting Literary and Ecological Landscapes of Renee Gladman's *Calamities.*" *Ploughshares*, September 30, 2018. http://blog.pshares.org/index.php/the-shifting-literary-and-ecological-landscapes-of-renee-gladmans-calamities/.

Dillon, Lindsey, and Julie Sze. "Police Power and Particulate Matters: Environmental Justice and the Spatialities of In/Securities in U.S. Cities." *English Language Notes* 54, no. 2 (2016): 13–23.

Diouf, Mamadou, and Ifeoma Kiddoe Nwankwo. *Rhythms of the Afro-Atlantic World: Rituals and Remembrances.* Ann Arbor: University of Michigan Press, 2010.

Doroteo, Jan. "Let Your Building 'Breathe' with This Pneumatic Façade Technology." *ArchDaily*, June 11, 2016. http://www.archdaily.com/789230/let-your-building-to-breathe-with-this-pneumatic-facade-technology.

Doyle, Jennifer. *Campus Sex, Campus Security.* Los Angeles: Semiotext(e), 2015.

Doyle, Jennifer. "Dirt Off Her Shoulders." *GLQ* 19, no. 4 (2013): 419–33.

Doyle, Jennifer. *Hold It against Me: Difficulty and Emotion in Performance Art*. Durham, NC: Duke University Press, 2013.

Doyle, Jennifer. *Sex Objects: Art and the Dialectics of Desire*. Minneapolis: University of Minnesota Press, 2006.

Drury, Nevill. *The New Age: The History of a Movement*. New York: Thames and Hudson, 2004.

Dudley, Donald L. "MCS: Trial by Science." In *Defining Multiple Chemical Sensitivity*, edited by Bonnye L. Matthews, 9–26. Jefferson, NC: McFarland, 1998.

Duncan, Isadora. "The Dance of the Future." In *What Is Dance?*, edited by Roger Copeland and Marshall Cohen, 262–63. Oxford: Oxford University Press, 1983.

Du Pisani, Jacobus A. "Sustainable Development: Historical Roots of the Concept." *Environmental Sciences* 3, no. 2 (2006): 83–96.

Edelman, Lee. *No Future: Queer Theory and the Death Drive*. Durham, NC: Duke University Press, 2004.

Eigen, Michael. *Damaged Bonds*. London: Karnac, 2001.

Eigen, Michael. *Toxic Nourishment*. London: Karnac, 1999.

Elias, Norbert. "Essay on Laughter." Edited by Anca Parvulescu. *Critical Inquiry* 43, no. 2 (2017): 281–304.

Elliott, Jane. "The Currency of Feminist Theory." *PMLA* 121, no. 5 (2006): 1697–703.

Emerson, Ralph Waldo. *Nature*. Boston: Beacon, 1985.

Emerson, Ralph Waldo. *The Portable Emerson*. Edited by Jeffrey S. Cramer. New York: Penguin, 2014.

Eng, David L. *The Feeling of Kinship: Queer Liberalism and the Racialization of Intimacy*. Durham, NC: Duke University Press, 2010.

Engelmann, Sasha. "Toward a Poetics of Air: Sequencing and Surfacing Breath." *Transactions* 40, no. 3 (2015): 430–44.

Ephron, Nora. *"Crazy Salad: Some Things about Women" and "Scribble Scribble: Notes on the Media."* New York: Vintage, 2012.

Erevelles, Nirmala. *Disability and Difference in Global Contexts: Enabling a Transformative Body Politic*. New York: Palgrave Macmillan, 2011.

Fanon, Frantz. *Black Skin, White Masks*. Translated by Charles Lam Markmann. New York: Grove, 1967.

Fanon, Frantz. *A Dying Colonialism*. Translated by Haakon Chevalier. New York: Grove, 1967.

Fay, Jennifer. *Inhospitable World: Cinema in the Time of the Anthropocene*. New York: Oxford University Press, 2018.

Federici, Silvia. *Caliban and the Witch: Women, the Body, and Primitive Accumulation*. Oakland, CA: AK Press, 2004.

Feigenbaum, Anna. *Tear Gas: From the Battlefields of World War I to the Streets of Today*. New York: Verso, 2017.

Ferguson, Kevin L. "Painting in the Dark: The Ambivalence of Air in Cinema." *Camera Obscura* 26, no. 2 (2011): 33–63.

Ferguson, Roderick A. *Aberrations in Black: Toward a Queer of Color Critique*. Minneapolis: University of Minnesota Press, 2004.

Feron, Étienne. "Respiration et action chez Lévinas." *Phénoménologie et Poétique* 3, nos. 5–6 (1987): 193–213.

Firestone, Shulamith. *Airless Spaces.* Los Angeles: Semiotext(e), 1998.

Firestone, Shulamith. *The Dialectic of Sex: The Case for Feminist Revolution.* New York: Farrar, Straus and Giroux, 1970.

Flanagan, Bob. "Book of Medicines." In Bellamy and Killian, *Writers Who Love Too Much,* 433–42.

Flanagan, Bob. *Fuck Journal.* New York: Hanuman, 1987.

Flanagan, Bob. *The Kid Is the Man.* Hermosa Beach, CA: Bombshelter, 1978.

Flanagan, Bob. *The Pain Journal.* Los Angeles: Semiotext(e) and Smart Art, 2000.

Flanagan, Bob. "S." *Frame/Work: The Journal of Images and Culture* 5, nos. 2–3 (1992): 24–30.

Flanagan, Bob. *Slave Sonnets.* Los Angeles: Cold Calm, 1986.

Flanagan, Bob. *The Wedding of Everything.* Los Angeles: Sherwood, 1983.

Flanagan, Bob, Sheree Rose, and Ralph Rugoff. "Visiting Hours." *Grand Street,* no. 53 (1995): 65–73.

Flatley, Jonathan. *Affective Mapping: Melancholia and the Politics of Modernism.* Cambridge, MA: Harvard University Press, 2008.

Foucault, Michel. *Histoire de la sexualité 3: Le souci de soi.* Paris: Gallimard, 1984.

Fradenburg, L. O. Aranye. "Breathing with Lacan's Seminar X: Expression and Emergence." In *Staying Alive: A Survival Manual for the Liberal Arts,* by L. O. Aranye Fradenburg, edited by Eileen A. Joy, 163–92. New York: Punctum, 2013.

François, Anne-Lise. *Open Secrets: The Literature of Uncounted Experience.* Stanford, CA: Stanford University Press, 2007.

Freedman, Estelle B. *Feminism, Sexuality, and Politics.* Chapel Hill: University of North Carolina Press, 2006.

Freedman, Janet L. *Reclaiming the Feminist Vision: Consciousness-Raising and Small Group Practice.* Jefferson, NC: McFarland, 2014.

Freeman, Elizabeth. *Time Binds: Queer Temporalities, Queer Histories.* Durham, NC: Duke University Press, 2020.

Freeman, Thomas B. "Death Perception: How Temporary Ventilator Disconnection Helped My Family Accept Brain Death and Donate Organs." *Narrative Inquiry in Bioethics* 5, no. 1 (2015): 9–12.

Freudenthal, Gad. *Aristotle's Theory of Material Substance: Heat and Pneuma, Form and Soul.* Oxford: Clarendon, 1995.

Friedan, Betty. *It Changed My Life: Writings on the Women's Movement.* New York: Random House, 1976.

Fuchs, Thomas. "The Feeling of Being Alive: Organic Foundations of Self-Awareness." In *Feelings of Being Alive,* edited by Joerg Fingerhut and Sabine Marienberg, 149–65. Boston: De Gruyter, 2012.

Garland-Thomson, Rosemarie. "Seeing the Disabled: Visual Rhetorics of Disability in Popular Photography." In *The New Disability History,* edited by Paul K. Longmore and Lauri Umansky, 335–74. New York: New York University Press, 2001.

Garland-Thomson, Rosemarie. "Staring Back: Self-Representations of Disabled Performance Artists." *American Quarterly* 52, no. 2 (2000): 334–38.

Ghosh, Amitav. "Petrofiction." *New Republic*, March 2, 1992, 29–34.

Gibson, Ross. "Breathing Looking Thinking Acting." *Humanities Australia* 4 (2013): 17–24.

Gifford, Terry. "Gods of Mud: Hughes and the Post-pastoral." In *The Challenge of Ted Hughes*, edited by Keith Sagar, 129–41. London: Macmillan, 1994.

Gifford, Terry. "Judith Wright's Poetry and the Turn to the Post-pastoral." *Australian Humanities Review*, no. 48 (2010): 75–85.

Gifford, Terry. *Pastoral*. New York: Routledge, 1999.

Gifford, Terry. "Pastoral, Anti-pastoral, and Post-pastoral." In *The Cambridge Companion to Literature and the Environment*, edited by Louise Westling, 17–30. Cambridge: Cambridge University Press, 2014.

Gill-Peterson, Jules. "The Miseducation of a French Feminist." *e-flux Journal*, no. 117 (April 2021). https://www.e-flux.com/journal/117/382426/the-miseducation-of-a-french-feminist/.

Gladman, Renee. *Ana Patova Crosses a Bridge*. Urbana, IL: Dorothy, 2013.

Gladman, Renee. *Calamities*. Seattle: Wave, 2016.

Gladman, Renee. *Event Factory*. Urbana, IL: Dorothy, 2010.

Gladman, Renee. *Houses of Ravicka*. St. Louis: Dorothy, 2017.

Gladman, Renee. Interview with the editors of *HAUS RED*. *HAUS RED* 2 (2019): 8–18.

Gladman, Renee. *Morelia*. New York: Solid Objects, 2019.

Gladman, Renee. "The Person in the World." In *Biting the Error: Writers Explore Narrative*, edited by Mary Burger, 46–48. Toronto: Coach House, 2004.

Gladman, Renee. *Prose Architectures*. Seattle: Wave, 2017.

Gladman, Renee. *The Ravickians*. Urbana, IL: Dorothy, 2011.

Gladman, Renee. "The Sentence as a Space for Living: Prose Architecture." *Tripwire: A Journal of Poetics*, no. 15 (2019): 91–110.

Glassman, Marc. "The POV Interview: Allan King, the King of Vérité." *POV: Point of View Magazine*, accessed December 4, 2020. https://web.archive.org/web/20201204111333/http://povmagazine.com/articles/view/the-pov-interview-allan-king.

Glissant, Édouard. *Poetics of Relation*. Translated by Betsy Wing. Ann Arbor: University of Michigan Press, 1997.

Glissant, Édouard. *Poétique de la relation*. Paris: Gallimard, 1990.

Glück, Robert. *Communal Nude: Collected Essays*. South Pasadena, CA: Semiotext(e), 2016.

Godart, Caroline. "Silence and Sexual Difference: Reading Silence in Luce Irigaray." *Journal of Diversity and Gender Studies* 3, no. 2 (2016): 9–22.

Goeman, Mishuana R., and Jennifer Nez Denetdale. "Native Feminisms: Legacies, Interventions, and Indigenous Sovereignties." *Wicazo Sa Review* 24, no. 2 (2009): 9–13.

Goodstein, Elizabeth S. *Experience without Qualities: Boredom and Modernity*. Stanford, CA: Stanford University Press, 2005.

Gordon, Avery F. "Something More Powerful Than Skepticism." In Holmes and Wall, *Savoring the Salt*, 187–236.

Górska, Magdalena. *Breathing Matters: Feminist Intersectional Politics of Vulnerability*. Linköping, Sweden: Linköping University Electronic Press, 2016.

Grammatikopoulou, Christina. "Theatre Minus Representation: Breath, Body, and Emotion in Antonin Artaud." *Interartive*, no. 81 (February 2016). https://interartive .org/2016/02/theatre-minus-representation-breath-body-and-emotion-in-antonin -artaud-christina-grammatikopoulou.

Greene, Liz. "The Labour of Breath: Performing and Designing Breath in Cinema." *Music, Sound, and the Moving Image* 10, no. 2 (2016): 109–33.

Greenfield, Amy. "The Kinesthetics of Avant-Garde Dance: Deren and Harris." In *Envisioning Dance on Film and Video*, edited by Judy Mitoma and Elizabeth Zimmer, 21–26. New York: Routledge, 2000.

Griefen, Kat. "Ana Mendieta at A.I.R. Gallery, 1977–82." *Women and Performance: a journal of feminist theory* 21, no. 2 (2011): 171–81.

Griffin, Farah Jasmine. "Toni Cade Bambara: Free to Be Anywhere in the Universe." *Callaloo* 19, no. 2 (1996): 229–31.

Grobe, Christopher. *The Art of Confession: The Performance of Self from Robert Lowell to Reality TV*. New York: New York University Press, 2017.

Grosz, Elizabeth. *Architecture from the Outside: Essays on Virtual and Real Space*. Cambridge, MA: MIT Press, 2001.

Grosz, Elizabeth. *Time Travels: Feminism, Nature, Power*. Durham, NC: Duke University Press, 2005.

"Guide to Consciousness-Raising." In *Women's Liberation in the Twentieth Century*, edited by Mary C. Lynn, 111–18. New York: John Wiley, 1975.

Gumbs, Alexis Pauline. *Dub: Finding Ceremony*. Durham, NC: Duke University Press, 2020.

Gumbs, Alexis Pauline. *M Archive: After the End of the World*. Durham, NC: Duke University Press, 2018.

Gumbs, Alexis Pauline. *Spill: Scenes of Black Feminist Fugitivity*. Durham, NC: Duke University Press, 2016.

Gumbs, Alexis Pauline, China Martens, and Mai'a Williams, eds. *Revolutionary Mothering: Love on the Front Lines*. Oakland, CA: PM Press, 2016.

Guy-Sheftall, Beverly. "Toni Cade Bambara, Black Feminist Foremother." In Holmes and Wall, *Savoring the Salt*, 115–26.

Halberstam, Jack. "Go Gaga: Anarchy, Chaos, and the Wild." *Social Text* 31, no. 3 (2013): 123–34.

Haller, Robert. *Flesh into Light: The Films of Amy Greenfield*. Chicago: University of Chicago Press, 2012.

Halpern, Orit. *Beautiful Data: A History of Vision and Reason since 1945*. Durham, NC: Duke University Press, 2015.

Halpern, Rob. "'Where No Meaning Is': Appropriation and Scandal in the Writing of Robert Glück." In Halpern and Tremblay-McGaw, *From Our Hearts to Yours*, 219–32.

Halpern, Rob, and Robin Tremblay-McGaw, eds. *From Our Hearts to Yours: New Narrative as Contemporary Practice*. Oakland: ON Contemporary Practice, 2017.

Halpern, Rob, and Robin Tremblay-McGaw. "'A Generosity of Response': New Narrative as Contemporary Practice." In Halpern and Tremblay-McGaw, *From Our Hearts to Yours*, 7–16.

Han, Clara. "On Feelings and Finiteness in Everyday Life." In *Wording the World: Veena Das and Scenes of Inheritance*, edited by Roma Chatterji, 191–210. New York: Fordham University Press, 2015.

Han, Clara, and Veena Das. "Introduction: A Concept Note." In *Living and Dying in the Contemporary World: A Compendium*, edited by Clara Han and Veena Das, 1–37. Berkeley: University of California Press, 2016.

Hanisch, Carol. "The Personal Is Political." In Sarachild, *Feminist Revolution*, 204–5.

Haraway, Donna J. *Staying with the Trouble: Making Kin in the Chthulucene*. Durham, NC: Duke University Press, 2016.

Harries, Martin. *Forgetting Lot's Wife: On Destructive Spectatorship*. New York: Fordham University Press, 2012.

Harris, Kaplan Page. "Avant-Garde Interrupted: A New Narrative after AIDS." *Contemporary Literature* 52, no. 4 (2011): 630–57.

Harris, Kaplan Page. "New Narrative and the Making of Language Poetry." *American Literature* 81, no. 4 (2009): 805–32.

Harrison, Timothy M. *Coming To: Consciousness and Natality in Early Modern England*. Chicago: University of Chicago Press, 2020.

Heathfield, Adrian. "Embers." In Rosenthal, *Traces*, 21–37.

Heine, Stefanie. *Poetics of Breathing: Modern Literature's Syncope*. Albany: State University of New York Press, 2021.

Heise, Ursula K. *Sense of Place and Sense of Planet: The Environmental Imagination of the Global*. Oxford: Oxford University Press, 2008.

Hinrichs, Roger A., and Merlin Kleinbach. *Energy: Its Uses and the Environment*. Boston: Brooks/Cole, 2013.

Hockey, Jennifer Lorna. *Experiences of Death: An Anthropological Account*. Edinburgh: Edinburgh University Press, 1990.

Hogan, Linda. *Dark. Sweet. New and Selected Poems*. Minneapolis: Coffee House, 2014.

Hogan, Linda. *Dwellings: A Spiritual History of the Living World*. New York: Norton, 1995.

Hogan, Linda. *The Woman Who Watches Over the World: A Native Memoir*. New York: Norton, 2001.

Holmes, Brooke. *The Symptom and the Subject: The Emergence of the Physical Body in Ancient Greece*. Princeton, NJ: Princeton University Press, 2010.

Holmes, Janet, and Cheryl A. Wall, eds. *Savoring the Salt: The Legacy of Toni Cade Bambara*. Philadelphia: Temple University Press, 2007.

hooks, bell. *Feminism Is for Everybody: Passionate Politics*. Boston: South End, 2000.

Howard, Yetta. "Introduction: Performing the Minority Body Archive across Time and Sheree Rose's Legacy in Underground History." In Howard, *Rated RX*, 1–21.

Howard, Yetta, ed. *Rated RX: Sheree Rose with and after Bob Flanagan*. Columbus: Ohio State University Press, 2020.

Howarth, Glennys. *Death and Dying: A Sociological Introduction*. Cambridge: Polity, 2007.

Hsu, Hsuan L. *The Smell of Risk: Environmental Disparities and Olfactory Aesthetics*. New York: New York University Press, 2020.

Hull, Gloria T. "What It Is I Think She's Doing Anyhow: A Reading of Toni Cade Bambara's *The Salt Eaters*." In Smith, *Home Girls*, 124–42.

Hume, David. "Of Suicide." Hume Texts Online, Royal Society of Edinburgh, accessed September 3, 2021. https://davidhume.org/texts/su/.

Hurley, Jessica. *Infrastructures of Apocalypse: American Literature and the Nuclear Complex.* Minneapolis: University of Minnesota Press, 2020.

Hyacinthe, Genevieve. *Radical Virtuosity: Ana Mendieta and the Black Atlantic.* Cambridge, MA: MIT Press, 2019.

Irigaray, Luce. "The Age of Breath." Translated by Katja van de Rakt, Staci Boeckman, and Luce Irigaray. In Luce Irigaray, *Key Writings*, 165–70. London: Continuum, 2004.

Irigaray, Luce. *Elemental Passions.* Translated by Joanne Collie and Judith Still. New York: Routledge, 1992.

Irigaray, Luce. *Être deux.* Paris: Grasset, 1994.

Irigaray, Luce. *The Forgetting of Air in Martin Heidegger.* Translated by Mary Beth Mader. Austin: University of Texas Press, 1999.

Irigaray, Luce. *L'oubli de l'air chez Martin Heidegger.* Paris: Éditions de Minuit, 1983.

Irigaray, Luce. *Marine Lover of Friedrich Nietzsche.* Translated by Gillian Gill. New York: Columbia University Press, 1991.

Irigaray, Luce. *Sharing the Fire: Outline of a Dialectics of Sensitivity.* New York: Palgrave Macmillan, 2019.

Irigaray, Luce. *To Be Two.* Translated by Monique M. Rhodes and Marco F. Cocito-Monoc. New York: Routledge, 2001.

Irigaray, Luce, and Michael Marder. *Through Vegetal Being: Two Philosophical Perspectives.* New York: Columbia University Press, 2016.

Jackson, Zakiyyah Iman. *Becoming Human: Matter and Meaning in an Antiblack World.* New York: New York University Press, 2020.

Jameson, Fredric. *Postmodernism, or, The Cultural Logic of Late Capitalism.* Durham, NC: Duke University Press, 1992.

Jaworski, Katrina. "The Breath of Life and Death." *Cultural Critique* 86 (2014): 65–91.

Jerng, Mark Chia-Yon. "A World of Difference: Samuel R. Delany's *Dhalgren* and the Protocols of Racial Reading." *American Literature* 83, no. 2 (2011): 251–78.

Johnson, Dominic. *The Art of Living: An Oral History of Performance Art.* New York: Palgrave, 2015.

Johnson, E. Patrick. "Black Performance Studies: Genealogies, Politics, Futures." In *The Sage Handbook of Performance Studies*, edited by Judith Hamera and D. Soyini Madison, 446–63. Thousand Oaks: Sage, 2006.

Johnson, E. Patrick. "'Quare' Studies, or (Almost) Everything I Know about Queer Studies I Learned from My Grandmother." *Text and Performance Quarterly* 21, no. 1 (2001): 1–25.

Johnson, Valerie Ann. "Bringing Together Feminist Disability Studies and Environmental Justice." In Ray and Sibara, *Disability Studies and the Environmental Humanities*, 73–93.

Jones, Amelia. *Body Art/Performing the Subject.* Minneapolis: University of Minnesota Press, 1998.

Jones, Ian Bryce. "Do(n't) Hold Your Breath: Rules, Trust, and the Human at the Keyboard." *New Review of Film and Television Studies* 16, no. 2 (2018): 162–83.

Jue, Melody. *Wild Blue Media: Thinking through Seawater*. Durham, NC: Duke University Press, 2020.

Juno, Andrea, and V. Vale, eds. *Bob Flanagan: Supermasochist*. New York: Re/Search People Series, 2000.

Kafer, Alison. "Bodies of Nature: The Environmental Politics of Disability." In Ray and Sibara, *Disability Studies and the Environmental Humanities*, 201-41.

Kafer, Alison. *Feminist, Queer, Crip*. Bloomington: Indiana University Press, 2013.

Kalanithi, Paul. *When Breath Becomes Air*. New York: Random House, 2016.

Kant, Immanuel. *Critique of the Power of Judgment*. Edited by Paul Guyer. Translated by Paul Guyer and Eric Matthews. Cambridge: Cambridge University Press, 2000.

Kant, Immanuel. *Groundwork for the Metaphysics of Morals*. Edited and translated by Allen W. Wood. New Haven, CT: Yale University Press, 2002.

Kaplan, E. Ann. *Climate Trauma: Foreseeing the Future in Dystopian Film and Fiction*. New Brunswick, NJ: Rutgers University Press, 2015.

Kastenbaum, Robert. *On Our Way: The Final Passage through Life and Death*. Berkeley: University of California Press, 2004.

Kastenbaum, Robert. "Psychological Death." In *Death and Dying: Current Issues in the Treatment of the Dying Person*, edited by Leonard Pearson, 1-27. Cleveland: Press of Case Western Reserve University, 1969.

Kastenbaum, Robert. *The Psychology of Death*, 3rd ed. New York: Springer, 2000.

Kauffman, Linda S. *Bad Girls and Sick Boys: Fantasies in Contemporary Art and Culture*. Berkeley: University of California Press, 1998.

Kean, Sam. *Caesar's Last Breath: Decoding the Secrets of the Air around Us*. New York: Little, Brown, 2017.

Kelley, Margot Anne. "'Damballah Is the First Law of Thermodynamics': Modes of Access to Toni Cade Bambara's *The Salt Eaters*." *African American Review* 27, no. 3 (1993): 479-93.

Kenner, Alison. *Breathtaking: Asthma Care in a Time of Climate Change*. Minneapolis: University of Minnesota Press, 2018.

Kiechle, Melanie A. *Smell Detectives: An Olfactory History of Nineteenth-Century Urban America*. Seattle: University of Washington Press, 2019.

Killian, Kevin. "Sex Writing and the New Narrative." In Bellamy and Killian, *Writers Who Love Too Much*, 292-95.

Kim, Annabel L. *Unbecoming Language: Anti-identitarian French Feminist Fictions*. Columbus: Ohio State University Press, 2018.

Kim, Myung Mi, and Cristanne Miller, eds. *Poetics and Precarity*. Albany: State University of New York Press, 2018.

Kong, Belinda. "Pandemic as Method." *Prism* 16, no. 2 (2019): 368-89.

Krauthamer, Barbara. *Black Slaves, Indian Masters: Slavery, Emancipation, and Citizenship*. Chapel Hill: University of North Carolina Press, 2013.

Kressbach, Mikki. "Breath Work: Mediating Health through Breathing Apps and Wearable Technologies." *New Review of Film and Television Studies* 16, no. 2 (2018): 184-206.

Kristeva, Julia. *Powers of Horror: An Essay on Abjection*. Translated by Leon S. Roudiez. New York: Columbia University Press, 1982.

Kuppers, Petra. *The Scar of Visibility: Medical Performances and Contemporary Art.* Minneapolis: University of Minnesota Press, 2006.

Kyle, Richard. *The New Age Movement in American Culture.* New York: University Press of America, 1995.

Lacan, Jacques. *Le séminaire de Jacques Lacan: Livre II, Les quatre concepts fondamentaux de la psychanalyse.* Paris: Seuil, 1973.

Lacan, Jacques. *Le séminaire de Jacques Lacan: Livre 23, Le sinthome.* Paris: Seuil, 2005.

LaFleur, Greta. *The Natural History of Sexuality in Early America.* Baltimore: Johns Hopkins University Press, 2018.

Laird, Paul R. "Musical Styles and Song Conventions." In *The Oxford Handbook of the American Musical,* edited by Raymond Knapp, Mitchell Morris, and Stacy Wolf, 33–44. Oxford: Oxford University Press, 2011.

Laplanche, Jean, and Jean-Bertrand Pontalis. "Fantasy and the Origins of Sexuality." *International Journal of Psychoanalysis* 49, no. 1 (1968): 1–18.

Lasky, Dorothea. "Poetry Is Not a Project." Brooklyn: Ugly Duckling Presse, 2011. https://issuu.com/uglyducklingpresse/docs/poetry_is_not_a_project_ebook.

Lau, Travis Chi Wing. "On Virality, Corona or Otherwise." *Synapsis,* May 15, 2020. https://medicalhealthhumanities.com/2020/05/15/on-virality-corona-or-otherwise/.

Leder, Drew. *The Absent Body.* Chicago: University of Chicago Press, 1990.

Lefebvre, Henri. *The Social Production of Space.* Translated by Donald Nicholson-Smith. Malden, MA: Blackwell, 1974.

Le Guin, Ursula K. *The Left Hand of Darkness.* 1976. New York: Ace, 2010.

León, Christina A. "Forms of Opacity: Roaches, Blood, and Being Stuck in Xandra Ibarra's Corpus." *ASAP/Journal* 2, no. 2 (2017): 369–94.

León, Christina A. "Trace Alignment: Object Relations after Ana Mendieta." *Post45 Contemporaries,* December 9, 2019. https://post45.org/2019/12/trace-alignment-object-relations-after-ana-mendieta/.

Lévinas, Emmanuel. *Otherwise Than Being, or Beyond Essence.* Translated by Alphonso Lingis. Pittsburgh: Duquesne University Press, 1998.

Lewis, Jayne Elizabeth. *Air's Appearance: Literary Atmosphere in British Fiction, 1660–1794.* Chicago: University of Chicago Press, 2012.

Liboiron, Max. *Pollution Is Colonialism.* Durham, NC: Duke University Press, 2021.

Lorenz, Renate. *Queer Art: A Freak Theory.* Translated by Daniel Hendrickson. London: Transcript Verlag, 2012.

Low, Trisha. *Socialist Realism.* Minneapolis: Coffee House, 2019.

Mackey, Nathaniel. "Breath and Precarity." In Kim and Miller, *Poetics and Precarity,* 1–30.

Mackey, Nathaniel. *Discrepant Engagement: Dissonance, Cross-culturality, and Experimental Writing.* Cambridge: Cambridge University Press, 1993.

Macnaughton, Jane. "Making Breath Visible: Reflections on Relations between Bodies, Breath and World in the Critical Medical Humanities." *Body and Society* 26, no. 2 (2020): 30–54.

Malabou, Catherine. "How Is Subjectivity Undergoing Deconstruction Today? Philosophy, Auto-Hetero-Affection, and Neurobiological Emotion." *Qui Parle* 17, no. 2 (2009): 111–22.

Malabou, Catherine. *The New Wounded: From Neurosis to Brain Damage*. Translated by Steven Miller. New York: Fordham University Press, 2012.

Malabou, Catherine. *Ontology of the Accident: An Essay on Destructive Plasticity*. Translated by Carolyn Shread. Cambridge: Polity, 2012.

Malkowski, Jennifer. *Dying in Full Detail: Mortality and Digital Documentary*. Durham, NC: Duke University Press, 2017.

Manning, Erin. *Always More Than One: Individuation's Dance*. Durham, NC: Duke University Press, 2013.

Manning, Erin. *Relationscapes: Movement, Art, Philosophy*. Cambridge, MA: MIT Press, 2009.

Marder, Michael. "Being Dumped." *Environmental Humanities* 11, no. 1 (2019): 180–93.

Marder, Michael. "Breathing 'to' the Other: Lévinas and Ethical Breathlessness." *Lévinas Studies* 4 (2009): 91–110.

Marks, Laura U. *The Skin of the Film: Intercultural Cinema, Embodiment, and the Senses*. Durham, NC: Duke University Press, 2000.

Marshall, Carmen Rose. *Black Professional Women in Recent American Fiction*. Jefferson, NC: MacFarland, 2004.

Masco, Joseph. *Nuclear Borderlands: The Manhattan Project in Post-Cold War New Mexico*. Princeton, NJ: Princeton University Press, 2006.

Massumi, Brian. "Notes on the Translation and Acknowledgments." In Gilles Deleuze and Félix Guattari, *A Thousand Plateaus: Capitalism and Schizophrenia*, translated by Brian Massumi, xvi–xix. Minneapolis: University of Minnesota Press, 1987.

Mathes, Carter A. "Scratching the Threshold: Textual Sound and Political Form in Toni Cade Bambara's *The Salt Eaters*." *Contemporary Literature* 50, no. 2 (2009): 363–96.

Mattern, Shannon. "A City Is Not a Computer." *Places*, February 2017. https://placesjournal.org/article/a-city-is-not-a-computer/.

Mbembe, Achille. "The Universal Right to Breathe." Translated by Carolyn Shread. *Critical Inquiry* 47, no. S2 (2021): S58–S62.

McCormack, Derek P. *Atmospheric Things: On the Allure of Elemental Envelopment*. Durham, NC: Duke University Press, 2018.

McGlotten, Shaka. "Black Data." Video and transcript of a lecture at the University of Toronto, February 13, 2014. http://sfonline.barnard.edu/traversing-technologies/shaka-mcglotten-black-data/.

McGowan, Todd. "Looking for the Gaze: Lacanian Film Theory and Its Vicissitudes." *Cinema Journal* 42, no. 3 (2003): 27–47.

McNamara, Nathan Scott. "It Just Made Perfect Sense: Dorothy, a Publishing Project." *Los Angeles Review of Books*, October 22, 2018. https://lareviewofbooks.org/article/just-made-perfect-sense-dorothy-publishing-project/.

McRuer, Robert. *Crip Theory: Cultural Signs of Queerness and Disability*. New York: New York University Press, 2006.

Menely, Tobias. "Anthropocene Air." *Minnesota Review*, no. 83 (2014): 91–101.

Merchant, Carolyn. *The Death of Nature: Women, Ecology, and the Scientific Revolution*. New York: HarperCollins, 1990.

Merewether, Charles. "Ana Mendieta." *Grand Street* 17, no. 3 (1999): 40.

Metz, Christian. *Impersonal Enunciation, or The Place of Film*. Translated by Cormac Deane. New York: Columbia University Press, 2016.

Michel, François-Bernard. *Le souffle coupé: Respirer et écrire*. Paris: Gallimard, 1984.

Miller, Nancy K. *Bequest and Betrayal: Memoirs of a Parent's Death*. New York: Oxford University Press, 1996.

Million, Dian. "Felt Theory: An Indigenous Feminist Approach to Affect and History." *Wicazo Sa Review* 24, no. 2 (2009): 53–76.

Mitchell, David T., and Sharon L. Snyder. "Is the Study of Debility Akin to Disability Studies without Disability?" *GLQ* 25, no. 4 (2019): 663–66.

Mitman, Gregg. *Breathing Space: How Allergies Shape Our Lives and Landscapes*. New Haven, CT: Yale University Press, 2007.

Mitropoulos, Angela. *Pandemonium: Proliferating Borders of Capital and the Pandemic Swerve*. London: Pluto, 2020.

Moller, David Wendell. *Confronting Death: Values, Institutions, and Human Mortality*. New York: Oxford University Press, 1996.

Moraga, Cherríe. "Preface." In Moraga and Anzaldúa, *This Bridge Called My Back*, xiii–xix.

Moraga, Cherríe, and Gloria Anzaldúa, eds. *This Bridge Called My Back: Writings by Radical Women of Color*, 2nd ed. New York: Kitchen Table, 1983.

Moro, Jeffrey. "Grid Techniques for a Planet in Crisis: The Infrastructures of Weather Prediction." *Amodern*, no. 9 (April 2020). https://amodern.net/article/grid -techniques/.

Moten, Fred. "The Case of Blackness." *Criticism* 50, no. 2 (2008): 177–218.

Moten, Fred. *The Little Edges*. Middletown, CT: Wesleyan University Press, 2015.

Mukherjee, Rahul. *Radiant Infrastructures: Media, Environment, and Cultures of Uncertainty*. Durham, NC: Duke University Press, 2020.

Mulvey, Laura. "Visual Pleasure and Narrative Cinema." In *Film Theory and Criticism: Introductory Readings*, 7th ed., edited by Leo Braudy and Marshall Cohen, 711–22. New York: Oxford University Press, 2009.

Muñoz, José Esteban. *Cruising Utopia: The Then and There of Queer Futurity*. New York: New York University Press, 2009.

Muñoz, José Esteban. "Vitalism's After-Burn: The Sense of Ana Mendieta." *Women and Performance: a journal of feminist theory* 21, no. 2 (2011): 191–98.

Murphy, Michelle. *Sick Building Syndrome and the Problem of Uncertainty: Environmental Politics, Technoscience, and Women Workers*. Durham, NC: Duke University Press, 2006.

Musser, Amber Jamilla. "Sheree Rose, the Maternal, and the Erotics of Care." In Howard, *Rated RX*, 122–27.

Nayar, Pramod K. *Ecoprecarity: Vulnerable Lives in Literature and Culture*. New York: Routledge, 2019.

Nelson, Alondra. "Introduction: Future Texts." *Social Text* 71 20, no. 2 (2002): 1–15.

Ngai, Sianne. "Shulamith Firestone's *Airless Spaces*." *Arcade*, August 31, 2012. http:// arcade.stanford.edu/blogs/shulamith-firestone%E2%80%99s-airless-spaces.

Ngai, Sianne. *Theory of the Gimmick: Aesthetic Judgment and Capitalist Form*. Cambridge, MA: Belknap, 2020.

Ngai, Sianne. *Ugly Feelings*. Cambridge, MA: Harvard University Press, 2005.

Nichols, Bill. "Fred Wiseman's Documentaries: Theory and Structure." *Film Quarterly* 31, no. 3 (1978): 15–28.

O'Brien, Martin. "Performing Chronic: Chronic Illness and Endurance Art." *Performance Research* 19, no. 4 (2014): 54–63.

Olson, Charles. "Projective Verse." In *Collected Prose by Charles Olson*, edited by Donald Allen and Benjamin Freidlander, 239–49. Berkeley: University of California Press, 1997.

Orlemanski, Julie. *Symptomatic Subjects: Bodies, Medicine, and Causation in the Literature of Late Medieval England*. Philadelphia: Pennsylvania University Press, 2019.

Orr, Jackie. *Panic Diaries: A Genealogy of Panic Disorder*. Durham, NC: Duke University Press, 2006.

Osterweil, Ara. "Bodily Rites: The Films of Ana Mendieta." *Artforum* 54, no. 3 (November 2015). https://www.artforum.com/print/201509/bodily-rites-the-films -of-ana-mendieta-55531.

Oxley, Rebecca, and Andrew Russell, eds. "Interdisciplinary Perspectives on Breath, Body and World." Special issue, *Body and Society* 16, no. 2 (2020): 3–29.

Parikka, Jussi. "The Sensed Smog: Smart Ubiquitous Cities and the Sensorial Body." *Fibreculture Journal*, no. 29 (June 2017): 1–23. https://twentynine.fibreculturejournal.org /fcj-219-the-sensed-smog-smart-ubiquitous-cities-and-the-sensorial-body/.

Parks, Lisa, and Nicole Starosielski. "Introduction." In *Signal Traffic: Critical Studies of Media Infrastructures*, edited by Lisa Parks and Nicole Starosielski, 1–30. Champaign: University of Illinois Press, 2015.

Patton, Venetria K. *The Grasp That Reaches beyond the Grave: The Ancestral Call in Black Women's Texts*. Albany: State University of New York Press, 2013.

Perera, Suvendrini, and Joseph Pugliese. "Introduction: Combat Breathing: State Violence and the Body in Question." *Somatechnics* 1, no. 1 (2011): 1–14.

Perez, Gilberto. *The Material Ghost: Films and Their Medium*. Baltimore: Johns Hopkins University Press, 1998.

Peters, John Durham. *The Marvelous Clouds: Toward a Philosophy of Elemental Media*. Chicago: University of Chicago Press, 2015.

Peterson, Jennifer. "Barbara Hammer's *Jane Brakhage*: Feminism, Nature, and 1970s Experimental Film." *Feminist Media Histories* 6, no. 2 (2020): 67–94.

Philip, M. NourbeSe. "The Ga(s)p." In Kim and Miller, *Poetics and Precarity*, 31–40.

Phillips, Adam. *On Kissing, Tickling, and Being Bored: Psychoanalytic Essays on Unexamined Life*. Cambridge, MA: Harvard University Press, 1993.

Piepzna-Samarasinha, Leah Lakshmi. *Care Work: Dreaming Disability Justice*. Vancouver: Arsenal Pulp, 2018.

Pinkerton, Kent E., Mary Harbaugh, MeiLan K. Han, Claude Jourdan Le Saux, Laura S. Van Winkle, William J. Martin II, Rose J. Kosgei, E. Jane Carter, Nicole Sitkin, Suzette M. Smiley-Jewell, and Maureen George. "Women and Lung Disease: Sex Differences and Global Health Disparities." *American Journal of Respiratory and Critical Care Medicine* 191, no. 1 (2015): 11–16.

Poe, Danielle. "Can Luce Irigaray's Notion of Sexual Difference Be Applied to Transsexual and Transgender Narratives?" In *Thinking with Irigaray*, edited by Mary C. Rawlinson, Sabrina L. Hom, and Serene J. Khader, 111–28. Albany: State University of New York Press, 2011.

Pollock, Griselda, ed. *Generations and Geographies in the Visual Arts: Feminist Readings*. New York: Routledge, 1996.

Povinelli, Elizabeth A. *Geontologies: A Requiem to Late Capitalism*. Durham, NC: Duke University Press, 2016.

Povinelli, Elizabeth A. "Hippocrates' Breaths: Breathing In, Breathing Out." In *Textures of the Anthropocene: Grain, Vapor, Ray*, edited by Katrin Klingan, Ashkan Sepahvand, Christoph Rosol, and Bernd M. Scherer, 4 vols., 2:31–40. Cambridge, MA: MIT Press, 2015.

Puar, Jasbir K. *The Right to Maim: Debility, Capacity, Disability*. Durham, NC: Duke University Press, 2017.

Puar, Jasbir K. *Terrorist Assemblages: Homonationalism in Queer Times*. Durham, NC: Duke University Press, 2007.

Puar, Jasbir K., Lauren Berlant, Judith Butler, Bojana Cvejić, Isabell Lorey, and Ana Vujanović. "Precarity Talk: A Virtual Roundtable." *TDR: The Drama Review* 56, no. 4 (2012): 163–77.

Quashie, Kevin. *The Sovereignty of Quiet: Beyond Resistance in Black Culture*. New Brunswick, NJ: Rutgers University Press, 2012.

Quinlivan, Davina. *The Place of Breath in Cinema*. Edinburgh: Edinburgh University Press, 2012.

Rahm, Philippe. "Meteorological Architecture." *Architectural Digest* 79, no. 3 (2009): 30–41.

Ray, Sarah Jaquette, and Jay Sibara, eds. *Disability Studies and the Environmental Humanities: Toward an Eco-Crip Theory*. Lincoln: University of Nebraska Press, 2017.

Ray, Sarah Jaquette, and Jay Sibara. "Introduction." In Ray and Sibara, *Disability Studies and the Environmental Humanities*, 1–25.

Read, Jason. *The Politics of Transindividuality*. Boston: Brill, 2016.

Reagon, Bernice Johnson. "Coalition Politics: Turning the Century." In Smith, *Home Girls*, 356–68.

Redfern, Christine. *Who Is Ana Mendieta?* New York: Feminist Press, 2011.

Reich, Wilhelm. *Selected Writings: An Introduction to Orgonomy*. New York: Farrar, Straus and Cudahy, 1960.

Richmond, Scott. *Cinema's Bodily Illusions: Flying, Floating, and Hallucinating*. Minneapolis: University of Minnesota Press, 2016.

Robertson, Lisa. *XEclogue*. Vancouver: New Star, 2012.

Rodríguez, Juana María. *Sexual Futures, Queer Gestures, and Other Latina Longings*. New York: New York University Press, 2014.

Rose, Arthur. "Combat Breathing in Salman Rushdie's *The Moor's Last Sigh*." In *Reading Breath in Literature*, edited by Arthur Rose, Stefanie Heine, Naya Tsentourou, Corinne Saunders, and Peter Garratt, 113–34. London: Palgrave, 2019.

Rose, Arthur. "In the Wake of Asbestos: Ship-Building and Ship-Breaking in Ross Raisin's *Waterline* and Tahmima Anam's *The Bones of Grace*." *ariel* 49, no. 4 (2018): 139–61.

Rose, Sheree. "Life Is Still Possible in This Junky World: Conversation with Sheree Rose about Her Life with Bob Flanagan" (interview by Tina Takemoto). *Women and Performance: a journal of feminist theory* 19, no. 1 (2009): 95–111.

Rosen, Elliott J. *Families Facing Death: Family Dynamics of Terminal Illness.* Lanham, MD: Lexington, 1990.

Rosen, Miss. "Ana Mendieta Fought for Women's Rights and Paid with Blood." *Vice*, April 30, 2018. https://www.vice.com/en/article/gym79y/ana-mendieta-fought -for-womens-rights-and-paid-with-blood.

Rosenthal, Stephanie. "Ana Mendieta: Traces." In Rosenthal, *Traces*, 6–19.

Rosenthal, Stephanie, ed. *Traces: Ana Mendieta.* London: Hayward, 2013.

Rothenberg, Laura. *Breathing for a Living.* New York: Hyperion, 2003.

Rothman, William. *The "I" of the Camera: Essays in Film Criticism, History, and Aesthetics.* 2nd ed. Cambridge: Cambridge University Press, 2004.

Rubin, Gayle. *Deviations: A Gayle Rubin Reader.* Durham, NC: Duke University Press, 2011.

Rudick, Nicole. "Press Pass: Dorothy." *Paris Review*, September 24, 2012. https://www .theparisreview.org/blog/2012/09/24/aunt-dorothy/.

Rudy, Jason R. *Electric Meters: Victorian Physiological Poetics.* Athens: Ohio University Press, 2009.

Russell, Marta, and Ravi Malhotra. "Capitalism and Disability." *Socialist Register* 38 (2002): 211–28.

Sandilands, Catriona. "Melancholy Natures, Queer Ecologies." In *Queer Ecologies: Sex, Nature, Politics, Desire*, edited by Catriona Sandilands and Bruce Erickson, 331–58. Bloomington: Indiana University Press, 2010.

Saoji, Apar Avinash, B. R. Raghavendra, and N. K. Manjunath. "Effects of Yogic Breath Regulation: A Narrative Review of Scientific Evidence." *Journal of Ayurveda and Integrative Medicine* 10, no. 1 (2019): 50–58.

Sarachild, Kathie. "Consciousness-Raising: A Radical Weapon." In Sarachild, *Feminist Revolution*, 144–50.

Sarachild, Kathie, ed. *Feminist Revolution.* New York: Random House, 1978.

Saul, Joanne. *Writing the Roaming Subject: The Biotext in Canadian Literature.* Toronto: University of Toronto Press, 2006.

Savell, Kristin. "A Jurisprudence of Ambivalence: Three Legal Fictions Concerning Death and Dying." *Cultural Studies Review* 17, no. 1 (2011): 52–80.

Scappettone, Jennifer. "Precarity Shared: Breathing as Tactic in Air's Uneven Commons." In Kim and Miller, *Poetics and Precarity*, 41–58.

Schechner, Richard. *Performance Theory.* Rev. and expanded ed. New York: Routledge, 2003.

Schlosberg, David. "Reconceiving Environmental Justice: Global Movements and Political Theories." *Environmental Politics* 13, no. 3 (2004): 517–40.

Schneider, Rebecca. *The Explicit Body in Performance.* New York: Routledge, 1997.

Schneider-Mayerson, Matthew. "The Influence of Climate Fiction: An Empirical Survey of Readers." *Environmental Humanities* 10, no. 2 (2018): 473–500.

Schneider-Mayerson, Matthew. "'Just as in the Book'? The Influence of Literature on

Readers' Awareness of Climate Injustice and Perception of Climate Migrants." *ISLE: Interdisciplinary Studies in Literature and Environment* 27, no. 2 (2020): 337–64.

Schneider-Mayerson, Matthew, Abel Gustafson, Anthony Leiserowitz, Matthew H. Goldberg, Seth A. Rosenthal, and Matthew Ballew. "Environmental Literature as Persuasion: An Experimental Test of the Effects of Reading Climate Fiction." *Environmental Communication* (2020): 1–16. https://doi.org/10.1080/17524032.2020.1814377.

Schuller, Kyla, and Jules Gill-Peterson. "Introduction: Race, the State, and the Malleable Body." *Social Text* 38, no. 2 (2020): 1–17.

Schuster, Joshua. *The Ecology of Modernism: American Environments and Avant-Garde Poetics.* Tuscaloosa: University of Alabama Press, 2015.

Schwartz, Louis-Georges. "Cinema and the Meaning of 'Life.'" *Discourse* 28, nos. 2–3 (2006): 7–27.

Sedgwick, Eve Kosofsky. *Tendencies.* Durham, NC: Duke University Press, 2013.

Sedgwick, Eve Kosofsky. *Touching Feeling: Affect, Pedagogy, Performativity.* Durham, NC: Duke University Press, 2003.

Sedgwick, Eve Kosofsky. *The Weather in Proust.* Edited by Jonathan Goldberg. Durham, NC: Duke University Press, 2011.

Sell, Mike. *Avant-Garde Performance and the Limits of Criticism: Approaching Living Theatre, Happenings/Fluxus, and the Black Arts Movement.* Ann Arbor: University of Michigan Press, 2005.

Seymour, Jane Elizabeth. "Revisiting Medicalisation and 'Natural' Death." *Social Science and Medicine* 49, no. 5 (1999): 691–704.

Seymour, Nicole. *Bad Environmentalism: Irony and Irreverence in the Ecological Age.* Minneapolis: University of Minnesota Press, 2018.

Seymour, Nicole. *Strange Natures: Futurity, Empathy, and the Queer Ecological Imagination.* Champaign: University of Illinois Press, 2013.

Sharpe, Christina. *In the Wake: On Blackness and Being.* Durham, NC: Duke University Press, 2016.

Sheldon, Rebekah. *The Child to Come: Life after Human Catastrophe.* Minneapolis: University of Minnesota Press, 2016.

Shotwell, Alexis. *Against Purity: Living Ethically in Compromised Times.* Minneapolis: University of Minnesota Press, 2016.

Shreve, Anita. *Women Alone: The Legacy of the Consciousness-Raising Movement.* New York: Viking, 1989.

Siebers, Tobin. "Disability and the Theory of Complex Embodiment." In *The Disability Studies Reader*, 4th ed., edited by Lennard J. Davis, 218–97. New York: Routledge, 2013.

Siebers, Tobin. "A Sexual Culture for Disabled People." In *Sex and Disability*, edited by Robert McRuer and Anna Mollow, 37–53. Durham, NC: Duke University Press, 2012.

Siltanen, Elina. "Conceptual Confession: Asymmetrical Emotion in Writer-Reader Relations in Trisha Low's *The Compleat Purge.*" *Journal of Modern Literature* 43, no. 4 (2020): 108–26.

Simmons, Kristen. "Settler Atmospherics." Member Voices, *Fieldsights*, November 20, 2017. https://culanth.org/fieldsights/1221-settler-atmospherics.

Simondon, Gilbert. *L'individu et sa genèse physico-biologique*. Paris: Millon, 1995.

Simondon, Gilbert. "The Position of the Problem of Ontogenesis." Translated by Gregory Flanders. *Parrhesia: A Journal of Critical Philosophy*, no. 7 (November 2009): 4–16.

Simpson, Leanne Betasamosake. "Land as Pedagogy: Nishnaabeg Intelligence and Rebellious Transformation." *Decolonization: Indigeneity, Education, and Society* 3, no. 3 (2014): 1–25.

Singh, Julietta. *Unthinking Mastery: Dehumanism and Decolonial Entanglements*. Durham, NC: Duke University Press, 2017.

Škof, Lenart. *Breath of Proximity: Intersubjectivity, Ethics and Peace*. New York: Springer, 2015.

Škof, Lenart, and Petri Berndtson, eds. *Atmospheres of Breathing*. Albany: State University of New York Press, 2018.

Sloterdijk, Peter. *Terror from the Air*. Translated by Amy Patton and Steve Corcoran. Los Angeles: Semiotext(e), 2009.

Smelcer, John E., and D. L. Birchfield, eds. *Durable Breath: Contemporary Native American Poetry*. Anchorage, AK: Salmon Run, 1994.

Smith, Barbara, ed. *Home Girls: A Black Feminist Anthology*. New York: Kitchen Table, 1983.

Smith, Sidonie, and Julia Watson. *Reading Autobiography: A Guide for Interpreting Life Narratives*. Minneapolis: University of Minnesota Press, 2001.

Sobchack, Vivian. *The Address of the Eye: A Phenomenology of Film Experience*. Princeton, NJ: Princeton University Press, 1992.

Solanas, Valerie. SCUM *Manifesto*. Oakland: AK Press, 2013.

Soto, Christopher. "CA Conrad: On the Film 'The Book of Conrad' and His Life in Poetry." *Lambda Literary*, September 10, 2015. http://www.lambdaliterary.org/features/09/10/ca-conrad-on-the-film-the-book-of-conrad-and-his-life-in-poetry/.

Spahr, Juliana. *This Connection of Everyone with Lungs*. Berkeley: University of California Press, 2005.

Spatz, Ben. *What a Body Can Do: Technique as Knowledge, Practice as Research*. New York: Routledge, 2015.

Stanford, Ann Folwell. "Mechanisms of Disease: African American Women Writers, Social Pathologies, and the Limits of Medicine." *NWSA* 6, no. 1 (1994): 28–47.

Stavridou, Anastasia D. "Breathing Architecture: Conceptual Architectural Design Based on the Investigation into the Natural Ventilation of Buildings." *Frontiers of Architectural Research* 4, no. 2 (2015): 127–45.

Stenner, Paul. "Being in the Zone and Vital Subjectivity: On the Liminal Sources of Sport and Art." In *Culture, Identity, and Intense Performativity: Being in the Zone*, edited by Tim Jordan, Brigid McClure, and Kath Woodward, 10–31. New York: Routledge, 2017.

Stewart, Kathleen. "Atmospheric Attunements." *Environment and Planning D: Society and Space* 29, no. 3 (2011): 445–53.

Stewart, Kathleen. *Ordinary Affects*. Durham, NC: Duke University Press, 2007.

Stimpson, Catharine R., Alix Kates Shulman, and Kate Millett. "*Sexual Politics*: Twenty Years Later." *Women's Studies Quarterly* 19, nos. 3–4 (1991): 30–40.

St. Jean, Wendy. *Remaining Chickasaw in Indian Territory, 1830s–1907*. Tuscaloosa: University of Alabama Press, 2011.

Svendsen, Lars. *A Philosophy of Boredom*. Translated by John Irons. London: Reaktion, 2005.

Swarbrick, Steven. "Nature's Queer Negativity: Between Barad and Deleuze." *Postmodern Culture* 29, no. 2 (2019). doi: 10.1353/pmc.2019.0003.

Tagle, Thea Quiray. "Becoming Abstract Together: Opacity's Ethical Intervention." *American Quarterly* 72, no. 4 (2020): 993–1010.

Taibbi, Matt. *I Can't Breathe: A Killing on Bay Street*. New York: Spiegel and Grau, 2017.

Taylor, Diana. *Performance*. Translated by Abigail Levine. Durham, NC: Duke University Press, 2016.

Taylor, Dorceta E. *The Environment and the People in American Cities, 1600s–1900s: Disorder, Inequality, and Social Change*. Durham, NC: Duke University Press, 2009.

Taylor, Dorceta E. *Toxic Communities: Environmental Racism, Industrial Pollution, and Residential Mobility*. New York: New York University Press, 2014.

Taylor, Jesse Oak. *The Sky of Our Manufacture: The London Fog in British Fiction from Dickens to Woolf*. Charlottesville: University of Virginia Press, 2016.

Tercier, John Anthony. *The Contemporary Deathbed Documentary: The Ultimate Rush*. New York: Palgrave Macmillan, 2005.

Thistlethwaite, Susan B. "God and Her Survival in a Nuclear Age." *Journal of Feminist Studies in Religion* 4, no. 1 (1988): 73–88.

Thompson, Evan. *Mind in Life: Biology, Phenomenology, and the Sciences of the Mind*. Cambridge, MA: Harvard University Press, 2007.

Thoreau, Henry David. *Walden and Other Writings*. Edited by Brooks Atkinson. New York: Modern Library, 1992.

Tierney, Matt. *What Lies Between: Void Aesthetics and Postwar Post-politics*. New York: Rowman and Littlefield, 2015.

Tompkins, Kyla Wazana. "Crude Matter, Queer Form." *ASAP/Journal* 2, no. 2 (2017): 264–68.

TPC Staff. "Doris Sung Creates Living Architecture Sensitive to Heat and Light." *Vice*, February 16, 2016. https://www.vice.com/en_us/article/z4qvq8/doris-sung-creates-living-architecture-sensitive-to-heat-and-light.

Tremblay, Jean-Thomas. "An Aesthetics and Ethics of Emergence, or Thinking with Luce Irigaray's Interval of Difference." *Criticism* 59, no. 2 (2017): 277–99.

Tremblay, Jean-Thomas. "Breath: Image and Sound, an Introduction." *New Review of Film and Television Studies* 16, no. 2 (2018): 93–97.

Tremblay, Jean-Thomas. "*Breathing: Chaos and Poetry*—Franco 'Bifo' Berardi." *Full Stop*, February 28, 2019. https://www.full-stop.net/2019/02/28/reviews/jean-thomas-tremblay/breathing-chaos-and-poetry-franco-bifo-berardi/.

Tremblay, Jean-Thomas. "How Sia Kept Breathing and Became a Formalist." *PopMatters*, January 27, 2016. https://www.popmatters.com/how-sia-kept-breathing-and-became-a-formalist-2495456003.html.

Tremblay, Jean-Thomas. "Poetics of Gender Self-Determination." *The Rambling*, no. 6 (November 26, 2019). https://the-rambling.com/2019/11/26/issue6-tremblay/.

Tremblay, Jean-Thomas. "Together, in the First Person." *Chicago Review*, November 9, 2020. https://www.chicagoreview.org/new-narratives-impersonal-voice/.

Tremblay, Jean-Thomas, and Steven Swarbrick. "Destructive Environmentalism: The Queer Impossibility of *First Reformed*." *Discourse* 43, no. 1 (2021): 3–30.

Tristani, Jean-Louis. *Le state du respir.* Paris: Les Éditions de Minuit, 1978.

Tucker, Jeffrey Allen. *A Sense of Wonder: Samuel R. Delany, Race, Identity, and Difference.* Middletown, CT: Wesleyan University Press, 2004.

Tullett, William. *Smell in Eighteenth-Century England: A Social Sense.* Oxford: Oxford University Press, 2019.

Ursell, Michael. "Inspiration." In *The Princeton Encyclopedia of Poetry and Poetics*, 4th ed., edited by Roland Greene, Clare Cavanagh, Jahan Ramazani, and Paul Rouzer, 709–10. Princeton, NJ: Princeton University Press, 2012.

Vincler, John. "Dwelling Places: On Renee Gladman's Turn to Drawing." *Paris Review*, August 28, 2018. https://www.theparisreview.org/blog/2018/08/28/dwelling-places-on-renee-gladmans-turn-to-drawing/.

Viso, Olga M. *Ana Mendieta: Earth Body: Sculpture and Performance, 1972–1985.* Washington, DC: Hirshhorn Museum and Sculpture Garden, 2004.

Voyles, Traci Brynne. *Wastelanding: Legacies of Uranium Mining in Navajo County.* Minneapolis: University of Minnesota Press, 2015.

Wah, Fred. "Is a Door a Word?" *Mosaic: An Interdisciplinary Critical Journal* 37, no. 4 (2004): 39–70.

Wah, Fred. "A Poetics of Ethnicity." In *Twenty Years of Multiculturalism: Successes and Failures*, edited by Stella Hryniuk, 99–110. Winnipeg: St. John's College Press, 1992.

Wah, Fred. *Scree: The Collected Earlier Poems, 1962–1991.* Vancouver: Talonbooks, 2015.

Walker, Janet, and Nicole Starosielski. "Introduction: Sustainable Media." In *Sustainable Media: Critical Approaches to Media and Environment*, edited by Janet Walker and Nicole Starosielski, 1–19. New York: Routledge, 2016.

Walters, Magdalene K. "What the HIV/AIDS Pandemic Can Teach Us about Covid-19." Think Global Health, May 13, 2020. https://www.thinkglobalhealth.org/article/what-hivaids-pandemic-can-teach-us-about-covid-19.

Weeks, Kathi. "The Vanishing *Dialectic*: Shulamith Firestone and the Future of the Feminist 1970s." *South Atlantic Quarterly* 114, no. 4 (2015): 735–54.

White, Orlando. LETTERRS. New York: Nightboat, 2015.

Wilentz, Gail. *Healing Narratives: Women Writers Curing Cultural Dis-ease.* New Brunswick, NJ: Rutgers University Press, 2000.

Wilkinson, Joshua Marie. "An Interview with Renee Gladman." *Tremolo*, no. 7 (July 2012). http://www.thevolta.org/tremolo-issue7-rgladman.html.

Williams, Linda. "Film Bodies: Gender, Genre, and Excess." *Film Quarterly* 44, no. 4 (1991): 2–13.

Willis, Ellen. *The Essential Ellen Willis.* Edited by Nona Willis Aronowitz. Minneapolis: University of Minnesota Press, 2014.

Willis, Susan. *Specifying: Black Women Writing the American Experience.* Madison: University of Wisconsin Press, 1987.

Wilson, Elizabeth A. *Gut Feminism.* Durham, NC: Duke University Press, 2015.

Wilson, Elizabeth A. *Psychosomatic: Feminism and the Neurological Body*. Durham, NC: Duke University Press, 2004.

Winnicott, D. W. *Reading Winnicott*. Edited by Leslie Caldwell and Angela Joyce. New York: Routledge, 2011.

Wittig, Monique, and Sande Zeig. *Brouillon pour un dictionnaire des amantes*. Paris: Grasset et Fasquelle, 1976.

Womack, Ytasha L. *Afrofuturism: The World of Black Sci-Fi and Fantasy Culture*. Chicago: Lawrence Hill, 2013.

York, Michael. *Historical Dictionary of New Age Movements*. Lanham, MD: Scarecrow, 2004.

Zeiba, Drew. "City Writer: Interview with Visual Poet Renee Gladman." *Pin-Up*, accessed September 3, 2021. https://pinupmagazine.org/articles/pinup-renee -gladman-interview.

Zhang, Dora. "Notes on Atmosphere." *Qui Parle* 27, no. 1 (2018): 121–55.

Zhang, Dora. *Strange Likeness: Description and the Modernist Novel*. Chicago: University of Chicago Press, 2020.

Zimring, Carl A. *Clean and White: A History of Environmental Racism in the United States*. New York: New York University Press, 2016.

hearing, 65. *See also* sensation

Heathfield, Adrian, 63

Heidegger, Martin, 21, 45

Heine, Stefanie, 29, 133, 168n99, 174n86

Heise, Ursula K., 24–25

Hinduism, 21, 71

History of Sexuality, The (Foucault), 69

HIV/AIDS, 17, 75, 82, 159–60

Hogan, Linda (Chickasaw), 96, 98–104, 112, 159; *Dark. Sweet. New and Selected Poems*, 99; *Dwellings: A Spiritual History of the Living World*, 99; "Gentling rhe Human," 100–101; "Morning's Dance," 102; "V. Who Will Speak?," 99; *The Woman Who Watches the World*, 103

holding environment. *See under* environment

Holmes, Brooke, 134

homelessness, 75

horror. *See under* cinema

hospital, 140–41, 194n42

hospitality, 99, 101–2, 104–5, 184n37. *See also* Hogan, Linda

Hsu, Hsuan L., 2, 30, 116, 163n6

Hull, Gloria T., 104

human immunodeficiency virus. *See* HIV/AIDS

Hume, David, 155–56

Hurley, Jessica, 109

hurricanes, 57

hypnosis, 87

"I can't breathe." *See under* breath and breathing

identity, 15–17, 20, 28, 120, 123–24, 136, 156. *See also* subjectivity

idiopathic environmental intolerance (IEI), 15–17. *See also* environment: illness

IEI. *See* idiopathic environmental intolerance

illness. *See under* environment

immersion, 53

imperialism, 2, 52, 93, 158–59, 180n96. *See also* colonialism

impersonality, 75–76, 82, 120

Indigenous feminism. *See* Native feminism

Indigenous people: ceremony, 99–100; concepts of racial difference, 164n23, 184n37; lung cancer, 5; matrilineality, 101–2, 184n37; settler state, 4–5; wildness and, 180n96. *See also* ceremony; colonialism: settler; healing; Hogan, Linda; Native feminism; plasticity

individual and individuation: consent and, 162; death and, 150; disability and, 17–21; gender and, 184n34; milieu and, 14, 36–37, 50, 59–60, 167n69; queerness and, 120. *See also* body; milieu; subjectivity

industrialism, 13, 44, 113, 167n65. *See also* pollution

inspiration, 22, 71, 75–76, 168n95

intention, 25–26, 135, 155–56

interpretation, 91, 120, 133–34, 137. *See also* critique and postcritique

intersectionality, 186n73

interval. *See under* temporality

Iraq, war in, 36–37

Irigaray, Luce, 21–22, 45–46

Jackson, Zakiyyah Iman, 104, 136

Jameson, Fredric, 133–34

jazz, 23, 101

Johnson, Dion, 6

Johnson, E. Patrick, 121

Jones, Ian Bryce, 24

Kafer, Alison, 68–69, 90

Kalanithi, Paul, 70–71

Kant, Immanuel, 44–45, 155–56

Kastenbaum, Robert, 145, 150

Kauffman, Linda S., 84

Kenner, Alison, 13, 15

Killian, Kevin, 73–75, 177n44

Kim, Annabel L., 14

kinesthetics, 53, 63. *See also* Greenfield, Amy

King, Allan: *Dying at Grace*, 141, 150–55, 194n42

kinship, 111–12, 120, 188n37

Korean War, 3

Kuppers, Petra, 68, 84

Lacan, Jacques, 42, 132

language, 3–5, 107–8, 131–33, 190n84

nature, 43–44, 55–59, 174n86. *See also* environment; pastoral and postpastoral

Nayar, Pramod K., 9–10

necropolitics and necropower, 2, 5, 21, 114, 122–23, 163n5. *See also* biopolitics and biopower

"negative refueling," 1, 5

Nepomniaschy, Alex, 16–17

Never for Ever (Bush), 33

New Age, 22, 69, 72–76, 87, 177n38, 178n48, 178n66

New England Conservatory, 41

New Museum, 83

New Narrative, 73–74, 114–15, 160, 177n38, 178n46, 178n48

New York City, 122

Ngai, Sianne, 44–45, 90, 95, 145, 193n16

Nine Variations on a Dance Theme (Harris), 53–54

normativity, 14–15, 120, 176n22

Notaro, Tig, 142–43

nourishment, 1–2, 65–66, 102

novel, 105, 115, 117–19, 136, 188n21. *See also* fiction

nuclear disaster, 5, 11, 33, 37, 109

O'Brien, Martin, 70

oil spills, 57–59

Olson, Charles, 22–23, 178n69

One Mississippi (TV show), 142–44

ontogeny, 14, 26–28

opacity, 120, 135–36, 159, 191n107, 191n109. *See also* Blackness

ordinary, 29, 111

orgone therapy, 81

Orlemanski, Julie, 134, 190n92

Osterweil, Ara, 52

otherness, 22, 81, 134, 136

Oxley, Rebecca, 28–29

pain, 3–4, 82–93, 182n152, 195n53

palliative care, 139–40, 144, 151–53, 155. *See also* care; death and dying; health care

Parikka, Jussi, 114, 117, 122

particles and particulate matter, 5–6, 15–16, 37, 65–66, 100, 111, 121, 123. *See also* Blackness; race and racism

particular. *See* "ecologies of the particular"

pastoral and postpastoral, 40, 42–45, 50, 54–57, 59, 64, 158–59. *See also* nature

pathology, 15–16, 68, 156

pedagogy, 44, 55, 59, 94, 111

Pentecostalism. *See* Blackpentecostalism

perception, 114–15, 163n7. *See also* sensation

Perez, Gilberto, 151

performance and performance art, 23, 25, 27–28, 29, 37–40, 47–52, 53, 57–59, 60–62, 70, 82–93, 110–12, 129, 176nn22–23. *See also* Bush, Kate; Flanagan, Bob; Greenfield, Amy; Mendieta, Ana; Rose, Sheree

Peters, John Durham, 171n9

Peterson, Jennifer, 54–57

petrofictions, 59

pharmakon, 30

phenomenology, 73, 77, 98–99, 125–30, 145, 150. *See also* death and dying: taxonomy of

Philip, M. NourbeSe, 101

Phillips, Adam, 89–90, 181n137, 181n141

philosophy, of breath and breathing, 21–22

photography, 41, 46–47, 151

phylogeny, 26–28

physiology, 21–22, 160–61, 168n99

plasticity, 103–4, 156, 185n56

Plato, 22

pneuma, 21, 81

Poe, Danielle, 46

poetry and poetics, 4–5, 22–23, 26–30, 36, 76–82, 87, 99–104, 177n33, 178–79n69

police. *See under* violence

pollution, 1–2, 9–10, 12–13, 36, 43–46, 76–78, 102–3, 116–17, 123. *See also* smog

pornography, 24

porosity, 1, 10, 74, 178n51

postcritique. *See* critique and postcritique

posthumanism, 84

prana, 21. *See also* yoga

precarity, 9–10, 23–24, 29–30, 158

privilege, disprivilege, 11, 16–17, 47, 141

"Projective Verse" (Olson), 22–23

projectivism, 22–23, 29, 76, 168n103

pronouns, 13, 138